Map showing the Penny Fares around Toynbee Hall.

The circles are half a mile apart.
The line ·——·—— connects the termini of
penny tram and 'bus fares from Toynbee Hall.

SCALE

½   1 mile.

Toynbee Hall
The First Hundred Years

Asa Briggs and Anne Macartney

Routledge & Kegan Paul
London, Boston, Melbourne and Henley

First published in 1984
by Routledge & Kegan Paul plc

14 Leicester Square, London WC2H 7PH

9 Park Street, Boston, Mass. 02108, USA

464 St Kilda Road, Melbourne,
Victoria 3004, Australia and

Broadway House, Newtown Road,
Henley-on-Thames, Oxon RG9 1EN, England

Set in Sabon 10 on 13 pt
by Input Typesetting Ltd, London
and printed in Great Britain
by The Thetford Press Ltd,
Thetford, Norfolk

Library of Congress Cataloging in Publication Data

Briggs, Asa, 1921–

Toynbee Hall, the first hundred years.
Includes bibliographical references and index.
1. Social settlements—England—London—Case studies.
2. Toynbee Hall (London, England)—History. I. Macartney,
Anne. II. Title.
HV4236.L66B74   1984   362.5'574'0942   84-11500

British Library CIP data available

ISBN 0–7102–0283–0

'Fear not to sow because of the birds'
Robert Browning

Contents

Illustrations

Visit of King George VI and Queen Elizabeth to Toynbee Hall to the New Building, November 1938

Toynbee Hall was bombed on 10 May 1941. The Warden's Lodgings and the Library were totally destroyed

East End victims of the bombing recovering at Bottingdean

Mallon rallying support. A meeting at Toynbee Hall to press for a new Education Act

Mallon with Lord Waverley, the Chairman of Toynbee Hall, and Clement Attlee, the President in 1947

Attlee with some members of the Toynbee Veterans' Club.

Mallon at his retirement reception in front of the bust of him by Jacob Epstein.

Pages 157-163

Dr A. E. Morgan, his wife, and some Toynbee Residents, *c.* 1955

Toynbee Hall in the 1950s

Huw Wheldon, a Toynbee Resident, entertaining local children at a Christmas party in the Lecture Hall

Ballet classes in the Lecture Hall at Toynbee

Music classes in the New Building

Special provision was made at Toynbee Hall for old people left behind after the population exodus from the area

The Warden, Walter Birmingham, and his wife Maisie, discussing with John Profumo the Royal Film Premier, *Othello* on 2 May 1966, to raise funds for Attlee House

Harold Wilson, Prime Minister, turning the first sod for the new Gatehouse, 23 July 1965

Attlee with the Archbishop of Canterbury at the opening of the Gatehouse, 30 March 1967

Her Majesty the Queen with John Profumo at the opening of Attlee House, 18 November 1971

The Queen Mother with Mrs Profumo, John Profumo and Lord Blakenham at the opening of Sunley House, April 1976

Some of the Sunley House children and helpers

The Children's Country Holiday Fund, a favourite activity of the Barnetts, is once again in operation from Toynbee Hall and organised with Anne Crisp and Bob le Vaillant

A satisfied customer

Overseas visitors with the Warden, Donald Chesworth

Some Toynbee Hall volunteers, 1983

Thrawl Street, the latest Toynbee Housing Association development (photograph by Peter Burton)

Toynbee Hall today (photograph by Peter Burton)

The scene in Whitechapel High Street: *c.* 1890, *c.* 1930, *c.* 1950, *c.* 1980

Preface

This is a book written for a centenary. The last detailed study of the history of Toynbee Hall by J. A. R. Pimlott appeared at the time of the Jubilee in 1934. Since then, Toynbee Hall, the East End, the country as a whole and the world have changed out of all recognition. So, too, indeed, has the writing of history and what is thought to be relevant to it. Yet there are curious parallels between the 1880s and the 1980s, as this book shows, and there are moments of stillness in the midst of uncertainty and confusion, particularly, perhaps in the East End, when it seems that *plus ça change, plus c'est la même chose*.

Persisting patterns of poverty, deprivation, squalor and racial separation characterise the area round Toynbee Hall. But so, too, does a distinctive combination of resignation and vitality. The area seems interesting – and significant – to those who choose to live there, to those who visit it, and even to those who live out of it. And it provokes fundamental questions about the facts and perceptions of poverty, the nature of community (and the lack of it), the visual as well as the social environment, and the relative roles of voluntary, local and national statutory policy in seeking not only to alleviate but to transform.

For these reasons, this is a book written not only as a centenary study, but as a personal contribution to the continuing history of an institution, Toynbee Hall, which has inspired respect and affection. It deals mainly with the past, but it is designed to assist in the task of determining what will be Toynbee Hall's future. The last chapter is deliberately called 'Unfinished Agenda': it might have been the title of the whole book.

As co-authors we have worked closely together on the text and on the research leading up to it, much of it in dusty archives. No chapter is entirely the work of one of us. We have also chosen together the pictures which we regard as an integral part of the history. We are deeply grateful to those people inside and outside Toynbee Hall to whom we have looked for evidence and who have been unfailingly helpful to us. It would be invidious to single out names, but we would have got nowhere at all without the outstanding assistance in the initial sorting of the Mallon archive of Cliff Tucker and Doris Greening and the initiative and encouragement of John Profumo, Lord Henniker and his Centenary Committee, the Warden Donald Chesworth, and the Council of Toynbee Hall. We would not have been able to get our text to our publishers without the typing assistance, not an easy task, of Tina Richards, Barbara Chambers and Margaret Stephens and we would not have been able to get our text from publisher to printer without the invaluable support of Elizabeth Fidlon.

When Henrietta Barnett, wife of the founder of Toynbee Hall, wrote her invaluable memoir of her husband, she welcomed the sixty reviews she received, 'many of them over a column long', but complained of her publisher, 'who is old, crabbed and indifferent to social reform of our sort'. Fortunately our own publisher's qualities have been quite different – patience with us, and enthusiasm for what we have been attempting to achieve.

We hope that our book will be read by many people who have never seen Toynbee Hall and, indeed, by many people who have never heard of it. But we know that there will be one group of well-informed readers scattered throughout the world – those who themselves are associated with urban Settlements, most of which look back to Toynbee Hall for inspiration. Henrietta Barnett's words about her publisher were written to perhaps the most remarkable of all the overseas pioneers, Jane Addams of Hull House, Chicago, to whom Henrietta was deeply attached and who first visited Toynbee Hall in 1887. And among the most curious and thoughtful visitors to Toynbee Hall are Japanese social workers who know just what settlements are and can be.

One of them, Shiro Abe, Director of the Yokosuka Christian Community Centre, recently paid a visit of pilgrimage not only to Toynbee Hall, but to Arnold Toynbee's tomb at Wimbledon where (in his own words) he 'scraped away' with his fingers 'the mess and debris in order to read the names inscribed there'. Arnold Toynbee, uncle of the famous twentieth-century historian, was born in 1852, and he is inevitably the first of many names to be mentioned in this book. Our very pertinent motto comes from Browning. It was a favourite of Samuel Barnett, the founder of Toynbee Hall, and once was prominent in his drawing room. In 1984 it needs no 'scraping away'. It is inscribed on the bronze tablet in Westminster Abbey which serves as his memorial.

Acknowledgments

The authors and publishers are grateful to the following for permission to reproduce plates: Tower Hamlets Local History Library, pages 13, 14, 15 (bottom) 43, 72 (top right), 90, 157 (bottom) and 163; Hampstead Garden Suburb Archive, pages 44 (bottom) and 75 (top right); Peter Burton, page 162; The Bodleian Library, page 12 (top and bottom left); *Punch*, page 12 (bottom right); The National Portrait Gallery, page 15 (top); Whitechapel Art Gallery, page 15 (centre); Hodder & Stoughton Ltd, page 72 (top left); Andre Deutsch Ltd, page 72 (top centre); the Hulton Picture Library, page 111 (bottom); Mr and Mrs Henry Smart, page 158 (top). All other plates are reproduced by permission of Toynbee Hall.

I
Time and Place:
The Victorian Prelude

1 The Time

Toynbee Hall celebrates its centenary in 1984, a twentieth-century year made famous in George Orwell's vision long before it began. The headline for the year 1884 in one of the best-known British chronologies reads more prosaically but with a hint of drama of its own – 'Parson's Steam Turbine, H. Maxim's Machine Gun'.[1] Toynbee Hall is not mentioned in it. In the section on 'politics, economics, law and education', however, the founding of the Fabian Society and the publication of Herbert Spencer's *Man versus the State* both find a mention. It is also noted that the play of the year was Ibsen's *The Wild Duck*. Another missing item is a reminder that Victorian England was neither a country of stable tranquillity nor of generally accepted and shared Victorian values. On 26 February 1884 a plot was discovered to blow up four of the principal railway stations of the metropolis – Victoria, Paddington, Charing Cross and Ludgate Hill.

One possible reason for the omission of Toynbee Hall from this chronology is that the events surrounding its foundation cover more than that one year. It was in the bleak autumn of 1883 that the first moves were made to establish it, and it was in January 1885 that the Hall was formally opened, with a students' conversazione. Moreover, when social chronologies are under review of a broader kind, 1884 figures as only one year – and that not the most exciting one – in a whole decade, the 1880s, which has often been picked out for its social and political drama. It was described as 'the end of an epoch' in a remarkable passage in Winston Churchill's life of his father where he was tracing the shifting patterns of old and new political preoccupations. 'Conscience was free, Trade was free. But hunger and squalor were also free'.[2]

The year 1883 has been identified as 'a year of groundswell', and it was then that Arnold Toynbee, the young Oxford historian after whom the Hall was to be named, died, an event which, it has been claimed somewhat pontifically, 'served to bring to light suddenly a whole world of sociological enthusiasm, of zeal and affection for the unfortunate, which had been steadily modifying the trend of politico-economical thought'.[3] And in the same year, when the Liberal minister, Sir Charles Dilke, was exploring 'the worst parts of London for himself', no less a person than the Conservative Marquess of Salisbury was pressing plans for a Royal Commission on Housing. He was to achieve his wishes in 1884, when a

Commission was appointed, an event picked out for special attention by the *Annual Register*.[4] Salisbury's important article on working-class housing appeared in the *National Review* on 5 November 1883,[5] and when in the same month Dilke dined at Windsor, 'the Queen talked Artisans' Dwellings.' So, too, did the Prince of Wales.[6]

It was in 1885, at the mid-point of the decade, when the Royal Commission had begun to meet, when Toynbee Hall was already a fact, and when the national electorate had been further expanded – the last great nineteenth-century landmark in franchise politics – that Joseph Chamberlain on the eve of the great Liberal split of 1886 noted how 'new conceptions of public duty, new developments of social enterprise, new estimates of the natural obligations of the members of the community one to another now come into view, and demand consideration.'[7] The relation between rich and poor was looming larger than the relation between voters and non-voters. And during the late 1880s there were dramatic signs of conflict. The year of Queen Victoria's Jubilee, 1887, was also the year of 'Bloody Sunday', 13 November, the unforgettable rioting in and near Trafalgar Square.

In the immediate background of the moves to establish Toynbee Hall earlier in the decade was the publication in mid-October 1883 of a remarkably effective penny pamphlet, *The Bitter Cry of Outcast London*, published anonymously under the auspices of the London Congregational Union. It said nothing that was new, and quoted more than once from a popular writer on London, the author of 'In the Workhouse – Christmas Day', George Sims, who had written brilliantly on the subject earlier in the year. Yet *The Bitter Cry* was immediately taken up and given full publicity in W. T. Stead's *Pall Mall Gazette* and in the *Daily News*. Almost at once, it was 'echoing from one end of England to the other', as much on account of Stead's sensational headlining of the pamphlet as on account of what the pamphlet itself said. Indeed, an American observer was led to speculate 'how much regenerating social activity would never have gone into East London if [Stead's] articles had not been written, and the tract had reached only the readers of such things'.[8]

The pamphlet itself pointed to 'a vast mass of moral corruption, of heart-breaking misery and absolute godlessness' in 'the very centre of our great cities', for 'only the merest edge of the great dark region of poverty, misery, squalor and immorality' had so far been touched by the Christian Church. 'Whilst we have been building our churches and solacing outsiders with our religion and dreaming that the millennium was coming, the poor have been growing poorer, the wretched more miserable and the immoral more corrupt.'[9] 'Is it not Time,' asked Stead in his articles on the pamphlet – that was the title of the first – 'to face one of the grimmest social problems of our time?' And, he went on to demand, 'Where is the leader of men, who will preach a new crusade against the crying evil of our times?'[10]

A few weeks after the publication of the pamphlet, and the Stead report on it, the Headmaster of Harrow, the Rev. Montagu Butler, held a copy of the pamphlet in his hand as he preached at St Mary's Church in Oxford.

> God Grant, [he told his congregation] that it may not startle only, but that it may be read and pondered by thoughtful brains, as well as by feeling hearts. . . . God grant also that *here*, in this great home of eager thought and enlightened action and generous friendship, the bitter cry of outcast London may never seem intrusive or uninteresting, but that year by year her choicest sons may be arrested by it.[11]

Time was moving at a faster pace than 'year by year' in Oxford, where there had been many signs of quickened interest in social questions earlier in 1883. Just over a fortnight after Butler's sermon, the Rev. Samuel Augustus Barnett, Vicar of St Jude's, Whitechapel, 'came as a prophet' and addressed a meeting of undergraduates and others, by invitation, in the room of his friend, Sidney Ball, a don then and later very hospitable to guests with a message. Barnett's theme was 'Settlements of University Men in Great Towns', and his audience included many young men later to achieve public distinction. Among them are said to have been Cosmo Gordon Lang, future Archbishop of Canterbury, J. A. Spender, future Liberal journalist, E. T. Cook, future editor of the *Daily News*, A. H. D. Acland, future Liberal minister, and Michael Sadler, future Master of University College and Vice-Chancellor of Leeds University.

There was no 'gush', Lang was to recall later, 'no exaggeration', 'only the call to come and see' and to join in 'sharing the life of that, to us, dim and strange other world of East London'. Instead of saying 'something must be done', Barnett quietly told his audience, it was more constructive to ask, 'What can I do?'[12]

For all its note of prophecy, the kind of appeal Barnett made with great success in Oxford was not a new one. As he put it simply, 'The revelations of recent pamphlets have fallen on ears prepared to hear.' He thought that while *The Bitter Cry* was 'sensational', 'the Time' was indeed ripe for action, not only in Oxford but outside – even in Cambridge, where already he had many allies. Nor was he alone in this. As the *Illustrated London News* was to put it just before the end of 1883, 'recent revelations as to the misery of the abject poor have powerfully touched the heart of the nation' and there probably never had been 'a time when the desire to alleviate their wretchedness was so widespread'.[13]

Barnett himself had long been familiar with what Mearns had to say – from his own experience. For him East London was not the other world. He had moved from London's West End, St Mary's, Bryanston Square, to become Vicar of St Jude's, a derelict church in the East End, as long ago as 1872, at the age of 28, and he had learnt there how to do things as well as to talk about them. His Bishop had told him when he moved to St Jude's that it was 'the worst parish in the diocese, inhabited mainly by a criminal population, and which has, I fear, been much corrupted by doles', and the first act of welcome Barnett met with from one of his parishioners was to be knocked down in Commercial Street and to have his watch stolen.[14]

It was through his zealous and courageous parish work at St Jude's that Barnett and his intelligent and energetic wife, Henrietta, whom he had married in 1873, had been drawn into community action. Barnett had served, for example, on the Whitechapel Board of Poor Law Guardians, had established an East London Branch of the University Extension Society, part of an enthusiastic nation-wide attempt to carry higher education to the large cities, had organised the Metropolitan Association for Befriending Young Servants, and had inaugurated not only a literary and discussion society in St Jude's but an annual art exhibition, the first of them in 1881 (with Watts pictures and Morris fabrics). He had also collected a Children's Country Holidays Fund. Finally, he had shown many distinguished visitors around the East End, including Sir Richard Cross, Disraeli's Home Secretary, in 1875.

All this activity preceded the beginning of the 1880s, a proof that the main themes of social history can no more be confined within decades than within years. And already by 1880, Barnett had attracted undergraduates to spend their vacations in the East End as well as more permanent settlers to live there long before Sidney Bell invited him to St John's. There was nothing new, in fact, about the idea of 'settlement', which has rightly been traced back to the late 1860s, another period of unrest, when the social historian J. R. Green, also an Oxford graduate, who deliberately preferred to work in the East End rather than the West End, was Perpetual Curate of St Philip's of Stepney.[15] The idea of Oxford revitalising the life of the great cities and of the nation belongs to the same decade also, and there were older origins still for the view put forward at that time by Edward Denison, son of a Bishop and for time an MP – and referred to by Barnett in his Oxford address – that the East End suffered from the absence of a class of well-to-do people with leisure, a 'resident gentry' who could help the less fortunate by living alongside them.[16]

Long before 1883, Barnett himself had established what proved to be invaluable links with Oxford, the university where he had himself studied as an undergraduate, and had met there Benjamin Jowett, the influential Master of Balliol, T. H. Green, the equally influential philosopher, whose liberalism, 'the very heart of the philosophical education of Oxford', pointed towards a gospel of active citizenship, and the dedicated historian, Arnold Toynbee, a pupil and friend of Green, who popularised the term 'industrial revolution' in lectures delivered in Oxford in 1881 and 1882.[17]

Toynbee, a regular visitor to St Jude's, mourned the death of Green in 1882 – 'I don't care very much what goes on in Oxford now Green is gone,' he told a friend[18] – but he himself died soon afterwards in March 1883 at the early age of 31. Almost at once, Barnett, Ball and Philip Lyttelton Gell, whom Barnett had met on his very first visit to Oxford and who later became Chairman of Toynbee Hall Residents, thought of commemorating his name in an East End settlement. They felt that the idea of doing so in a course of lectures, an idea favoured by some of Toynbee's friends and his widow – and one which was followed – was completely inadequate by itself.[19] It was not through talk but through action, they maintained, that Toynbee's name should be perpetuated. One of the key phrases in his papers had appeared in the middle of a lecture which he had given to the Cooperative Congress in Oxford in May 1882: it was the duty of education, Toynbee stressed, not to deal with 'the individual man', but with

> the *citizen*, with a view to showing what are his duties to his fellow-men and in what way union with them is possible. The mere vague impulse in a man to do his duty is barren without the knowledge which enables him to perceive what his duties are, and how to perform them.[20]

The Barnetts were just as deeply committed to active citizenship, with equal emphasis on the noun and the adjective. The religious impulse would be fully satisfied only if it operated within its social context through the 'opening of channels between eternal sources and everyday needs'.[21] 'The soul,' Toynbee wrote, 'demands not a refuge, but a resting place.'[22] 'Citizenship,' wrote Green, 'makes the moral man,' and the moral man was more than an individual. He was a person.[23] Yet Toynbee went further and held also that the middle class, 'not merely the very rich', had sinned against the poor, 'offering charity not justice', and that it was the duty of the middle class 'to devote our lives to your service', while Barnett himself more pithily maintained that 'the sense of sin has been the starting point of progress.'[24]

For Barnett, at least, however, sin was not the only starting point. Nor was 'earnestness', though he tried to invoke 'every form of earnestness' in Oxford when he appealed to dons and undergraduates to turn their eyes towards London's East End. Knowledge was the greatest ally, as Barnett put it in his address in Oxford.

> The fact that the wealth of England means only wealth in England, and that the mass of the people live without knowledge, without hope, and often without health has come home to *open minds* [our italics] and consciences.

The other world had to be penetrated, not moralised over. 'He who has, even for a month, shared the life of the poor, can never rest again in his old thoughts.' Thinking was involved as well as feeling.

Barnett was not content in 1883, therefore, to recommend what he called 'the machinery' of religious missions as a mode of approaching London's East End. His angle was very different from that of Evangelicals anxious to convert the poor or of Tractarians calling them to worship. He wanted not only 'settlement', but sharing of experience, not only contact, but community. 'A sense of unity – like other things – wears better – when it comes unconsciously.'[25] And everything was ready, given the will. There were large houses to be found in the East End. Directors could be appointed there and maintained by colleges, and around them 'graduates and undergraduates would gather'. They would make the house where they lived their home, and they would make contact not only with Churches but with 'the various charitable agencies . . . the clubs and centres of social life . . . all the bodies engaged in local government'.

Relationships would be reciprocal. 'Nothing that can be learnt of the University is too good for East London' and the university settlers would justify their presence by 'having something to give'. Yet they would learn too, for it was 'by living in East London that Arnold Toynbee fed the interest which in later years became such a force in Oxford'.

The settlers would have to start by being 'friendly to their neighbours'. 'Parties will be frequent, and whatever be the form of entertainment provided, be it books or pictures, lectures or reading, dancing or music, the guests will find that their pleasure lies in intercourse.' Meanwhile, 'elder settlers' might take up 'official positions' as Vestrymen and Poor Law Guardians (as Toynbee himself had done in Oxford, when he certainly could not be described as 'elder'). The possibilities were limitless. 'It has not entered into men's imaginations to conceive the change for good which might be wrought if men of culture should undertake the education of the people.'

Barnett himself wanted involvement, therefore, not merely compassion, and the involvement had to be based on knowledge, not on guilt. 'The needs of East London are often urged, but they are little understood.' Its inhabitants were 'at one moment assumed to be well-paid workmen, who will get on well if they are left to themselves; at another . . . outcasts starving for the necessaries of living'. It was 'impossible but that misunderstanding should follow ignorance, and at the present moment the West End is ignorant of the East End'.

Barnett pleaded for a true picture, less 'sensational' than that of *The Bitter Cry*, for 'much talked-of East London' was, in fact, 'made up of miles of mean streets', whose inhabitants 'were in no want of bread or even of better houses', so that visitors there from the West End might find themselves saying that they were 'disappointed that the people don't look worse'. Barnett had no patience with people who went to the East End for 'mystery' or for thrills. He knew, of course, that there were many different categories of poor in the East End with whom the 'settlers' would have to deal – notably casual labourers, who were in need, first and foremost, not of the *necessaries* for life, as the artisans were, but of the necessaries for *livelihood* itself. 'It will be something, if they . . . give to the one class the ideal of life and stir up in the other those feelings of self-respect, without which increased means of livelihood will be useless.' And in the process, they could do 'a little to remove the inequalities of life'.

One passage, more dramatic than anything in *The Bitter Cry*, stands out.

> What will save East London? asked one of our University visitors of his master. The destruction of West London, was the answer, and, insofar as he meant the abolition of the space which divides rich and poor, the answer was right. Not until the habits of the rich are changed, and they are again content to breathe the same air and walk the same streets as the poor, will East London be saved.

There were other elements in the Barnett approach, as he described it in 1883, which had a longer pedigree. Barnett was worried about what he thought were 'false' remedies for action in the East End and elsewhere. In particular, he disliked 'indiscriminate' charity, 'the careless giving which has made the poor poorer or . . . has tempted them to improvidence and hypocrisy'.[26] The desire 'to suppress the spirit of pauperism' had been a main motivation during the 1860s, when the Charity Organisation Society (COS) was founded in 1869 to combat 'mendicity' in the metropolis and to oppose any liberalisation in practice of the poor law of 1834, and J. R. Green had been one of the influences behind it.[27] Moreover, the first local Charity Organisation Committee had been set up in Barnett's first parish, St Mary's, Bryanston Square, and Barnett's wife had worked closely with Octavia Hill, the housing reformer, who was one of its stalwarts.[28]

Barnett himself mentioned the Charity Organisation Society in his 1883 address as one of the organisations to which the 'settlers' might belong – as 'visitors' to the homes of the poor, meticulously separating (through personal encounter) the 'deserving' from the 'undeserving'. It was always the view of the Charity Organisation Society that 'intimate knowledge' was a necessary prerequisite for effective help to the poor, and that 'handing out' charity, without investigating their 'deserts' did more harm than good to the human spirit. Twentieth-century social casework has its origins in this approach.[29]

There was a second 'false' remedy abroad in 1883, many social observers maintained, a remedy which had not been proffered much during the 1860s but which had recently become far more attractive to the working classes – secular socialism. It has been argued, indeed, that it was the upsurge of socialism which drew into the field of social action many of the people, particularly clergymen, who were to organise and to support Toynbee Hall. They were facing a challenge and found an answer in social, if not socialist, Christianity. 'Religion was alive again,' George Bernard Shaw was to write more than a decade later in the Preface to his *Pleasant Plays*, 'coming back upon men, even clergymen, with such power that not even the Church of England itself could keep it out.'[30] There were clergymen seeking social change long before 1883,[31] but now there was a new reason why they should be heard. It was not only that conditions in East London were, in the view of George Sims, 'a national scandal'; they were beginning to seem a national threat. It was in 1883 that Karl Marx died – and his death was noted in the *Annual Register* – and 1884 was the year when the Fabian Society was founded, with its very different brand of socialism. So, too was H. M. Hyndman's Social Democratic Federation. It was within this context that Frank Harris could warn his middle-class readers that 'if you suffer the poor to grow up as animals, they may chance to become wild beasts and rend you.'[32]

Barnett himself was influenced more by hope than by fear. He has often been described as a Christian Socialist, and Henry Scott Holland, who undoubtedly was, could portray Toynbee, too, as a 'radiant and beautiful figure' in the same mould. Yet Barnett was always at pains to distinguish between 'theoretical socialism' and what he called 'practicable socialism', the title of an article he wrote in 1883 itself and subsequently of two books in which various of his earlier pieces were collected:[33] He always wanted to apply a feasibility test.

> All real progress must be by growth [he insisted]. The new must be a development of the old, and not a branch added on from another root. A change which does not fit into and grow out of things that already exist is not practicable change; and such are some of the changes now advocated by socialists.[34]

Toynbee, who had believed that 'the poorest class needs to be raised in the interest of all classes', distinguished sharply between what he called 'Tory Socialism' and 'Continental Socialism' and expressed 'abhorrence and detestation of the materialistic ideas of the 'Continentals'. What were necessary instead, he argued, were 'plans of social reform directed to secure the material independence of the workman' and an ideal for workmen and employers alike. 'To a reluctant admission of the necessity for State action,' he concluded – Barnett would have left out the adjective – 'we join a burning belief in duty, and a deep spiritual ideal of life.'[35]

The term 'socialism' was often used vaguely during the 1880s, so that when the *Oxford Magazine* asked the question in 1883 (after a highly successful Oxford lecture by William Morris), 'Is the new Oxford movement to be a Socialistic one?' it did not touch on any issues in socialist theory. It replied rather that the answer would be yes if the questioner was implying that 'the most living interest of Oxford' had shifted to social questions.[36] Nor was Oxford alone. At such a time, not only Joseph Chamberlain but Lord Salisbury could be accused of preaching socialism. Indeed, when the latter published in the very month that Barnett visited Oxford, November 1883, his article in the *National Review* demanding housing improvement as a matter of national urgency, he was accused, for all his traditionalist political views, of plunging suddenly into 'the turbid water of State Socialism'.[37]

It is no wonder that Alfred Milner, who was one of Toynbee's closest friends, and who, like Salisbury, repudiated then, as later, all talk of *laissez-faire* as a guide to national policy, called the word 'socialism' 'that most vague and misleading of all the catchwords of current controversy'. It often meant no more than 'State intervention' or what began to be called 'collectivism', equally misleadingly contrasted with 'individualism'.[38] It was all that Herbert Spencer did not want in *Man versus the State*.

Yet however vague the term was in 1883, there was, nevertheless, no doubt about the significance of the distinctions Barnett and Toynbee drew. They both wanted social harmony, not social conflict, and they both believed that progress depended not on force but on education. 'The social problem is at root an educational problem . . . without more knowledge, power might be a useless weapon and money only a means of degradation.'[39]

In a period of low profits, of high unemployment, of disturbed social relationships – and these were obvious and much publicised features of the time – they were both particularly aware, too, that great cities, with their huge burden of seemingly intractable problems, were places of danger to order, and that they would remain so until 'centres of civilisation' could be created in them. They were less interested in extending the role of the state, therefore – though they recognised the need to do this – than in opening up a new theatre of citizenship. Philanthropy was not enough, they maintained, if it did not narrow social distance. At the same time, in the words of Gell, political and social programmes were of no use unless 'they took account of the social complexities of human life and character'.[40] Formulae or slogans were not enough.

After the meeting at St John's College, Oxford, and further meetings there, one of them addressed by the bookbinder son of a dock labourer, Frederick Rogers (and attended by undergraduates from Cambridge), events moved fast. Oxford, wrote the *Oxford Magazine* enthusiastically, had turned at last 'from playing at the Middle Ages in Churches or at a Re-Renaissance in cupboards' to 'a new faith with Professor Green for its founder, Arnold Toynbee for its martyr, and various societies for its propagation', and Barnett himself spoke at the Oxford Union in December 1883, to propose the motion, carried unanimously, that 'in the opinion of this House the condition of the poor in our large towns is a national disgrace': the motion also called for voluntary, municipal and state action.[41]

In the same month, an informal meeting was held at Balliol at which it was resolved to found a University Settlement in East London, if possible in co-operation with other colleges. It was known that St John's, Wadham and New College were interested, and at a second Balliol meeting – this time a general one – in February 1884, which was presided over by the Reverend the Hon. W. H. Fremantle, Barnett's old vicar at St Mary's, Bryanston Square, it was decided to go ahead and establish a London settlement.

At the same meeting a strong action committee was set up which included Sidney Ball of St John's, A. H. D. Acland, A. L. Smith and W. H. Forbes of Balliol, and T. H. Warren, a future President of Magdalen. The field of action was, of course, to be the 'other world' of London, East and West, and a powerful London group of supporters who included the Liberal MP, James Bryce, C. S. Loch, Secretary of the Charity Organisation Society, and Milner, proceeded with energy and good fortune to discover that a disused boys' school within a few yards of St Jude's, Whitechapel, was for sale. Now was obviously the time, and the Committee bought the property for £6,250, a satisfactory price 'in view of the facilities afforded by the completion of the Inner Circle [underground railway] to Aldgate'. After reporting back to Oxford (and Cambridge, where a parallel Committee for the Study of Social Questions had been set up), plans were authorised for demolition of the school and for the building of a new settlement house, and work began in July 1884.

Cambridge, which Barnett considered 'more cautious than Oxford', 'duller and gooder', was slower to act than Oxford in terms either of 'money or men'.[42] Yet the early Cambridge supporters of 'settlement' included Professor James Stuart, pioneer of university extension, who had felt the urgency of associating the university with the great centres of population, Professor J. R. Seeley, the historian, Austen Chamberlain, Joseph Chamberlain's son, then a prominent figure in the Cambridge Union, and the Duke of Clarence, then a first-year undergraduate; and given this influential backing of the Barnett scheme in 'the other place', the word 'University' in the title of the Settlement Association was quickly changed to the word 'Universities'. Powerful London supporters now included the Duke of Westminster and A. J. Balfour, a future Conservative Prime Minister.

The Association became a registered joint stock undertaking in July 1884 – with four objects:

(a) to provide education and the means of recreation and enjoyment for the people in the poorer districts of London and other great cities; to inquire into the condition of the poor and to consider and advance plans calculated to promote their welfare;
(b) to acquire by purchase or otherwise and to maintain a house or houses for the residence of persons engaged in or connected with philanthropic or educational work;
(c) to provide in whole or in part for the salary or maintenance of any person or persons engaged in promoting the aforesaid objects; and
(d) to receive and apply donations and subscriptions from persons desiring to promote the objects aforesaid or any of them and to hold funds in trust for the same.[43]

The four objects were far broader than those of a religious mission – Anglican, Methodist or Congregationalist – and for this reason there were Fellows and undergraduates both in Oxford and Cambridge who supported a different remit – 'the preparation of character for . . . the reception of the religion of Christ'.[44] Already at the end of January 1884 an Oxford initiative, not from Balliol but from Keble, pointed to the possibility of a distinctively religious settlement, and Oxford House was duly set up during the autumn of 1884 in Bethnal Green. Its first lay head, James Adderley, who was soon to be ordained, had listened with enthusiasm to Barnett, but he shared the view of one of his successors, H. Henley Henson, later Dean of Durham, that 'Church and Settlement should be directly associated.'[45]

Toynbee, however, and Barnett after him, were out of sympathy with this approach: they were more interested in Green – and in Ruskin – than in Pusey – or Shaftesbury – and they had worked together in a lively, if minuscule, Church Reform League, set up by Toynbee, Milner and Gell in 1879.[46] Of Toynbee, Milner wrote that while he was 'intensely conscious of the all-pervading presence of the Divine', he was 'incredulous of miracle and indifferent to dogma',[47] while Barnett, speaking for himself after he had been appointed first Warden of Toynbee Hall in February 1884, told his brother that he would now leave 'the hard wearing detail of parish work to efficient curates' while enjoying the fellowship of 'the salt of the earth in the shape of Oxford men'.[48] The latter, he felt, were 'soldiers of the nineteenth century'.

There were ironies, however, in the immediate history of Oxford House and Toynbee Hall and of some of the other religious mission settlements, including the Congregationalist Mansfield House, opened in 1890. Adderley at Oxford House – and later – was a militant socialist, who was to go 'on errands between the Bishop of London and John Burns', the Labour Leader; strong though his religious faith was, he was equally strong in his political opinions, asking himself what he thought of as the fundamental linking question, 'Am I prepared to take . . . Christ's pains to make myself the friend of the suffering poor and to seek the causes of their poverty, not merely to get frightened at the results?'[49] Barnett, who was undenominational in his outlook, left other people to look for 'causes', and, though he had political views of his own, he deliberately kept Toynbee Hall open to men of all views, a decision of fundamental importance for its future. Meanwhile, the Congregationalists were not without their problems when they turned from writing about 'outcast London' to doing something about it. When a stone was laid in 1896 at Mansfield House, in memory of T. H. Green, the Congregationalist periodical, the *British Weekly* objected strongly to what it called a 'studious ignoring of the religious side of the Settlement'.[50]

Toynbee Hall came into existence, then, not only in a time of social turmoil, but in a time of transition, when the religious motive by itself, so strong for centuries in the organisation both of philanthropy and education, was beginning to drive not a whole generation but a diminishing minority of activists, and the minority was to diminish even more in the last twenty years of the century. Whereas sixteen out of the first eighty Toynbee residents went into the Church or were already clergymen, during the next twenty years only two entered the Church. Barnett himself stands out in the middle of the transition, and it was not a coincidence that in 1888, Mrs Humphrey Ward, niece of Matthew Arnold, published her controversial novel, *Robert Elsmere*, which described the modern priest who could no longer believe in miracles and who founded a sect in the East End which preached a *mélange* of Christianity, Positivism, and the social gospel.[51] It was dedicated to Green and was reviewed by Gladstone, and its remarkable success led Mrs Ward to open a Settlement of her own, mainly Unitarian, University Hall.

Matthew Arnold, who died just before the novel was published, had blessed the Toynbee Hall Residents, all of whom, he said, would have their names written in the Book of Life.[52] Yet Barnett himself was unhappy about the element of rivalry, as he saw it, which had been introduced as new Settlements in the East End were opened which professed a specifically religious purpose. According to his wife Henrietta, he continued to feel 'a deep, very deep pain' that 'the call to the East' was not a united crusade.[53]

Arnold Toynbee

(*left*) How it began: *The Bitter Cry*

The

Bitter Cry
of
Outcast London

With a
Cartoon

By kind permission of the Editor of

"Punch"

PRICE ONE PENNY

Published by James Clarke & Co.
13 and 14, Fleet Street, London, E.C.

THE BITTER CRY
OF
OUTCAST LONDON.

AN INQUIRY INTO THE CONDITION OF THE ABJECT POOR.

THERE is no more hopeful sign in the Christian Church of to-day than the increased attention which is being given by it to the poor and outcast classes of society. Of these it has never been wholly neglectful, if it had it would have ceased to be Christian. But it has, as yet, only imperfectly realised and fulfilled its mission to the poor. Until recently it has contented itself with sustaining some outside organisations, which have charged themselves with this special function, or what is worse, has left the matter to individuals or to little bands of Christians having no organisation. For the rest it has been satisfied with a superficial and inadequate district visitation, with the more or less indiscriminate distribution of material charities, and with opening a few rooms here and there into which the poorer people have been gathered, and by which a few have been rescued. All this is good in its way and has done good; but by all only the merest edge of the great dark region of poverty, misery, squalor and immorality has been touched. We are not losing sight of the London City Mission, whose agents are everywhere, and whose noble work our investigations have led us to value more than ever, but after all has been done the churches are making the discovery that seething in the very centre of our great cities, concealed by the thinnest crust of civilization and decency, is a vast mass of moral corruption, of heart-breaking misery and absolute godless-

(*below*) 'Seeing's Believing' - *Punch*, 1 December 1883

'SEEING'S BELIEVING.'—1883
Mr. P. 'Quite right, Sir Charles! *That* means business!!'

Henrietta Octavia Rowland and Samuel Augustus Barnett at the time of their marriage in 1873

Parish workers at St Jude's, Whitechapel

Toynbee Hall, designed by Elijah Hoole

(*below left*) The exterior of Toynbee Hall (*Builder*, 14 February 1885)

(*below*) The drawing room and the dining hall (*Architect*, 14 February 1885)

A portrait of Barnett by G. F. Watts

The *Pall Mall Gazette*, 28 April 1886, shows Barnett explaining the meaning of art at the annual exhibition at St Jude's, Whitechapel

The Whitechapel Art Gallery and the Passmore Edwards Library

2 The Place

When Barnett persuaded his Oxford audience – and a bigger group of sympathisers – to found Toynbee Hall in the heart of the East End, Toynbee's friend, Milner, who, despite his later interest in Toynbee Hall, would have preferred a series of academic lectures in Toynbee's memory, complained,

> As for Barnett, he is simply a professional grabber for the East End. Why the Dickens should the thing be specially for the East End? Any other of the towns that received Toynbee well, that he was fond of, have more claim.[54]

It was a biased judgment, and it was not shared by other friends of Toynbee, like Bolton King, who advanced money to Barnett at this critical juncture.[55] There were just as good reasons in the 1880s for focusing attention on the East End as the nation's problem centre as there had been for focusing attention on the great industrial cities of the provinces forty years before. Then, people who were concerned with the present and future shapes of society had been drawn to Manchester; and even in 1860, when the young Positivist Frederic Harrison set out to explore, he left behind 'the confused and monstrous' city of London, and turned to the 'enormous weight, mass and power of selecting the manufacturing districts', still selecting that 'vast, palpitating industrial city' for special attention.[56] Now, in the 1880s, the socially aware had to search and understand London, 'the world city' and the social contrasts which dominated it.[57] 'A city,' wrote Arthur Sherwell in his *Life of West London* – and he was thinking of a great metropolis – 'is like a great, hungry sea, which flows on and on, filling up every creek, and then overspreads its borders, flooding the plains beyond.'[58]

Between 1871 and 1901 the population of Greater London was growing faster than that of any provincial conurbation and faster by far than that of the national population as a whole: indeed, its growth was compared with that of a cancer as well as, more picturesquely, with that of a coral reef. Between 1891 and 1901 – after its government had been reformed in 1888 with the founding of the London County Council (LCC) – its total increase (867,165) was the greatest decennial increase of the century. Lord Rosebery, the first chairman of the LCC found no thought of pride associated with London. 'Cobbett called it a wen. If it was a wen then, what is it now? A tumour, an elephantiasis.'[59]

It was not so much the growth in London's numbers that stood out, as the migration, internal and external, that made the growth possible, the increased social segregation that went with growth, and the continuing presence of poverty in the midst of vaunted wealth and urban improvement; and while some of the implications of these trends were most easily traced in the developing suburbs of the metropolis – 1883 was the year of the first Cheap Trains Act, and the suburbs were London's social safety valve – the East End was the huge area in London where the most gloomy effects of almost every trend were visible.

The inner ring of 1½ miles ending at the Regent's Canal, described by Booth as a girdle of poverty, consisted of most of Shoreditch, Bethnal Green (excepting the Victoria Park end), all Whitechapel, St George's, Wapping, Shadwell and Ratcliff, with the inlying portions of Mile End.[60] Yet these districts, often treated as a unity, were quite different from each other. Only 4 per cent of Whitechapel's population was made up of labourers, while the figure for St George's was 9 per cent; and whereas the makers of food and clothes accounted for 24½ per cent of the population of Whitechapel, they accounted for only 12 per cent in Bethnal Green and 9 per cent in Shoreditch. Each district had its own 'peculiar flavour', as Charles Booth put it. 'One seems to be conscious of it in the streets. It may be in the faces of the people or in what they carry . . . or it may lie in the sounds one hears or in the character *of the people*.'[61]

Behind the 'peculiar flavour' there was peculiar history. Huguenots, 'gentle and profitable strangers' from France, had settled in Spitalfields in the late seventeenth century, no fewer than 13,000 of them in Spital Square and its immediate vicinity. And later the Irish had formed their own colonies of a very different kind. Whitechapel, the area within which St Jude's parish and Toynbee Hall were situated, had long been a major centre of Jewish immigration; and when between 1870 and 1914 thousands of Jews, most of them from Eastern Europe, came to England to seek refuge, a large number of them, over half, settled in the East End.[62] They fled from pogroms and persecutions, and there were few of them who spoke English. Their communities were characterised by 'extreme poverty' and distinctive ways of life, well described by Beatrice Webb, who was working for Booth, in a remarkable section of his 'grand inquest', and more dramatically or melodramatically by Jack London a little later in his *People of the Abyss*.[63] The population of aliens living in Whitechapel in overcrowded premises increased further from 24.1 per cent at the 1891 census to 31.8 per cent ten years later.[64]

Despite the building of new model dwellings in 1887 – critics thought them more like warehouses than homes – the MP for Bethnal Green told the House of Commons in 1900 that the housing situation had got worse not only in his constituency but elsewhere – even in parts of suburbia – during the twenty years since 1880, and that while the rents of the poorest were far higher, the area of high rents had been itself extended.[65] Not surprisingly, there was terrible overcrowding, and not surprisingly too Jewish immigration was blamed for it.[66] The East End was a place of endemic racial prejudice, therefore, as well as poverty, particularly during the first decade of the twentieth century. Bethnal Green was a predominantly Christian area, avoided by Jewish residents of Whitechapel 'because we were afraid of being beaten up'.[67]

There was crime in the area as well as prejudice; and it was after Toynbee Hall opened that the case of Jack the Ripper – on its doorstep – hit the headlines. And prejudice came into comments on this case too: the murders, it was said, were 'foreign to the English style in crime'. For Stead, still on the look out for new topics, this was the new topic of the hour, 'the only one topic today throughout England'.[68] In fact, 'low life journalism' had never neglected this theme.

For most observers during the 1880s poverty took pride of place, and the extent of poverty in the East End was researched systematically for the first time in the 1880s and 1890s by Charles Booth, 'a Liverpool gentleman' who was first drawn to the task by the Barnetts in 1878. His leading questions were – Who were the people of England? How did they really live? What did they really want? Was what they wanted good, and if so, how was it to be given to them? As he searched for the answers, Booth learned much from contacts, debates and lectures at Toynbee Hall. Indeed, it was due to the help of early residents at Toynbee Hall, notably Ernest Aves, who according to Mrs Booth, had 'a natural gift of fair-mindedness beyond any that I have ever met', that Booth was able carefully to collect statistics over a long period of time.[69]

The author of *The Bitter Cry*, Booth maintained, 'had not mentioned the causes of poverty', and if the causes were to be identified in the future, this would depend on 'counting heads and examining afresh in the light of such counting what people thought they already knew'. In 1883, the year Barnett introduced the idea of a Toynbee Hall to Oxford, Booth had at his disposal the reports of the National Census of 1881. Yet he was not content with social arithmetic, facts to which he could give 'a quantitative value'. He was already 'studying the ways of the people'. He was aware of and profoundly interested in what he called 'the clash of contest, man against man and men against fate', which he watched with his own eyes in the East End. It had all 'the absorbing interest of a battle-field', or to change the metaphor, of 'a rush of human life as fascinating to watch as the current of a river'. East London had lain 'hidden from view behind a curtain on which were painted horrible pictures'. And Booth characteristically changed his metaphor yet again.

> Did these pictures truly represent what lay behind, or did they bear to the facts a relation similar which the pictures outside a booth at some country fair bore to the performance or show within. This curtain we have tried to lift.[70]

For Booth, Whitechapel with all its problems was 'the Eldorado of the East' and the great market in Petticoat Lane, on the edge of Toynbee Hall, was 'one of the wonders of London, a medley of strange sights, strange sounds and strange smells'. In nearly all cases, the Jews were the sellers and the Christians the buyers, so that it was the 'exchange of the Jew, but the lounge of the Christian'. To be best appreciated, 'Brick Lane', another place of buying and selling, 'complete with its steam bath' – had to be seen at night with its 'flaring lights', its piles of 'cheap comestibles' and 'the urgent cries of the sellers'. And Booth went on to admire the vitality revealed not only in the streets but in the activities of the East End clubs – 115 of them – which also presented 'a bright and lively scene'. 'Coarse though the fabric be' in the East End, 'it is shot through with golden threads of enthusiasm.'[71]

Religion, Booth thought, played a part in East End life which was 'difficult to define', although there were 'at least a hundred agencies of religious or philanthropic character'. He had once heard a man say, thinking of the evils which surrounded him, 'If there is a God, he must be a bad one.' Many people went to church only on New Year's Eve, the great watchnight. Church attendance, indeed, did not figure among 'the recognised proprieties of life', and there was often little interest either in school attendance, a form of 'social discipline' which was subject to compulsion after 1876.[72] Booth appreciated just as much as the Barnetts did that Toynbee Hall was facing a challenge whatever it set out to do, a challenge which could be more effectively met, if it were to be met at all, from a Settlement rather than from a church. Significantly two successive vicars at Christ Church, Spitalfields, a large and substantially Jewish parish, spotlighted in the Jack the Ripper case, had 'broken down' as a result of their daily work in the most difficult of conditions.[73]

Booth's imagery was as novel as his formidable statistics, which showed that 35 per cent of the population were at all times living more or less 'in want', or his conclusion that 'the question of those who actually suffer from poverty should be considered separately from those of the true working classes, whose desire for a larger share of wealth' was 'of a different character . . . it is not by welding distress and aspirations that any good can be done.' Most earlier writers on the East End had been content with impressions rather than with facts; when they set out to explore 'the other world', they used the same kind of rather stale metaphors that explorers employed when they travelled through 'darkest Africa'. Booth tried not only to compute but to get inside different cultures: indeed, he felt an affinity with some of them. His wife believed that he was more relaxed roaming through the East End than staying in his own estate with its 'quiet and beauty'. 'He likes the life and the people,' she wrote, 'and the food! which he says agrees with him in kind and time of taking better than that of our own class.' She might have added that not every statistician would have dwelt as her husband did on 'the love of dancing in the streets' which 'bursts out whenever it has a chance'. 'Let a barrel organ strike up a waltz at any corner,' Booth noted, 'and at once the girls who may be walking past, and the children out of the gutter begin to foot it merrily.'[74]

While, then, Booth thought of the East End as *terra incognita*, the place that 'needed to be written on our social maps', he realised that he was dealing with people as well as a place, with people worthy of attention, and not just 'savages' living in 'dens', 'swamps' or 'deeps'.[75] It was not fear that drew him to the East End any more than it was fear that drew Barnett, who shared his image of the battlefield, claiming, indeed, that more lives were 'lost' in the East End in any year than in any battlefield.[76] Curiosity and concern were the forces that drew him. The East End, Booth recognised, had its own ways of life which were not only in general distinguishable from those of the West End, but, when placed under a microscope, were distinguishable also from each other.[77]

Booth's descriptions were very different, therefore, from those of his namesake, the Salvation Army General, William Booth, who compared East Enders with 'African pygmies' or those of the scientist, T. H. Huxley, who compared them with 'Polynesian savages'. In places, too, his analysis was more profound than that of Barnett, who, for all his receptivity, once described East London as 'joyless, a mass of starving, wretched, hopeless human beings', with 'some of its most vigorous inhabitants making no secret of their war against society'.[78]

Moreover, the kind of computation and of exploration that Booth carried through had a universal as well as a national significance. 'The facts which I have used to classify the inhabitants of London,' he wrote confidently, 'could be applied to any city – to Paris or Moscow, New York or Melbourne, Calcutta or Hong Kong.'[79] 'East Ends' were of increasing interest and concern during the 1880s in other great cities of the world, including new cities across the Atlantic.[80] And there, too, there were statisticians at work as well as clergymen.[81]

For this reason, the Settlement movement was likely from the start to be an international one. As early as 1886, Dr Stanford Coit, the American Ethical Society leader, who had heard of Toynbee Hall from an even earlier American visitor, Howard D. Bliss, entered into residence in Toynbee Hall for three months before returning to start a similar, though more modest, experiment in one of the worst quarters of New York's East Side; and before the end of the decade Jane Addams, in co-operation with Ellen Starr, founded what was to become the most famous of all American settlements, Hull House in Chicago.

When Coit moved from Park Avenue to the East Side, the Irish truck man who transported his furniture, told him, 'You don't really mean to move to Forsyth Street. I just moved out of there myself. It ain't a fit place to live for the likes of you or me.'[82] The remark should be set alongside that of a foreman in Whitechapel in 1886, 'the majority has not the stamina to make even a good scavenger.'[83] But Barnett, like Coit, had his answer.

> God's spirit has been imprisoned in phrases about the duty of contentment and the sin of drink . . . Old teaching will have to be put into new language, giving shown to consist in sharing and earning to be sacrificed. For some time it may be to the glory of a preacher to empty rather than to fill the Church as he reasons about the Judgement to come.[84]

A well-known writer on London's East End, who cared little for preaching or for prophecy and probed far less deeply in his analysis than Charles Booth – Sir Walter Besant – none the less has left a vivid description of London's late-nineteenth-century East End which made its way round the world. Besant, who often lectured at Toynbee Hall, was directly concerned with the implications of economic, social and cultural change both in his novels – *All Sorts and Conditions of Men* had appeared in 1882 – and in books like *East London*, which appeared in the year of his death, 1901. He was directly involved also in the foundation of the People's Palace of the East End which was opened by Queen Victoria in 1887.

The East of London, Besant wrote, was an area with a 'population . . . greater than that of Berlin or Vienna, or St Petersburg, or Philadelphia'. It was 'a city full of churches and places of worship, yet there are no cathedrals, either Anglican or Roman'. It had 'sufficient supply of elementary schools', but it had 'no public or high school', and it had no colleges for higher education and no university.

> The people all read newspapers, [he went on] yet there is no East End paper except of the smaller and local kind. . . . In the streets there are never seen any private carriages; there is no fashionable quarter. . . . One meets no ladies in the principal thoroughfares. People, shops, houses, conveyances all together are stamped with the unmistakeable seal of the working class.

And Besant left his most telling comment for the last: 'Perhaps the strangest thing of all is this: in a city of two millions of people there are no hotels: that means, of course, that there are no visitors.'[85]

That was after Toynbee Hall had brought in its first Residents and Booth had published his statistics; and also after the opening of the Hall and the Booth volumes, the story teller, Arthur Morrison in his *Tale of Mean Streets*, when he asked 'Who knows the East End?' could still echo J. R. Green, who had described 'a London about which the ordinary Londoner is totally ignorant . . . the London beyond Aldgate Pump'.[86] Concerning one point in the answer to this question, Booth, at least, was as clear as Barnett. What was needed was not a still, but a moving, picture. 'As in photographing a crowd, the details of the picture change continually.' 'In many districts the people are always on the move; they shift from one part of it to another like fish in a river.' Yet both Booth and Barnett were aware they 'did not usually go far' and that however great the changes from one year to the next, 'the general effect is much the same, whatever moment is chosen'.

The East End was always there, whether it was observed – or photographed – or not. Yet there was always a problem in the encounter between West and East when efforts were made to talk as well as to observe. The gaps in communication were wide. It was not only that 'beyond Aldgate Pump' was different: there was also what William Morris called 'this great class gulf' separating even the people who tried hardest to bridge it.[87] Forty years before Toynbee Hall, an early Inspector of Schools had argued that

> the inner life of the classes below us in society is never penetrated by us. We are profoundly ignorant of the springs of public opinion, the elements of thought and the principles of action among them – these things which we recognise at once as constituting our own social life.[88]

And the sense of 'impenetrability' persisted when it was realised that it was not only 'elements of thought' and 'principles of action' which were different, but values also. 'I doubt if any real conversation between members of two classes is possible,' wrote a conscientious district nurse to whom the East End was very familiar in 1911.[89] *From Their Own Point Of View*, written three years earlier, was the title of another of her books.[90]

Most East Enders doubtless did not see their own ways of life – or their 'plight' – in the same terms as the people who talked to them or even tried to entertain them. Yet the most sensitive observers were always well aware of this. 'I am not sure that we would feel greatly complimented,' wrote William à Beckett in what he described as a 'book of gossip' in 1900, 'were the costers of Shoreditch and Hackney to organise a society to provide the upper class with amusements suitable to their station.'[91]

It was always easy to go further than à Beckett and pass from such comment to satire. Indeed, à Beckett himself in the best *Punch* tradition began his chapter on East End entertainment brightly with the observation that 'when the Season is coming to an end in the West End it is the fashion to consider the claims of the East'; and when Toynbee Hall was founded the *Spectator* was not alone in trying to dismiss the whole 'settlement' project as 'hazardous and chimerical' on the grounds that the inhabitants of East London were scarcely likely to be 'regenerated by the efforts of undergraduates and the sight of aesthetic furniture and Japanese fans'. More seriously, too, it suggested that fashion was involved and that 'the spasm of public emotion which some eighteen months ago produced so much hysterical talk about 'Outcast London', seemed 'almost to have passed away' by the time Toynbee Hall was founded.

Yet there was a touch of fear behind the satire in its further remark. The prospect of 'boys, whose own ideas are still unsettled' 'beguiling East Enders with the rhodomontade of debating societies' was positively harmful.[92] Toynbee Hall was always to have two kinds of critics – those East Enders who distrusted its presence and those 'West Enders' who both made fun of it and feared that it might succeed.

Barnett, however, was consistent in his purpose. The people he drew to the East End, he reiterated with insistence, came 'not as missioners' but 'to settle, that is, to learn as much as to teach, to receive as much as to give'.[93] And he and Henrietta could be satirical in their own way when they described some of the young ladies who visited Toynbee Hall in its earliest days, 'seeking cultivation' and quoting Browning on all occasions. 'They made one long to shake them', Henrietta wrote, concluding more seriously, 'they killed by bad manners the belief that education made for equality.'[94]

Yet Toynbee Hall easily survived such displays of bad manners. In 1912 Milner, then Viscount Milner, who had expressed doubts about its foundation, was to become Chairman of its Council.

> Knowledge begets sympathy [he told an audience gathered there in December of that year], and sympathy is the golden key which opens a way to the solution of many problems that are a hopeless puzzle to the mere theorist. . . . If our methods of handling economic and social problems have become humanized and promise a richer harvest of results, that change is largely due to the sociological workshops such as this and to the influence of the men who have graduated in them.[95]

3 The building

Toynbee Hall as a building was very different from any other building in its vicinity, and in the year Barnett died – one year after Milner's oration – it was to be described as 'a spot hallowed by wonderful memories'. Through its deliberately dignified form it, too, had its message, as did later Henrietta Barnett's garden suburb. Elijah Hoole, its London architect, envisaged an edifice like 'a manorial residence' in 'nineteenth-century Elizabethan style', although it is fair to add that he had taken an interest earlier in his life in model dwellings for the poor.[96] In fact, the building was influenced most by Oxford and Cambridge colleges, and although it was in red brick and Box stone, it had 'ecclesiastical doors, dog-tooth patterns and mullions' and a quadrangle.[97] It was quite different from the Boys' Industrial School which it replaced.

Pevsner compared it favourably with the 'gloomy and barrack-like' Peabody buildings, and claimed also that it was 'a slight improvement' on the Industrial Buildings in Wentworth Street.[98] Yet he did not comment on its purpose or on its interior. The dining room was decorated by one of the first Residents, C. R. Ashbee, and his class. They painted sunflowers around modelled medallions of a stylised tree, and crests of Oxford and Cambridge colleges. There was also a drawing room where Ashbee was to leave a piano and bookcase in Arts and Crafts style.[99]

The residential accommodation consisted of a number of sets of two rooms and bed sitting rooms, where twenty Residents would live neither in extremes of luxury nor of austerity, but in what Barnett described to his brother as 'space, comfort and quiet'.[100] There were, of course, public rooms also, designed for lectures, classes and social activities.

The buildings were not completed by Christmas Eve 1884, when one of the first

Residents, C. H. Grinling, of Hertford College, slept in Toynbee Hall for the first time, and Barnett was not to move to the Warden's Lodge at the gateway until 1892. Grinling was to stay in the Hall until September 1885, by which time the work was finished and the first tea parties had been held in the drawing room, described by one visitor as 'filled with a strange medley of upholstery', the walls

> hung with Japanese designs of very beautiful creation . . . but somewhat out of keeping with the substantial stone mullions and lattice panes of the windows, hung with heavy, warm-coloured curtains, and fitted with softly cushioned seats, conveniently low.[101]

There was nothing else like this in the East End, not even College Buildings in Wentworth Street (with open corridors leading to small flats, shared lavatories, and no running water in each room). Yet there was far more of a historic heritage than contemporaries – or historians – had usually recognised. In the sixteenth century the area was described as 'a tranquil paradise' with 'plain meadows with brooks running through them'. Stepney had its medieval church, St Dunstan's; the Trinity Almshouses in Mile End Road, planned for '28 decayed masters and commanders of ships or the widows of such', were attractive early seventeenth-century buildings; there were many examples of eighteenth-century building, secular and ecclesiastical, at its best; and among nineteenth-century buildings All Saints, Poplar, must find a place, along with Wilton's Music Hall in Grace Alley, built in 1858.[102] There had been significant changes in use also, reflections of a changing social history. The Église Neuve of the Huguenots, built in 1742, had been let to the Methodists in 1809 and in 1891 became an orthodox 'Spitalfields Great Synagogue'.

Besant left out much of this heritage when he described East London. Different generations, many of them from distant parts of the world and speaking no or little English, were to see it in different ways – or if they were too preoccupied, or too apathetic – not to see it at all, amid all the surrounding squalor. The Jews were the last to arrive before Besant wrote. 'They packed into slums that the British, and even the Irish were trying to quit, and settled into those few occupations that had been sanctioned in the ghetto.'[103]

Yet this was a ghetto that some of them were to come to love, and it was of the literary heritage, not of the architectural heritage, that one grateful Jewish immigrant of the 1930s was to write in a poem, 'Shakespeare and Whitechapel';

The name Shakespeare drew me to London,
When I was a hunted Jew.
A sea-mew in a thick fog
Into the Thames I flew.

A sea-mew in a thick fog,
I flew into London town,
And I found my way to Whitechapel
Which had become my own.[104]

The story of Toynbee Hall, which begins with the Barnetts – and they, too, were immigrants – has this as its setting. The interplay of personalities and ideas would not have been the same at any other time or in any other place.

The building of Toynbee Hall was only the start, however. In 1901 a new 'Whitechapel Art Palace' was opened by Lord Rosebery, the Liberal leader, 'consecrated for all time to the service of popular art'. Another of Barnett's dreams was thereby realised. The *Daily Chronicle* was not alone in contrasting it with 'the bleak, cheerless St Jude's schoolroom', where he had opened an art exhibition arranged by Barnett twenty years before.[105] The school had been taken over in 1893 by the School Board, which gave Barnett the chance to press for a new building, and the new Upper Room was said to be 'one of the very best picture galleries in all London'. 'Life without industry is guilt' was the message on the cover of an early exhibition catalogue, 'Industry without art is brutality'.[106] And so Ruskin was called in to bless one of the first new buildings of the twentieth century. An older guide, Plato, was brought in too. 'The young citizens must not be allowed to grow up amongst images of evil, lest their souls assimilate the ugliness of their surroundings. Rather they should be like men living in a beautiful and healthy place.'[107]

II
Samuel Barnett and his Friends, 1884–1913

Samuel Barnett – Canon Barnett from 1895 – was Warden of Toynbee Hall from its foundation until 1906. During that time he was the inspiration of all the immensely varied activity that went on there. It was his spirit that bonded the equally wide diversity of men and women who made use of the Settlement and that gave unity to the extraordinary diffusion of effort.

Barnett was physically unimpressive, and Beatrice Webb, in a typically unsparing description, portrayed 'a diminutive body clothed in shabby and badly assorted garments . . . small black eyes set close together, sallow complexion, and a thin and patchy pretence of a beard'. Yet even the critical Beatrice was drawn sympathetically to Barnett's questioning mind, 'passing suddenly and unexpectedly into emotional enthusiasm or moral indignation, and then melting back again into the calmness of an argumentative intelligence'. She noted, too, 'an utter absence of personal vanity' in him and 'an almost exaggerated Christian humility'.[1] She may have been attracted, too, by a touch of mysticism in him. In nature, he would say, there is no outline. And in thought there were ideas too large for definition.

Barnett had the great gift of communicating with those who met him not as representatives or as types, but as individuals with special experience, interests, concerns and gifts of their own, whatever their social background; and although he was capable of impressing his listeners when in the pulpit or on the platform, he was at his best not in sermons or in speeches but in one-to-one relationships, as in an Oxford tutorial. The point was made in different language in his obituary in *Stepney Welfare*.

> Living in one of the poorest and most crowded parts of London, he never lost sight of the individual in the mass; he could make his way through the forest, but he thought of the trees; he planned and travelled for a great community, but 'one by one'.[2]

In particular, he set aside time to meet each Resident and Associate of Toynbee Hall individually.

> He never grudged you his time [J. A. Spender, who had been present at the famous meeting in St John's College in 1883, wrote of him]. He never seemed to be bored or tired or superior or condescending. Whatever problem you brought him, whether your private affairs or your tangled thoughts, he gave you the whole of his wise, subtle and original mind.[3]

And it was the mind of a 'seer', the name given to him at Toynbee Hall, so that he could relate his knowledge of people to a vision of a future society, the society that might be.

Harold Spender, J. A. Spender's brother, made a different and perhaps bigger point when he suggested that Barnett's church, which had sent him to Whitechapel in 1873, to Bristol in 1893 and to Westminster in 1906, 'failed to follow or to understand what Barnett tried to do at Toynbee – and outside'. It never 'quite registered'. 'They were shocked at the breadth of his appeal, the fact that he was always seeking a point of unity.' 'Some of them, indeed, did their best to drive him, as they drove Wesley, outside their fold. It was only his own good patience . . . that kept him within.' Barnett was made a Canon, first at Bristol in 1893, where he was able to work while retaining his Wardenship, then at nearby Westminster in 1906, when he became in consequence President of Toynbee Hall, a new office, instead of Warden. The canonries were well deserved. Yet according to Spender, they were not enough. Barnett should have been canonised. 'The Church of England missed one of its great chances. God sent them a St Francis and because he did not wear a cowl and cord they threw him out.'

Meanwhile, Spender went on, with Toynbee Hall as the centre, it was not Churchmen, but 'Statesmen, Civil Servants, Landlords, Journalists and Workmen' who had carried Barnett's teaching into 'practical life'.[4] The first of them to secure a place in the Cabinet was Captain John Sinclair, a regular soldier, later Lord Pentland, who became Secretary of State for Scotland in the Liberal Government formed in 1905 a few months before Barnett ceased to be a Warden. At least one critic of Toynbee, George Lansbury, himself an East Ender – and a Christian Socialist – thought that Barnett's 'picked men', as Spender called them, included too many 'careerists', men who went to the East End full of enthusiasm and zeal for the welfare of the masses and discovered the advancement of their interests.[5] Yet this was far too general a statement, and no-one, including Lansbury, ever said that it applied to Barnett himself.

Unlike most saints, Barnett had a wife. There is a fascinating letter from J. R. Green, Barnett's great predecessor as an East End 'settler', to a close friend, which begins portentously, 'The general question is "What sort of a wife *ought* you to marry?" Without any doubt, one who can sympathise in your pursuits, one who can help you forward in your work.'[6] Henrietta Barnett, no saint herself, was the perfect partner for Samuel, so perfect that he could write to her in 1872, before they were married, that he could not conceive how there could be another woman in the world 'who will so meet my wants and stimulate my powers.' And she could write of him long after his death and after she had finished his biography, 'I have loved living with my husband's spirit as I wrote his life and painted his character.'[7]

Henrietta was not only long to survive her husband – he died in 1913, she in 1936 – but to write this still definitive account of her husband's character and work. By then she deserved a biographer herself, the kind of biographer who would do justice to her as wife and widow; and there were friends, who knowing both Samuel and Henrietta, were well qualified to judge. For Cosmo Lang, then Archbishop Lang, who spoke at her funeral, 'the ideals and plans which glowed in the fervent imagination of the wife were clarified and defined and disciplined as they passed through the mind of the husband,'[8] and he is said to have remarked in private that 'Samuel was but the mouthpiece of Henrietta and had the courage of her opinions'. 'Again and again' wrote T. E. Harvey, Barnett's successor as Warden and one of Henrietta's own friends, on her death – and he had been a pall bearer at Barnett's funeral – 'her insight and her will power harnessed men and women to tasks which would otherwise have been untouched, tasks that needed doing.' Harvey, like Beatrice Webb describing Samuel, began with her physical characteristics – her 'great, grey eyes' and 'her magnetic personality sweeping imperiously in its train the thoughts and wills of young and old'.9

J. J. Mallon, outstanding among twentieth-century Wardens of Toynbee Hall, was to describe the partnership of the Barnetts as 'uniquely suited'.

> For forty years they thought and worked together, stimulating, balancing and supplementing one another, unlike in so many of their most notable qualities, yet with the texture of their life so closely interwoven that their work and ideas belonged each together.10

It is fascinating to compare such a partnership with that of the Webbs, remembering that Beatrice Potter, as she then was, met Barnett before she met either Sidney Webb or Henrietta. Indeed, it was thanks to Barnett that Beatrice began to find her 'way easily in the East End', and it was after talking to him and Henrietta at an autumn lunch in 1885 that she wrote that 'strong women' had a great future between them in the study of social questions: 'they *are not* just inferior men.'11

There was never anything inferior about Henrietta, who loved to speak her own mind; and late in life she presented her own assessment of Toynbee Hall, where men, not women, were the first chosen settlers, at her eighty-first birthday party, complete with cake and eighty-one candles, held in the Hall in 1932. It was an assessment close to that of Harold Spender, pronounced thirteen years before, 'Has the effort failed?' she asked, before giving her own reply. 'Let the answer be in the swarming men now in the high places of this country who owe all their knowledge of the working classes to their Toynbee days. You find them everywhere.'12 By then, however, Henrietta was as much associated in the public mind with Hampstead Garden Suburb as with Whitechapel, and daily life in the East End was a distant memory. Her assessment has what would now be called an 'elitist' flavour about it, and in retrospect she could marvel at her husband's faith when he believed in the possibility of overcoming through education 'the degradation of the majority of the population of our parish'.13

At the time, however, during the early years of Toynbee Hall, the Residents' sense of finding there a 'ladder to future fame' was less strong than their immediate sense of sharing in a broader fellowship; and Henrietta herself was not afraid of being laughed at behind her and her husband's backs for trying to make it possible.14 Gell, then in residence in Toynbee Hall insisted that 'in a democratic country nothing can be achieved except through the masses of the people', and it was his view that the main role of the Residents was to work like a leaven.

> The primary object of Toynbee Hall [he wrote in 1886] is not to collect men together to do a certain piece of work, but rather to live a certain kind of life. The enterprises

of its members may be scattered and various, but their social life is one. . . . The unity at which we aim is the unity of spirit, and diversity of occupations suited to the diverse gifts of its members.[15]

The language, like the image of the leaven, is biblical, and the statistics of early Toynbee Hall reinforced it. Out of the eighty Residents who lived at Toynbee during the first ten years, some staying for a few months, others for years, sixteen were already clergymen, while another became a rabbi. It is significant also that many of the first activities of the settlers followed on without any break in continuity from activities already carried out in the parish of St Jude's.[16] Thus, the annual art exhibitions, for example, continued as before – with exhibitions of photography added – but they attracted a bigger audience – as many as 55,300 in 1886 as compared with 9,000 in 1881 and 20,000 in 1882. The Children's Country Holiday Fund, a favourite idea of Henrietta, gained in strength also with the help of Residents, one of whom became Secretary: over 17,000 children were sent to the country in 1888. And the Shakespeare Society and the Elizabethan Society, the latter originating in a reading party organised by the Reverend W. Bartlett in March 1884, each remained active. They both owed much to Sidney (later Sir Sidney) Lee, who is chiefly remembered by posterity as editor of the *Dictionary of National Biography* in which so many 'Toynbee' names were to figure.

There was one activity which it was easier to organise after the Settlement was opened than it had been in the parish – activity amongst the Jews who were more willing, it was sometimes claimed, to accept the presence of Toynbee Hall than the Christians: 'with us,' Willy Goldman was to write decades later, 'the Rabbis dominated one part of our life as the schoolteacher dominated the other.'[17] Within twenty years of Toynbee Hall's foundation, one quarter of the students there were Jews, and the Jewish presence in Whitechapel seemed established for ever.

One Toynbee Resident in particular, Henry Samuel Lewis, stood out as a friend and advisor of the growing local Jewish community, whether or not they were interested in education. He would meet early mornings in the quadrangle off Toynbee Hall any Jews who were destitute or in distress, and his reputation was such that it was said that among the only intelligible words which newly arrived Jews could utter in the presence of the immigration officers were 'Mester Lewis'. By being a Settlement and not a mission, Toynbee Hall was well equipped to provide indispensable help to uprooted newcomers. Indeed, Barnett was 'firmly opposed not only to the methods employed by conversionist agencies but also to the theory that underlies such efforts'.[18]

The most striking strand of continuity before and after 1884 was in education, although here too a significant increase in scale was associated with a larger vision of what could be done. Already in 1882, Barnett had envisaged 'a kind of East London College', and before and after 1884 he and his colleagues in Whitechapel concentrated – it seemed to them quite natural – first on higher, not on basic, education, and, second, not on vocational or professional education, but on general education. Barnett wanted to 'widen the horizons' of East Enders, not to enable them to adapt to the East End as it was. And he succeeded, even if he never succeeded in turning his college into a 'University of the East End' as some of his students and colleagues wished. It was a student, indeed, who elaborated in 1886 –

in what J. A. R. Pimlott has rightly called 'an almost Wellsian manner' – [19] Barnett's dreams for the future in an article in the *Toynbee Journal and Students' Union Chronicle*, a magazine started in October 1885. Barnett had already produced a leaflet which included the words, 'The ideal of many connected with Toynbee Hall is that it may grow into an East London University,' and looking forward to 1932, the student author enthusiastically set the future scene:

> The old Hall still stands, but around it has been built a circle of university buildings, with dwellings for four hundred students, mostly clerks and workmen from the cooperative factories of the neighbourhood, who usually come here at the age of sixteen and remain here six years. . . . No-one is so poor that he cannot afford the College education; the living is very simple and the food vegetarian. Forty professors and tutors belong to the University. The most different branches are attended to, but a course on citizenship is obligatory.[20]

The author with that genuinely Wellsian confidence in education which was to run through Wells's *Anticipations* (1901), one of his most prophetic books, went on to predict that most of the positions in the national Offices for Statistics, Trade and Agriculture (note the omission of Industry) would be occupied in 1932 by the graduates of the University of East London. Wells would not have approved completely, however, of the Toynbee author including in his 1932 scenario a 'little Gothic chapel' to 'serve for the worship, every evening, of a religion of humanity'. There was a pre-Wells, pre-Barnett, Positivist touch here, reminiscent of the disciple of Auguste Comte, Frederic Harrison, who was himself a regular visitor to Toynbee Hall. In youth he had turned to Manchester: in age he turned to London.

The *Journal* in which the article was written disappeared long before the vision might be realised. Indeed, it disappeared in 1888. Yet its place was taken then by a *Toynbee Record* which, while claiming to be purely domestic, soon included articles on a wide range of subjects as the *Journal* had done. In 1902, for example, there was an article by Barnett called 'A College for the Humanities', the opening sentence of which ran 'Is there anything new?'[21]

By then, 'extension lectures' were not as successful as they had been during the 1880s. First offered in 1877, they continued to present during the 1880s and early 1890s what the Christian socialist F. D. Maurice, founder of the Working Men's College in 1854, had called a union of 'labour and learning'.[22] Indeed, after the founding of Toynbee Hall, the numbers enrolled in them rose dramatically from just over 300 in 1883 to 582 in 1886, largely because the students were now given a 'fixed home'; and by the early 1890s 130 different subjects were being taught in what Charles Booth called 'a very varied bill of fare' and numbers of students reached a peak figure of over 1,000.[23] It was claimed that half the early students were residents of East London and Hackney, 20 per cent from North London, 10 per cent from South East London and 5 per cent from the West. An early *Toynbee Record* described the majority of them as schoolmasters, schoolmistresses and clerks – a familiar clientèle in the history of adult education – and one to whom Barnett attached particular importance although then, as later, pride was taken in the fact that 'there was a considerable and increasing proportion of artisans, especially in science courses.'[24]

In education, as in other activities, the early Toynbee Hall was appealing deliberately 'to the best working men and women . . . leaving it in their hands to transmit ideas worth preserving to those whose habits and thoughts are less in accord with our own';[25] and if there was any elitism it was here, and deliberately here. Yet the idea of a bridge was always more striking within this context than the idea of a ladder.

> No doubt [an early report put it] good work can be and has been done by direct contact with the classes holding the lowest moral standards, but there is a disregard of economy of labour in such dealings, and vitality seems to pass out of the worker so quickly without a corresponding gain.[26]

It was Barnett's hope, from the start, that the Extension students would not be mere passive recipients of knowledge. 'The Warden of Toynbee Hall,' he wrote in the early 1890s, 'is not the Head of an Educational Institute, he is director of enthusiasm disciplined for the service of East London.'[27] An effort was made 'to unite them', therefore, like the Residents, through something of 'a common life', and in 1887 a student's hostel was opened which it was hoped might become the first college where, as in an ideal Oxford, there would be an opportunity for friendship between lecturers and students. They would share both in the learning process and in social life, and they would be called upon to search diligently together for 'a better and nobler interpretation of the principles upon which English society must rest'.[28]

It was within the context of an ideal University geared specifically to the needs of working people in the East End and functioning as the cultural centre of the community, that the first hostel of Toynbee Hall was named Wadham House in honour of Barnett's old Oxford college. It was said to be self-supporting and made no appeal for funds.[29] The second college, opened a year later, was called just as appropriately Balliol House, after the Oxford college most directly involved in Toynbee activities.[30] Thereafter, Barnett hoped, a 'long succession of Colleges' would 'grow up in Whitechapel naturally and to meet a felt need, just as Colleges sprang up at Oxford and Cambridge in the Middle Ages'.[31]

Barnett believed, as did the founders of the Extension Lectures Movement, that the universities of the nineteenth century had deviated from their medieval ideal and had closed their doors to poor students. His university, therefore, was to be 'a great democratic university, as popular and far-reaching as the medieval universities were, when the poor students crowded in thousands round the feet of great scholastic teachers'.[32] It was in the same spirit that at the official opening of Balliol House on 10 March 1891, Asquith, the future Liberal Prime Minister, spoke of the 'democratizing of the Universities', complaining that in the great national institutions of Oxford and Cambridge, which embodied English history, 'learning and culture which were not to be obtained elsewhere . . . had become in time the patrimony of a particular class of society.'[33] Toynbee Hall was not just to be an offshoot of Oxford and Cambridge, therefore. Through its success it was believed that it would highlight the unsatisfactory provision for students in the old universities and remind them of their original purpose and function.

If Oxford and Cambridge had lost sight of their ideal, most of the Board School teachers who went through 'training' had, in Barnett's opinion, been given no ideal at all to hold before them: they had been drilled rather than inspired to learn. For this reason elementary school teachers who were also students played a key role in Barnett's educational strategy. He called them 'true leaders of the people' and in another place 'men and women to whom is entrusted the power once held by priests'. Many of them, he insisted, had not even received a proper training. He objected strongly to the limited modes of their preparation to be teachers, which he called 'a never ending and monstrous round of cramming', and urged that they should not be taught in monotechnic colleges but in universities.[34]

As early as 1883, he had written to L. R. Phelps, a Fellow and later Provost of Oriel, and an old friend of Toynbee, asking him to extend an invitation from his college to a group of pupil teachers from East London, and the idea was put into practice by Balliol in 1885, when groups of pupil teachers were enabled to spend two or three weeks of their summer vacation at the college. They are said to 'have thrown themselves heart and soul into the work'.[35] Barnett was not content, however, with mere 'peeps behind the curtain' and successfully supported the establishment of Day Training Colleges at universities (with the help of A. H. D. Acland, former Bursar of Balliol, who won a Liberal seat at the election of 1885).[36] He also organised appeals to raise money for scholarships for pupil teachers to attend them. All in all, eighty pupil teachers were assisted to go to Oxford and Cambridge between 1892 and 1903.[37]

There were many testimonials to the early Extension Lecture Classes and the activities associated with them. The bookbinder, Frederick Rogers, for example, the workingman who had become Secretary of the local Extension Centre in 1878 and who had addressed a meeting at St John's College, Oxford, in 1883, had particular praise, like many of his fellow students, for S. R. Gardiner, who lectured in political and social history.[38] J. M. Dent, who was eventually to publish books, not just to bind them, first attended classes in 1886 and was, in his own words, 'literally lifted into a heaven beyond my dreams'. 'My whole being,' he went on, 'had been transformed.'[39] It was under the influence of his Toynbee Hall experience that Everyman's Library was to be launched, after careful planning in 1906, when no fewer than 152 volumes were published.[40]

A fascinating third testimonial was collected by J. J. Mallon in 1945. John Fox (later Sir John Jacob Fox CB FRS DSc), the son of Russian Jewish immigrants of the East End, then an office boy, started studying at Toynbee Hall at the age of 16 in 1890, his first encounter with science, while his brother Robert was listening keenly to the historian Oscar Browning, another Toynbee lecturer.[41] It was one of the first 'settlers', E. B. Sargant, who had started lectures on electricity on Sunday mornings in 1885, a change from such subjects as 'The Intuitions of Ordinary Life', 'What is the Connection between Morality and Metaphysics?' and 'Schemes for Bettering the Relations between Capital and Labour'. There was, in fact, a very wide repertoire of lecturers, with political economy to the forefront as Toynbee would have wished.

In order to stimulate the intellectual interests of the Extension students and to enlarge their experience, overseas expeditions were organised. Barnett himself was a great believer in the educational value of travel, and in August 1887 a small party of eight students, the first of the so-called 'Toynbee pilgrims', paid a short visit to Belgium. The following Easter, a further party of eighty-one, led by Bolton King, a Mazzini enthusiast, who had been the

Secretary of the Oxford Committee which brought Toynbee Hall into existence, paid a short visit to Florence. Many of the members of the party were schoolmasters and schoolmistresses in elementary schools who had never been abroad before; some of them were clerks or civil servants, usually tied to their desks.[42] While on their journey, which included Antwerp, Brussels, Lucerne, Milan, Pisa and Florence, they were seen in Venice (under the care of 'a deaf old female chaperone') by John Addington Symonds, historian of the Renaissance. He observed that while they looked 'very sleepy after a long day's sightseeing' they were 'creditable to England, expressive of English force and grit'.[43]

Thomas Okey, a Spitalfields basket maker, who went on to become the first Professor of Italian at Cambridge,[44] was one of the key figures in the group, which acquired the title of the Travellers' Club in 1889 and which had as its aims the planning of an annual expedition, the organisation of related lectures, and the collection of associated books, articles and photographs. 'Its objects,' the Club stated firmly, 'are educational, not merely to promote pleasant trips,' and its basis was 'mutual helpfulness'.[45] Spain and Germany were among the countries visited by the end of the century, with required preparation for the former visit including the reading of some fifty books in Spanish and English, including *The Bible in Spain* as well as *Don Quixote*, and for the latter James Bryce's *Holy Roman Empire*. Bryce, a keen traveller himself, was a friend of Barnett – and of T. H. Green – and Liberal MP for Tower Hamlets, the local constituency when Toynbee Hall was founded.

Given the amount of reading required of the students, not all of whom attended the Extension classes, they must have been 'very sleepy' even before they left the country, but for most of them the visits made everything worth while. And action often followed travel. Dent, for example, was so impressed by Florence, 'a city built before industrialisation had destroyed a whole spirit of beauty', that he planned a whole series of volumes on medieval towns.[46]

Greece was visited in 1894, a difficult trip to plan, and Iceland, favourite haunt of William Morris, in 1896; and in 1902 a Workmen's Travelling Club was founded – with cheap fares – the forerunner of the Workers' Travel Association.[47] It was open only to members of trade unions, co-operative societies and friendly societies, and while its visits were necessarily of short duration the importance to workers of knowledge of the world and of its past, as well as of its present, was stressed on every occasion.[48]

Knowledge – and sympathy – could be advanced by debate as well as by travel and in small discussion groups as well as in formal classes; and it was with Barnett's blessing that a whole range of societies chose Toynbee Hall as their rendez-vous – among them the East London Antiquarian Society, the Philosophical Society, the Toynbee Hall Natural History Club, which itself planned excursions, and the Adam Smith Club, 'which humbly aims at the recall of economic principles from those outer spheres of Jupiter and Saturn to which ardent reformers would needlessly banish them'.[49] Toynbee, who once wrote that 'the bitter argument between economists and human beings has ended in the conversion of the economists', would certainly have approved.[50]

The clubs often attracted distinguished lecturers, and so also on Saturday nights did the Hall as a whole. 'Popular Lectures' held there then drew in large audiences, mainly of working men. So, too, did Thursday Smoking Conferences, when, it was claimed, 'permission to smoke . . . enjoyed by the large majority' helped 'doubtless to keep us all on a more friendly and familiar footing'.[51] They had their origins in a club organised by James Bryce when he fought and won the Tower Hamlets constituency in 1880. From the start in social debate there was some difficulty in getting 'the Conservative view of political questions fairly advocated, the bulk of the audience being Radical in sympathies'.[52]

There was no doubt, however, about the variety of lecturers and debaters. Margaret Nevinson, a Toynbee supporter, who with her husband had answered Barnett's appeal to take up residence in Whitechapel, recalled later how

> all the most eminent in literature, art and politics came to pour their wisdom to the poor of Whitechapel: Leslie Stephen, Arthur Sidgwick . . . Henry Sidgwick, Charles Booth etc. and had often the pleasure of meeting them at Toynbee Hall. Other celebrants [*sic*] of the day to be met there were Mrs Humphrey Ward, Holman Hunt . . . and the doomed Oscar Wilde.[53]

She might have added the Dean of Westminster, the lawyer A. V. Dicey, the young and ambitious Liberal politicians Asquith and Haldane, and the socialist Tom Mann.

Not all Toynbee Hall activities were educational, however. The Residents were drawn at once into local community life, and by 1889 six of them were managers of elementary schools, one was a Poor Law Guardian, four were serving on committees of the Charity Organisation Society, one was Secretary to a Sanitary Aid Sub-committee, three were on and involved with an important friendly society, the Ancient Order of Foresters. Some of them were participating in more than one such activity.

The Sanitary Aid Committee is said to have achieved 'the removal of a number of specific nuisances' – Residents made good sanitary inspectors – and to have promoted 'greater vigilance both on the part of the landlords and of the local authorities with regard to the condition of tenement houses'.[54] Of secondary importance, however, it was claimed that it had provided Residents with 'the opportunity of becoming acquainted with the lives of the people and of entering into friendly relations with them'. Practical action included the forming of a company to build a block of flats 'with some regard to beauty'.[55] Paradoxically perhaps, despite this flat phrase, environmental questions seemed easier to tackle than education, and it was not until 1891 that two Residents were elected to the one statutory educational authority in the area, the London School Board. J. Murray Macdonald, later MP for East Falkirk Burghs, failed in 1885 although the full weight of a Barnett Committee was placed behind him. His leaflets, prepared in Toynbee Hall, demanded secondary education, better training of teachers, night classes in Board Schools and, at the same time, 'economy in management'.[56]

The failure led Barnett to start an Education Reform League, seeking to improve the quality of elementary education, and in 1885 one of the Residents, E. B. Sargant, organised a Pupil Teachers' Association setting out to give this important group improved facilities both for education and for recreation. The language of the latter Association revealed the sources of inspiration – 'by the agencies of cricket, rowing, and debating clubs, to kindle amongst them [the pupil teachers] that *esprit de corps* which so strengthens the *morale* of our higher public schools'. The italics were Gell's.[57] Yet this was more than rhetoric. In

1892 funds were raised (with Dr Percival of Rugby School as one of the sponsors) for pupil teachers' scholarships to Oxford and Cambridge. Twelve were chosen, of whom ten, somewhat surprisingly, went to Cambridge. A year later the Drapers' Company provided another six scholarships. The examination consisted of an English essay and, forbiddingly, translation at sight from Greek and later authors, and the examiner was Oscar Browning.

Browning, whose biography has recently appeared, was never a Resident at Toynbee. Nor does he seem to have been a member of the Association. Yet Residents were always at the centre of the stage and Associates were always in the wings.

The average stay for a Resident at Toynbee during the early period of its history was two to three years, although some stayed considerably longer. Bolton King, a founder member and energetic University Extension Lecturer, stayed for seventeen years, while Henry Ward, a batchelor, who arrived in 1886 – reputedly for a weekend – stayed at Toynbee for thirty. He was an engineer, and after his election to the LCC in 1891 went on to become Vice-Chairman in 1906. He was a great benefactor, and gave no less than £100,000 to the London Hospital on condition that strict anonymity was preserved. Yet after he left Toynbee Hall he was very well known for his superb Rolls Royce which was often commandeered by Barnett.

The idea of Residency remained crucial. There were to be 'relays of men arriving year by year from the Universities in London to study for the professions or to pursue their independent interests there, free from the ties of later life'; and whatever their dissimilarities, they were expected to be 'possessed by the common desire to share their good things with their neighbours'. The Associates, who were to back them up, were elected by the Warden and the Residents.[58]

The ideal of participatory citizenship influenced the internal government of Toynbee Hall itself. The Residents set up a Grand Committee, which considered all issues, big or small, relating to the life of the Hall, including membership, for which the necessary qualification was three months' residence, followed in this case also by election by the Committee. It has been claimed that during Barnett's Wardenship there were only two issues on which the Warden and the Committee disagreed – Sunday tennis and dancing. A ban was put on both. In such circumstances the Council of the Hall was of relatively minor importance, although it included influential names and was presided over until 1897 by Gell. In any case, Barnett's opinion there was always decisive, and it was firmly stated in the twelfth *Annual Report* that it had been 'the glory of Mr Gell's reign that the powers of the Council have been so rarely exercised and that the position of the Settlement is in all ways so strong'.[59]

One interesting early Resident who did not fit easily into the pattern was C. R. Ashbee, remembered in history as architect, designer and writer, and the founder of the Guild of Handicraft in 1888. Ashbee arrived at Toynbee Hall two years earlier 'as a sop to my own conscience', from King's College, Cambridge, and at once resented the Oxonian 'lordly charm' of the Sub-Warden, Thory Gardiner, who had been Barnett's Curate of St Jude's: 'your Balliol man looks down upon King's much as King's looks down upon the rest of the world.' Yet Ashbee was happy at first, far from 'the quagmires of Society', and liked both Barnett and Toynbee as people, and it was not until the following year, after he had set up the School of Handicraft there, that he left Toynbee Hall to forge his own life in quite different places.[60]

Ashbee made fun of the 'broadness' or the eclecticism of Toynbee Hall and the attempt to associate people of different persuasions, 'saints' and 'sinners':

> Yes, mingle here those elements so contrary,
> The man of Balliol and the missionary,
> Two full-blown curates shall adorn my page
> Three crawling in the caterpillar stage
> Now mortals like ourselves, but soon to shine
> In cope and cassock, each a Broad divine
> True to this doctrine (if they know no other)
> Don't hurt the feelings of your Skeptic brother.
> Drop not a word that might be thought unpleasant
> By those who follow Comte or Mrs Besant.[61]

Years later, after his own Guild, a very different institution, had folded in 1907, he was to write a novel, *The Building of Thelema*, in which he recalled Toynbee Hall tea parties 'where everybody is invited and everybody comes' and 'everybody always does the wrong thing'. For him, such teas were Punch and Judy shows, and Barnett, the Rev. Simeon Flux, a dubious prophet when he preached that while there were many religions there was only one mortality.[62] Yet years later still, Ashbee made his peace with Toynbee Hall, and that is why a piano, a present to his wife, still stands in the dining room.

A vivid, if chronologically somewhat unreliable, account of early Toynbee Hall has been given by a man who was an Associate, not a Resident, the journalist Henry W. Nevinson, in his reminiscences *Last Changes, Last Chances*. Nevinson had briefly been a member of F. D. Hyndman's recently founded Social Democratic Federation before he joined the Barnetts, but he disliked its doctrinal basis. 'Toynbee Hall,' he wrote years later, 'promised better. It was not hampered by theories, and it appealed to a more cultivated intelligence. Of course, in those early days, it was the scene of some absurdity and some self-righteousness.' This was 'not so much among the inmates or neighbours', he went on, living like himself in Petticoat Lane 'among bugs, fleas, old clothes, slippery cods' heads and other garbage'. It was rather among 'the solemn people who came down to encourage our "noble enterprise"' and talked pompously about 'shedding the light of University teaching among "the dark places of the world"'. Nevinson himself held readings in Milton's *Paradise Lost*, to which large numbers of men and women came 'all the way from dull and deserving districts' (like Dalston Junction and Hackney Marshes) to attend.[63]

Nevinson's comments on other lecturers at Toynbee are as vivid as Beatrice Webb's pen portraits. Gardiner was 'one of the ugliest men ever seen. A face like an old fox . . . coat and trousers bagged and bulged in every curve or angle; but within it all the calmest, gentlest soul, and the humblest.' Grant Allen was 'all sugar. He had a lot to say and says it well; is more tolerant of contradiction than most.' Walter Pater is 'sturdier than I expected, with the look of a French colonel in face and bearing. . . . Whilst reading he shut his eyes when a common lecturer would have looked at the audience.' Philip Wickstead, who developed a theory of value different from that of Marx and Mill, was 'excellent on Dante, and, I suppose, quite as good on economics, though I never understood his doctrine'. 'Henry Nettleship of Oxford . . . could be modest in Latin, and while crossing crowded Bishopgate with me continued to argue the extreme uncertainty of immortality.'[64]

Few writers could have ensured the immortality of the people they were describing as firmly as Nevinson. And two years before the great Dock Strike of 1889, 'the fight for the docker's tanner', a fight into which Toynbee Hall was drawn inevitably, he colourfully described Beatrice Webb (then Beatrice Potter) and how he went with her to the docks to witness the routine struggle for work outside the dock gates:

> May 11, 1887: At Cartwright Buildings by 7.15. Met Miss Potter and Miss Pycroft, with a man who had dropped from policeman to dock labourer for one small slip. He showed us the dock labourers going into London Dock; the clanging bell, the chain, the police, the ticket-holders, the short struggle for the two vacancies, the following search for work, down to the cage, a large enclosed shed, where casuals wait till two o'clock on the chance of an odd job. Out of the 100 or so, generally two are taken on. When one of the turned-away began to lament his lot to us, the others shut him up sharp. They say the strong men often get the tickets and sell them for two pence each. One threw his hat at the distributor, otherwise there was no violence. Talked a good deal to Miss Potter, and again was forced to marvel at that clear analytic mind. 'The province of the statistician', she said, 'is to establish empirical laws, of the personal observer ultimate laws. The social observer should have no prepossessions,' (I think that was the word) 'but should collect from the statistician and personal observer, such as School Board people or rent-collectors, and build his laws by help of imagination from cases he has himself inspected.'

'I am afraid there is something a little hard about it all,' Nevinson wrote. 'Unhappily, man has bowels of compassion, and the individual case appeals so much more to compassion than an undefined and unimaginable "class".'[65]

The final Nevinson contrast is related to the difference between what has been called a Beatrice Webb view of society – and the possibilities of transforming society through national policy – and an Octavia Hill view of society, which looks less to fundamental change in structure or policy than to mediatory action based on detailed and direct knowledge of 'problem' individuals and families. 'Massing people together', according to Helen Bosanquet, made it more difficult to understand their needs.[66] Because of its strategic position in the East End and its links with Westminster and Whitehall, Toynbee Hall was at the centre of argument about the practical implications of such a difference of approach, and there was never unanimity. There were always some Residents at the Hall who were more in sympathy with the Webbs; and Barnett himself, who in the late 1880s was becoming impatient with some of the 'impossible' Charity Organisation Society folk . . . who were 'refusing to do anything except to clothe themselves in the dirty rags of their own rightness',[67] described an interesting Poor Law Conference held in April 1890 when 'Sidney Webb and sixteen others' pressed for a well considered measure 'to provide for the aged and sick'.[68]

In 1887, when Nevinson wrote, Beatrice Potter was working ardently for Charles Booth; and both Booth's personal connection with Toynbee Hall and the Dock Strike of 1889 must figure prominently in Toynbee Hall's history. For Beatrice, who responded willingly to his challenge, Booth was 'perhaps the most perfect embodiment of the mid-

Victorian spirit – the union of faith in the scientific method with the transference of the emotion of self-sacrificing from God to Man',[69] and through Booth both the renown and the status of Toynbee Hall were greatly raised.

Although Barnett is said to have begun by 'pouring cold water' on Booth's project, saying first that it would be impossible to collect the information which Booth was seeking and, second, that if it were to be collected there would be doubts about its value, as early as 1888 the *Annual Report* of Toynbee Hall referred to Booth's investigation as a 'bold experiment'. It also noted the contribution made to the investigation – an account of the furniture trade – by Ernest Aves, a Toynbee Hall Resident, and praised 'the attempt to render the Hall more and more a repository of systematical facts, relating to the complex life and varied social and economic problems that East London presents'.[70] In 1889 it referred to what might be called Booth's 'instantaneous photograph of the 908,000 inhabitants of East London' and praised the way in which he had made 'the dry figures live by descriptive matter and special articles'.[71]

Barnett developed his own opinions in the light of this changing experience. In 1895, for example, he emerged openly as a 'friendly critic' of the Charity Organisation Society and attached far more importance in public thereafter to the role of the State, leaving far behind him Herbert Spencer's *Man versus the State* which had appeared in the year when Toynbee Hall was founded.[72] Behind the scenes, of course, he had often been more blunt, referring earlier in that very same year to 'the chaff of the clumsy methods of the Charity Organisation Society'.[73] He distinguished sharply between the different causes of poverty, too, drawing attention to the consequences of unemployment and old age. To deal with the former he advocated State intervention, including training farms, and to deal with the latter he was at one with Booth in demanding old age pensions. He even had the temerity to ask – in defiance of all the logic of the COS – 'Is thrift always so virtuous?'[74]

Not surprisingly, when he asked such tantalising questions, he incurred the terrifying wrath of C. S. Loch, who now described him, not without justification, as 'a declared opponent to the whole policy of the Society', of which he still remained a member.

> With Mr. Barnett [Loch told a COS meeting] progress is a series of reactions. He must be in harmony with the current philanthropic opinion of the moment or perhaps just a few seconds ahead of it. . . . He sails close to the philanthropic winds . . . having changed once or more than once he may yet change again.[75]

It was an unfair verdict, given that Barnett not only deliberately chose to remain for the whole of his life a member of the Whitechapel COS Committee, but encouraged Residents to be associated with it. Moreover, as a Poor Law Guardian he stood behind the policy of refusing outdoor relief, not, however, on deterrent grounds. Indeed, if Loch complained of Barnett's change of position, Barnett in turn complained of the rigidity of the COS, as did the economist Alfred Marshall, an Associate of Toynbee Hall, who in his evidence to the Royal Commission on the Aged Poor, set up in 1893, accused its members of belonging to 'the old world'. 'Their basis consists exclusively of those people who used to be the governing classes but are not the governing classes now.'[76]

Marshall put his hopes in the improvement of 'the vast masses of men who, after long hours of hard and unintellectual toil, are wont to return to their homes with bodies exhausted and with minds dull and sluggish'. And Barnett was a source of inspiration for him.

The *Toynbee Record* for 1913 summed up Barnett's style as well as his change of stance.

> The intensity of his sense of what was right and just never made him intolerant or self-assertive and when criticism exposed weakness in his plans or methods, and when he felt that the old plans and methods had served their purpose, he was always ready, as he said, to lead a revolution against himself.[77]

Loch was never so prepared, although by 1913 when he attended Barnett's funeral he had seen all his own remedies castigated.

By then, too, a new Labour Party had 79 MPs at Westminster. As early as 1899 Barnett had noted that there was no longer 'the old demand for University leaders', that there was 'a vast increase in the supply of other teaching', and that 'the relation of workmen to society has changed, and things are new.' 'There is nothing harder for us old pilots,' he went on, 'than to give up the old methods, but I am sure it must be done.'[78] Two years earlier still, he had also told his brother that he suspected that Christ would appear 'out of the Nazareth of secularism rather than out of the Jerusalem of the Church'.[79]

It is not surprising, therefore, that in 1902 he wrote to his brother that it was possible to detect 'under the dark surface of working-class opinion . . . the forces [that were] to rule the future',[80] and two years later he was complaining that 'the Liberal Party had nothing to offer'.[81] Indeed, just before the great Liberal victory at the 1906 General Election, a victory which brought the new Labour Party to national prominence for the first time, he observed that the 'Liberal Party' had grown old and that men like Bryce and Asquith, his old friends, to whom he had hitherto looked, seemed 'worn and weary'.[82] He did not appreciate at that time, of course, that within less than three years Asquith would be Prime Minister, nor, perhaps, that when his own obituary notices were being written the *Nation* would describe him [Barnett] as 'the most representative Liberal of his time'.[83]

Interest in independent Labour politics was slower to develop than interest in other branches of the labour movement, although it was significant that the first Chairman of the Labour Representation Committee set up in 1900 was one of the first Toynbee Hall supporters – Frederick Rogers, then a member of the LCC. It was inevitable, however, that situated as it was, Toynbee would be drawn not only into its discussion of working-class issues but into the disputes which went with them. It was important, just because of this that it was not tied to any political group. Indeed, its non-political alignment made it an invaluable forum. The point often had to be stressed, as in 1898, when Lord Salisbury referred disparagingly to the 'advanced opinions' of Toynbee Hall.

> The place has not gone uncriticized [wrote Barnett in the *Report* on that year], but no one with any knowledge of it, be he crusted Tory who is inclined to shout 'Dangerous', or impatient Socialist who is ready to shout 'Rosewater for the Plague!' can with truth level against it the charge of having been sensational, extreme or partisan.

The first Residents of Toynbee Hall
Front Row (*on ground*): T. G. Gardiner,
E. B. Sargant, T. H. Nunn, R. N. Blandy
Middle Row: Bolton King, Mrs Barnett,
S. A. Barnett, R. E. Mitcheson, C. H. Grinling,
G. Parker
Back Row: H. G. Rawson, V. A. Boyle,
J. Murray Macdonald, B. Whishaw, (name
unknown)

Barnett's friends: *centre*, The Reverend W. Robinson, Dean of Balliol House;
clockwise, starting at top, Harold Spender, G. L. Bruce, H. Llewellyn Smith, Frederick Rogers, Harry Ward, Bolton
King

Programme.

* * *

From 7.45 to 8.30.

Drawing Room	Reception by Canon and Mrs Barnett.

Exhibits.

Lecture Hall	Illustrations of Spanish Art.	*(Mainly from The South Kensington Museum.)*
Dining Room	Toynbee Travellers' Club.	Photographs, &c.
Balliol House *(Common Room)*	Collections made by the Members of the Toynbee Natural History Society.	
New Block (Room B)	The Year's Work of the Sketching Club.	
Exhibition Buildings *(First Floor)*	Nursing and Ambulance.	Arranged by the Toynbee Nursing Guild and the St. John's Ambulance Association.

* * *

Special Fixtures.

8.30	(a) Ambulance Display	On the Tennis Court.
	(b) Exhibition of Lantern Slides	New Block, Room A.
8.45	Musical Drill by a Squad from the Old Northwiches' Club.	In the Quadrangle.
9.0	Exhibition of Lantern Slides	New Block, Room A.
9.30	(a) Ambulance Display	On the Tennis Court.
	(b) Exhibition of Lantern Slides	New Block, Room A.
9.45	Musical Drill by a Squad from the Old Rutlanders' Club.	In the Quadrangle.
Occasionally	Echoes from Past Times by The Phonograph	Wadham House. *(Common Room.)*
"	Demonstrations of The New Photography *(Röntgen Rays)*	Exhibition Buildings *(First Floor.)*
Library.	Laboratories.	Wadham and Balliol Houses.

* * *

Music.   Refreshments.

* * *

TOYNBEE LITERARY ASSOCIATION.

SESSION, 1897-98.

The Literary Studies Sub-Committee request the pleasure of your Company at the Opening Meeting of the Toynbee Literary Association, to be held at Toynbee Hall, on Tuesday, October 12th, 1897, when Mr. J. C. BAILEY will deliver an address on

"SIR WALTER SCOTT,"

to be followed by songs and recitations from his works, given by friends of the Association.

Refreshments, 8 p.m.   Address, 8.30 p.m.   Songs, etc., 9 p.m.

FUTURE ARRANGEMENTS:

Nov. 9th.—"Shakespeare" Evening. Programme by Members of Toynbee Shakespeare Society.

Dec. 14th.—Social Evening.

A. C. HAYWARD, *Hon. Sec.*

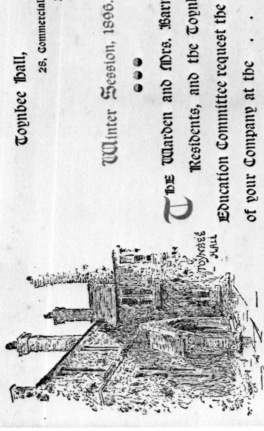

Toynbee Hall,
28, Commercial Street,
E.

Winter Session, 1896.

* * *

The Warden and Mrs. Barnett, the Residents, and the Toynbee Hall Education Committee request the pleasure of your Company at the · · · ·

Opening + Conversazione,

On Saturday, October 3rd.

7.45 to 10.30.

FOR PROGRAMME SEE OVER.

TOYNBEE HALL,
28, COMMERCIAL STREET,
WHITECHAPEL, E.

SUNDAY EVENING LECTURES.

SUNDAY, MARCH 7th, 1897.

GREAT REFORMERS IN CHURCH & STATE:

"John Wesley,"

BY

AUGUSTINE BIRRELL, Q.C., M.P.

COMMENCE AT EIGHT.

ADMIT BEARER.   *Residents and admitted males in a course of Addis.*

TOYNBEE HALL,
28, COMMERCIAL STREET, WHITECHAPEL, E.

SATURDAY POPULAR LECTURES.

SATURDAY EVENING, DECEMBER 11th, 1897.

"THE MAGIC MIRROR,"

BY

Professor SILVANUS THOMPSON, D.Sc., F.R.S.

ADMIT BEARER.   COMMENCE AT EIGHT

The men's nursing class

The chemistry class

The Toynbee Hall Orchestra

Thomas Okey's Italian class

The Toynbee Hall Library which later formed the core of the National Central Library

Residents of Balliol House, a Hall for students. Barnett is in the middle of the second row. Morant, then Censor of Studies at Balliol House, is the tallest figure in the third row

Balliol House

The Match Girls, whose strike in 1888 won the sympathy and support of leading Toynbee Residents

The fight for the dockers' tanner: the Great Dock Strike of 1889

Outdoor activities in the
quadrangle: Henrietta
Barnett at the 1897 Jubilee
Flower Show. There were
9,000 visitors in two days.

An evening concert, 1900

Asquith unveiling a
Herkomer portrait of
Henrietta and Samuel
Barnett in 1908

There were 'many minds at work in many directions', but 'one heart'.[84]

Co-operation was the first working-class cause to appeal to the heart of Toynbee Hall and to be received sympathetically there. As early as 1887, indeed, Edward Greening, who believed in co-operative production as well as in co-operative distribution, paid a warm tribute to 'friends from the Working Men's College and Toynbee Hall' who looked to 'the older Co-operators for advice'.[85] A fire at the premises of the Co-operative Wholesale Society, by destroying the large board-room, had left London Co-operators without a suitable place for meetings in London and had given Toynbee Hall the opportunity of lending them its lecture-room for meetings and its drawing-room for tea. And there, month by month, Residents could meet, if they wished, 'representatives of "the aristocracy of the working-classes" from all parts of England'.[86]

There had long been links between Christian Socialists and Co-operators, and it was Acland, who had organised an important Co-operative Conference held in Oxford in 1882, which introduced Oxford dons to Northern Co-operators. It was he, too, who introduced Benjamin Jones, the leading London Co-operator, to Barnett. He became a Toynbee Associate in 1886, and thereafter, particular attention was paid by Toynbee Hall to persuading the London Co-operators to devote greater attention to the educational side of their movement through classes held both in Toynbee Hall and at the headquarters of the Co-operative Wholesale Society in Leman Street. In the 1889 *Annual Report*, for example, we read of a 'valuable series of conferences' which had been held during the past winter, 'at which members of various trades' had learnt, 'not only more of the Co-operative idea, but also of the difficulties that their forerunners had had to meet and which they themselves must be prepared to face'.[87]

Cigar-makers, stick and cane-dressers and cabinet-makers were among the trades attending these meetings, and in 1888 a Co-operative Aid Association, was launched with a view to providing loans for co-operative production societies in the East End, some of them associated with groups who belonged not to 'the aristocracy of labour' but to unorganised and exploited production. This was a distinctive Toynbee Hall venture. So, too, was an exhibition of co-operative products organised at Lord Aberdeen's house. The fact that co-operative production was not in general successful for long – only the Bass Dressers, founded in 1889, was to survive – was less important than the fact that through this activity Toynbee Hall was drawn not only into education – or research – but into action.

As Toynbee Hall became the meeting place of occupational unions like the Co-operative Bass Dressers, the Stick Makers, the Boot Makers, the Cigar Makers and the Mantle Makers, it was inevitable that it would be drawn into the industrial disputes resulting from the first attempts by previously unorganised workers in these trades, to achieve acceptable working conditions. It was not only that the Toynbee Hall Council was 'glad to offer them rooms for their meetings'.[88] It helped them also to shape their strategies, and to appeal to a sympathetic public.

The case of the Stepney Bass Dressers illustrates the sort of trying struggle with which Toynbee Hall Residents felt that they must identify themselves in a period when the boundaries between co-operation and trade unionism were sometimes blurred. Bass is a fibre used in making ropes and brooms, and the dressers had a hot and nasty occupation.

They had taken a workshop in Stepney, in which ten of them were employed, and their Masters who had tried to lock them out were forced to give way as soon as the Co-operative Society appeared in the field and to allow the men to return to work with an increase of 20 per cent on their previous wages.

> The Masters who were most resolute in refusing to employ 'union' men a couple of months back are now seeking for labourers in vain [The Hall reported]. . . . The Bass Dressers' Workshop shows how co-operation and trade-unionism may work together for their mutual advantage. A supper was subsequently held for the Bass Dressers at Toynbee Hall rather to celebrate a victory than for mutual encouragement in their contest.[89]

Some of the best-known Toynbee Residents, like Vaughan Nash and Llewellyn Smith, who arrived there in 1888, began to devote their attention more widely to the organisational activities and struggles of the trade and benefit societies in East London. And once again the timing was ripe. More trade-union banners were made in 1889 in an East End Workshop specialising in their production than in any other year in history.[90]

The matchgirls' strike of 1888 came first. Matchgirls had been described by Dickens as 'the worst of the ill-paid workers in the East', yet in a more recent article they had been called 'very industrious and remarkably well behaved' as well as happy.[91] They were, in fact, miserably paid and subject to dangerous conditions of work; and terrifying 'phossy-jaw' gave its name to the fiery dispute which started in 1888 after four girls who had described their pay and work to Annie Besant, the social reformer, were dismissed from their jobs.[92] Three Residents of Toynbee Hall, Llewellyn Smith, A. P. Laurie and A. G. L. Rogers, and one Associate, A. S. Stevenson, set up an independent enquiry of their own and wrote three highly influential letters to *The Times*. The girls, they pointed out, 'receive during a great part of the year a wage so small as to be totally insufficient to maintain a decent subsistence'. Yet

> even the question of low wages, important as it is, is but a part of the wide question of the whole relation between employers and employees. . . . To say nothing of the want of sympathy which we have observed on the part of the directors, and the dislike and fear on the part of the girls, the present strike offers unanswerable evidence of the deplorable conditions which exist in the factory.[93]

The last of these letters appeared on the day the dispute terminated – following the intervention of the London Trades Council. It was a victory for the matchgirls which, in Annie Besant's words, 'far exceeded expectations',[94] although disputes in the trade were by no means over.

The dockers' strike of 1889 had quite different characteristics. This was a year of relative prosperity, and though the dockers' claims were modest – 'the dockers' tanner', a minimum wage of sixpence an hour – they were in a far better position to back them up than the matchgirls. Indeed, two years earlier their claims had been put forward eloquently by Ben Tillett in an address significantly called. when published, *A Dock Labourer's Bitter Cry*.[95]

Barnett was in Switzerland with the Toynbee Travel Club when the strike started, but he returned instantly. 'My feelings are with the men,' he wrote to his brother, 'but how to give these feelings expression is more than I know.'[96] In fact, his feelings were already well known, for in articles and sermons he had frequently challenged critics of trade unionism with hard-hitting frankness.

> The workmen through the Trade Unions are said to sacrifice the common interest to that of their class interest [he had noted]. They raise wages, careless as to whether trade suffers, and . . . 'go easily' . . . limit the output regardless of the loss of wealth incurred. Such criticism might sometimes [he admitted] be well-founded, but the same charge could be made on like grounds against other classes. Capitalists form trusts and provide companies which for their own people raise the price of the necessities of life against workmen – professional men refuse to take work unless others of the same profession are also employed – a barrister will not see a client unless a solicitor is first consulted. . . . In all these instances classes, other than the industrial classes, put their own interest before the common interest.[97]

Why should working men to whom solidarity was a necessary ideal be lampooned by other groups for whom it was not? Barnett's attitude to the strike, supported by the *Church Times*, was less patronising, therefore, than that of the socialist H. M. Hyndman, who conceived of this and similar disputes as 'unconscious strugglings towards socialism'.[98]

As far as the facts themselves were concerned, Barnett had often argued forcefully against the prevalent system of 'casual' labour, both in the docks and elsewhere, describing it as 'the hardest problem of East London'.[99] Moreover, he believed that it would be impossible to raise the quality of life in East London so long as it persisted. 'East London,' the *Toynbee Record* complained, 'is more a labour warehouse than most places.' 'A glance at it is sufficient to show that it is primarily a labour receptacle, and life in it makes it clear that only by an after thought and half-heartedly is it a community.' For this very reason, the *Record* went on,

> the workmen's associations deserve the warm support and sympathy of all those who are concerned for our civic life, since their influence cannot fail to arouse and keep up the public spirit for which the dry bones of municipal London have waited so long. Arnold Toynbee's appeal to co-operators to apply themselves to the education comes with peculiar force to every detachment of the industrial army in this city of many inhabitants and few citizens.[100]

Once the strike began, several Toynbee Residents and Associates, including Nash, Llewellyn Smith, Rogers, and A. P. Laurie, who had just moved (with Barnett's blessing) to a house in Stepney Green, offered their assistance to the dockers without reserve, assistance which was gratefully received. And already by then they were trusted. There was 'no high-brow condescension' in their dealings, Tom Mann, the Labour leader, recalled in his memoirs. 'Quite a number of young men residing there, or in one way or another identified with Toynbee Hall had rendered considerable help during the strike.'[101] They had helped to organise and administer relief for the dockers and their families, and had persuaded outsiders of the justice of the dockers' case.[102] It was Nash, too, who is said to have arranged for the intervention of Cardinal Manning.[103]

When the heat of the struggle was over, the Central Strike Committee were entertained to supper at Toynbee Hall on 21 September 1889, and the strike leaders, John Burns, Ben Tillett, Tom Mann and sixty others, paid tribute to Toynbee Hall not only by their presence but by their conversation. Barnett, anxious to preserve some semblance of Toynbee Hall impartiality, insisted that 'the House itself has not taken sides'.[104] Yet he admitted that 'individuals among the Residents have taken sides strongly'.[105] Paradoxically, the sympathies of many of the national trade-union leaders were not fully with the dockers. Beatrice Webb could report that George Shipton, the Chairman of the Parliamentary Committee of the Trades Union Congress and Secretary of the London Trades Council, was 'strongly adverse to the men' and held that 'the way the strike was started was illegitimate. No responsible official of a trade union which had trades of its own to protect would trust employers in that fashion.'[106] As for Tillett, he claimed in his *Memoirs* that his inspirational leadership as a trade unionist owed much to a course of lectures he had heard at Toynbee Hall by the future Archbishop Lang on 'the strategy and tactics of Napoleon's wars'.[107]

The subsequent spread of trade unionism in London has been well documented by historians, and at the time the *Toynbee Record* of December 1889 reported triumphantly that 'the Dockers' Union is a fact. Some 30,000 men have received their tickets and are learning the control of common action.'[108] The contemporary official history of the strike was written by two old Toynbee Residents, Llewellyn Smith and Vaughan Nash. Mann described it as 'the best account'.[109].

A magisterial statement by one of the Residents in the *Toynbee Record* of October 1890 tried to establish long-term perspectives and argued that trade unionism had value chiefly as a transitional agent – 'While not representing in any sense an industrial ideal, its very existence proving rather that the ideal has not been reached, Trade Unionism appears to be an almost inevitable stage in the gradual evolution of a better industrial order.' Yet it had 'special features' of a positive kind also, among them 'unselfishness', 'orderliness', and the power to influence those workers who had hitherto been judged 'incapable of organisation'. Trade unionism, therefore, he held to be 'progressive' –

> It not only prepares the way for the establishment of Boards of Arbitration and Courts of Conciliation, but it educates men for the adoption of a more co-operative form of industry. The best Trade Unionists do not regard their Unions simply as fighting bodies, but as organisations that have the germs within them of a real education and 'leavening force'.[110]

After the dock strike was over, a number of Toynbee men even became branch members of the Dockers' Union, and a few accepted positions as officers. Aves, for example, became the first President of the Trafalgar Branch which met for several years at Toynbee Hall. Its first meeting in 1889 was held there, with Barnett in the chair, and two hundred dockers were present.[111] Soon afterwards, Ben Tillett spoke there on the future of the Union.[112]

Co-operation was now relegated to a position of lesser importance in Toynbee expectations.

> It is in the increasing strength of the Trades Unions and in the hope of bringing Co-operators and Trade Unions more closely together rather than in the hopeful anticipation of separate action on the part of the former that sympathies are now apt to dwell with most satisfaction,

the *Annual Report* proclaimed soon afterwards.[113] Yet trade unionists were always encouraged to turn to education as much as to organisation. If they would remember to combine not only for strength but for enlightenment they could become 'a great moral as well as industrial force'.[114] They would have to learn, however, 'both to wield power that combination gives, and to recognise the limitations of that power, and the bounds that justice as well as wider economic laws impose'.[115]

It was recognised, however, that 'one of the most serious difficulties with which the trade union leaders had to contend with' was 'want of leisure'.

> They are well aware that unity and cohesion amongst their members are all important, and that to bring this about social and educational opportunities must be afforded. They know that while men are ignorant of one another, and of the movement in which they have instinctively enrolled themselves, its history, its possibilities, and the relation which it has to bear in public life, their societies cannot flourish. But what is to be done? They have no time to make arrangements for discussions, classes, lectures, social gatherings and the rest.[116]

Toynbee Hall could contribute in this situation.

Around this time Toynbee Hall was providing accommodation for branch meetings of the Typographers, Railway Servants, Dock Labourers, Women Cigar Makers, Fellowship of Porters, Clothiers, Cutters and Pressers, Stickmakers, Jewish Cabinet Makers, Jewish Bakers and East End Tailors; and an inter-union conference was held in 1890 to discuss on 'neutral ground' 'the utility of strikes' (with a number of Dock Directors present).[117] In the same year, too, an 'Oxford Conference on Trades Unionism' organised by the Oxford Committee of Toynbee Hall, attracted an audience of more than 500. It was chaired by Acland and Leonard Courtney and the speakers included leading politicians, workers' representatives and representatives of the employers.[118]

Barnett urged trade-union leaders to meet at Toynbee Hall to discuss their aspirations as well as their grievances, and many of them responded. He also acted as an arbitrator, 'interfering no less than fourteen times' in one year, according to Henrietta, in relations 'between master and men or women with peace-making consequences'. There was further Toynbee Hall action, too, of a direct kind in the busmen's strike of 1891, when Llewellyn Smith and Laurie attended a mass meeting at the Old Vic where the unanimous decision was taken to demand a reduction of hours from sixteen to ten. And when John Burns went on to ask them to organise a strike in the East End they gladly responded. There was no doubt that they were acting as individuals when they organised picketing – highly efficiently – and when the strike ended successfully within a week, they, amongst others, had the satisfaction of being described by the Chairman of the General Omnibus Company as 'unscrupulous ruffians'.[119]

For all the excitement of the early 1890s there were signs by the end of the decade that Toynbee Hall could not realise all the aspirations of its founder. It was not only that the trade unions, once organised, went their own way. The educational vision was difficult to realise also. Thus, while the eighth *Annual Report* expressed the hope that Wadham and Balliol would 'provide a nucleus in which some of the social unity that marks college life at Oxford and Cambridge can be secured in East London',[120] there were always difficulties in attracting sufficient serious students to fill the rooms available for them and in 1897 they were described as 'somewhat in the experimental stage'. Barnett's own vision was certainly not to be realised in this form, and by the end of the century they were mentioned as 'annexes' to the Hall. Balliol House, where there was 'a turbulent and rebellious tradition amongst the students',[121] was to close down in 1913 and Wadham House lasted only a few years longer.

Research was more soundly based. Thus, as early as 1892, a Commission consisting of Toynbee representatives and local MPs was organised at Toynbee Hall to examine the problems of unemployment. Three years later, under the auspices of the Toynbee Trust, a statistical enquiry into the same subject was carried out by Dr. A. V. Woodwall. At the end of the decade Seebohm Rowntree asked for guidance both from Barnett and Booth for his inquiry into poverty in York. Many Toynbee Residents were to distinguish themselves in allied fields of research. Cyril (later Sir Cyril) Jackson, for example, who had been elected to the School Board in 1891, carried out a notable survey of 'Boy Labour' – a subject to gain in importance ten years later – and H. R. P. Gamon of 'London Police Courts', a subject already topical as 'hooliganism' appeared to be increasing. The Hall gained much in this line of research through club work, some of it associated with old boys of local schools, like the Old Northeyiter Club in Limehouse, organised by Jackson. And there was interest too in the Sociological Society which would make possible, it was hoped, 'the understanding of social causes and effects which only patient investigation can give'.[122] In this ferment of research Barnett certainly saw part of his vision realised. Asquith, like Clement Attlee ten years later, described Toynbee Hall as a 'social laboratory'.[123]

> This is not a time to preach reform and, as Theudas did, lead hundreds into the wilderness in the vain hope of at once establishing a better order [wrote Barnett in 1897]. It is out of date to start new institutions, whether for old or young.[124]

Yet new activities could be launched inside institutions, and there was one other interesting development at Toynbee Hall in the late 1890s – the launching of the East London Tenants' and General Protection Committee in 1899. Mansfield House had pointed the way since 1891. Every Tuesday evening the Honorary Solicitor and other members of the Committee spent two to three hours at Toynbee Hall for the purpose of giving legal advice to people who were too poor to pay for professional assistance.[125] This 'Poor Man's Lawyer' scheme was to establish itself: G. O. Roos was the first lawyer, the first of many lawyers who were offered a very special glimpse of the East End. Many of the persons seeking assistance were of 'Russian, Polish or other foreign extraction, who besides being entirely ignorant of English laws and customs' had little, if any knowledge of the language. 'Frequently,' it was reported in 1912 'the applicant' knew that he had 'signed a paper' and little else. The scheme, established largely as a result of the work of Dr A. E. Western, was perhaps the most popular venture Toynbee Hall had ever attempted.[126]

University Extension, which had been a major component in Barnett's educational programme, had lost some of its appeal by the end of the century. In this case, however, Barnett himself had never been blind to its shortcomings. Even when Extension numbers at Toynbee were at their peak in the late 1880s, Barnett was far from complacent –

On Friday I went to the University Extension meeting and by fatuity let myself in
for paying £10. The Society wants the sight of another peak. It has reached the
height it saw ten years ago and is now deceived in thinking itself at the top.[127]

Even though the Toynbee Extension Centre charged less than other London centres (1
shilling), it still remained beyond the reach of workmen earning on average 20 shillings a
week; and those who managed to find the money had to cut out other activities. As he
became aware of such obstacles to progress, Barnett became more radical in his own
opinions.

Thursday we had the annual dinner of University Extension students. Sixty sat down.
The price, three shillings, of the dinner, excluded all but our rich and gave a certain
sense of falseness to the proceedings. What a trouble this money is and how gradually
all things work together to make us socialists.[128]

By the late 1890s, although other educational classes were flourishing and the civil
servant Sir George Kekewich could describe Toynbee's extension work as 'some of the most
important done', University Extension work at Toynbee had gone into a marked decline.
'Some of the things we believed in are gone,' Barnett wrote, 'we have twenty-two when we
used to have a hundred.'[129] He recognised that some sort of change was necessary, and it
was at this critical juncture that he was approached by Albert Mansbridge, founder of the
Workers' Educational Association, described in detail in the next chapter. Four years before
the WEA was founded, however, a trial run of tutorial classes, involving a two-year sequence
of systematic study, had been introduced in connection with University Extension Lectures
at Toynbee Hall in October 1899. There were ten students. Mansbridge himself was to
acknowledge later that the idea of tutorial classes had arisen in London with the first twelve
students of Toynbee Hall. 'Oxford and Rochdale developed it, and laid down the lines of
its work.'[130]

The most important educational initiatives of Toynbee Hall before the development of
the WEA were associated with the system of national education rather than with voluntary
action. It was Barnett's reputation as an educationist – and an educationist without dogma
– which drew to Toynbee Hall, first, Sir John Gorst, the Conservative MP and Vice-President
of the Committee of Council in charge of education from 1895 to 1902, and, second, his
Private Secretary, Sir Robert Morant, the dynamic educational reformer. Hitherto, Acland
had been the main ally of Barnett. Now Gorst, who lived at Toynbee for a time, and later
visited it every week when the House was sitting, became a close friend, and Morant also
took up residence at Toynbee in order to join in discussions on secondary education, the
structure of the new Board of Education, formed in 1899, and the Education Act of 1902,
which abolished the Board Schools. The discussions went on 'backwards and forwards',
wrote Barnett, 'till we feel we are in the Cabinet'.[131]

The two of them discussed both objectives and tactics, with Barnett, whom Gorst
thought of as his mentor, contributing as much as the other two. 'As I get older,' he wrote,
'I feel that everything a Government can do is second to what it can do for Education.'[132]
Yet all around him he saw deception. The educational ladder about which others boasted

was, in his view, only a slender handrail with only a few boys and hardly any girls climbing the stairs.

> There is small chance of any child, say one against sixty, getting firmly on to the first round. Then the gap between the first standard and sixth in elementary school is very large. In many districts there is no second round . . . and such scholarships as exist are generally too small to enable the parent to help the child.[133]

Barnett wanted bigger scholarships to secondary schools and more of them. He also wanted paid work for children under 14 to be prohibited and the half-time system abolished. He also demanded that continuation schools should be made available in every district with compulsory attendance up to 16. Finally he came to believe in co-education, arguing that it would promote consideration and courtesy. Gorst, who was to dedicate his book, *The Children of the Nation*, to the new Labour MPs in the House of Commons, recognised the 'great political importance' of the 'destitute class' in the cities and urged that on those grounds alone there should be major reforms.

On the eve of the Education Bill of 1902, largely engineered by Morant, Barnett praised Gorst who, in his opinion, had 'really done well considering that his Government is against Education and that the Liberal Party is jealous of Conservative success or at any rate suspicious'.[134] He was also able to report Cabinet asides, 'When proposals for better Education were urged, Salisbury growled "Made in Germany", but most got through.'[135] When the 1902 Act was passed – abolishing the School Boards but opening the way to the expansion of secondary education – Toynbee Hall had played an important part. Indeed, for J. J. Mallon, the future Warden, it was 'the greatest of Toynbee Hall's services to education'.[136]

Barnett agreed with the Webbs that the abolition of the School Boards, on which Toynbee Hall men had served devotedly, was a fair price to pay for a major educational reform. Indeed, he insisted that the assumption of responsibility for state education by the County Councils would not involve a desertion of 'Liberal principles' –

> Liberal principles are variously defined but their essence is trust in the people. Thirty years ago the Liberal Party determined to trust the people with the provision of education. They created School Boards as the only means by which the people could exercise their trust. . . . But during the years many changes have occured. . . . The County Councils have been created, few men and women of the same eminence as in the past offer themselves as School Board candidates. The Boards have developed a sense of rights . . . a sort of Board policy almost as distinct as a Church policy. Many of the School Boards sit to represent the claims of the Church or of dissent or of temperance or of workmen or of leaders and there are only a few who have a keen interest in education. The discussions are often, therefore, about rival claims and not about what makes an educated community. School Boards indeed do not express the mind of the people; they express what sections of the people want education to do for their own objects but they do not express the underlying common thought of the community on education.[137]

Viewing local government as the most accessible agency for the promotion of citizenship, Barnett argued that it should be 'exalted and endowed with particular responsibilities'. It took up 'the legacy left by Parliament' and brought home to every member of the community the fact that 'he is himself a governor of his country and a responsible member of society.'[138] Barnett outlined the means by which local government vested with overall responsibility could act in the best democratic interest:

> A county council, for instance, which would include the control of education, of housing, and of poor relief would be in its own area a little Parliament. The members would decide the policy and control the experts who carry out the policy. There would be, for instance, a committee for education. . . . They would listen to the different policies advocated by their experts, the different methods by which degrees of education could be co-ordinated, the different ways by which voluntary schools might be made efficient.[139]

It was a source of pride to Barnett when Residents or Associates were elected to the LCC or to the borough councils, particularly Stepney, to which three Residents were elected in 1899; and he was concerned too in the successful public libraries movement to take local advantage of the Public Libraries Acts, and in the Stepney Council of Public Welfare, presided over by Lang, then Bishop of Stepney. It was from Toynbee Hall that a lively and effective campaign was organised to persuade local voters to take advantage of new public library legislation in 1888. Two-thirds of the Whitechapel electors were canvassed, and in a poll of 1890 the pro-library party not only won but secured four times as many votes as their opponents. Passmore Edwards provided funds for the building and a new library was opened in 1892. A similar campaign at Hackney, also masterminded from Toynbee Hall, did not succeed.[140]

Yet not everything in Barnett's Toynbee Hall was a matter of mobilising local concern, as with the Guardians or the LCC or of deliberately relating the concerns of the East End to the wider issues of national politics. There were many 'out of the ordinary' events which do not fit in easily into any pattern. Thus, Toynbee Hall contributed to the Olympic Games movement as a result of the stay there of a young Frenchman, Pierre de Coubertin, then in his early thirties. His biographer records that he was deeply impressed by 'the sympathetic intermingling of peoples of different backgrounds at Toynbee Hall' and by the 'keen intelligence' of the Whitechapel workers who attended classes and debates. He dreamed of a different version of international fellowship and played the leading part in the revival of the Games in Athens in 1896. As Baron Pierre de Coubertin he remained President of the Olympic Games Committee until 1925.[141]

Another young foreigner with a future, Guglielmo Marconi, arrived in England in 1896, and although he did not stay at Toynbee Hall, it was there that he gave the first demonstration of the new wireless system which he had just patented. It was a surprise demonstration at the time, announced as it was to a fascinated audience in the course of a lecture by William Preece, Engineer-in-Chief of the Post Office.

In the words of a contemporary report,

> What appeared to be two ordinary boxes were stationed at each end of the room, the current was set in motion at one, and a bell was immediately rung in the other. To show that there was no deception Mr Marconi held the receiver and carried it about, the bell ringing whenever the vibrations at the other box were set up.

Preece told his audience that he had had the greatest possible pleasure in telling Mr Marconi that day that the Post Office had decided to 'spare no expense' in experimenting with the apparatus in which he personally had the greatest faith. 'If the experiments were successful,' he went on, 'it would be of inestimable value to our ships, for it would provide an easy way of communicating with lightships and lighthouses.' There was no thought, then, of course, of wireless as a medium of 'mass communication', although like Marconi, Barnett in the Chair 'hoped that it would bring mankind together and make for peace and goodwill'.[142]

An equally unusual experience, though its significance, like that of wireless, can be appreciated fully only in retrospect, was unchronicled at the time. In 1902, when William Bowman was a resident in Balliol House, he met a 'stranger' at a Toynbee Hall debate on 'Our Foreign Policy' at which John Morley, the Liberal MP and biographer of Gladstone, was a guest.

> There were half a dozen East Enders present [Bowman wrote later], including a stranger who, although shabby, was rather better dressed than his colleagues. Afterwards, I learned that he was called Richter, and although we did not know it, it was, in fact, Lenin. . . . He was not an impressive figure and few outside his own friends would have looked twice at him. His shabby clothes helped to detract from his appearance, but he was evidently an intellectual. One could hardly imagine him to be a leader even if his personality expressed a considerable amount of audacity.

Unfortunately, Lenin himself left no account of the occasion, but, according to Bowman, he took part in the debate, speaking in broken but intelligible English, and Morley replied to him.

> 'What is the use of you coming to the East End [he asked Morley] and talking about your foreign policy? Who there understands or cares about it? Go down to Limehouse or Shadwell and see how the people live. Their slums, bad food, low wages, impoverishment, degradation and prostitution! That's where your foreign policy should lie. They are the victims of your capitalist organisation which is just as powerful and cruel as the force of arms. What does your Government's foreign policy consist of? I'll tell you. You, together with other capitalist nations, look round the world until you find a delectable place and then you send your Christian missionaries out there. They preach to the natives, 'Dear brother,' they say, "there is nothing on this earth worth living for. Look to Heaven and prepare to wear the golden crown and play the harp that awaits you." Then, when you have got the poor black man looking into the heavens, you send your armies and you take their land away from them. That's your foreign policy!'

'John Morley sat through this impassioned diatribe', a not unfamiliar kind of diatribe in Toynbee Hall either in style or content, 'watching the speaker intently', before replying that he was, 'very surprised to hear that the workmen of the East End are not interested in our foreign policy' and that he did not believe it.

> 'I am accustomed to addressing large audiences of workmen in the North of England, who are just as much interested in the subject as I am, and I have to be very careful what I say to them, or they will soon pick me up. Nevertheless I should like to see you in another place. Perhaps the day will come when the House of Commons will

have men like you expressing their views, but whether that will be good or bad I won't venture to guess.'

'The debate became warm and the evening was prolonged'. At the end, John Morley shook hands with a little group of Russians, who had accompanied Lenin and who were then taken to the dining hall for refreshments.

A few days later, Dean Robinson, the Dean of Balliol House, told Bowman that he had invited Richter for tea and asked Bowman to join him. The three of them duly met at tea, a characteristic Toynbee Hall Tea at which, after introductions, the maid brought in a trolley laiden with buttered muffins and an assortment of cakes. Encouraged by the Dean, Lenin, 'who seemed hungry', ate a huge meal: the muffins interested him, he had never eaten them before.

After the tea things had been cleared, Robinson produced a jar of tobacco, and after filling their pipes, the three men drew their chairs around the fire. Lenin almost at once launched out into an attack on British imperialism, which 'seemed to be his religion and life's blood'.

> You took South Africa [he said], because of its gold and its diamonds. You took India because of its starving millions and low costs of production. Great Britain has become rich and indolent by robbing these countries of the results of their labours and possessions; but the day will come when they will rise up against you and you will have to live on your own industry or else starve. The Imperialist British Empire will dissolve.

'That's not true,' said the Dean, 'but it's too big a subject to discuss here today. What's your attitude to religion?' 'I have no use for any religion,' the Russian replied. 'I regard it as an opiate used by the capitalist classes to dope the people.' 'I entirely disagree,' replied the Dean, 'you could not say it about the Christian religion which has done more to uplift the working classes than any other movement.'

There was obviously no room for agreement here, but in response to a direct question from Lenin, Bowman told him that the Toynbee Hall Students 'in the main would be sympathetic to some of his views but would differ from the methods he advocated'. They believed improvements could be obtained by education and peaceful methods, by evolution and not revolution. 'History has shown,' replied Lenin, 'that no great change has ever been brought about without the shedding of blood and revolution. I am convinced this is absolutely necessary, and the toiling masses will continue in their slavery unless these methods are used.' 'I have enjoyed this talk,' Lenin said, 'but now my time is up and I must go. I am going to visit my friends down in Limehouse.' He shook hands, thanked Robinson very sincerely for his hospitality, and went out. 'None of us realised,' wrote Bowman, 'that we had been entertaining the world's greatest revolutionary.'[143]

There was a touch of radical pride, if not of revolutionary commitment, in Barnett's comments on the result of the general election of 1906, which A. J. Balfour believed reflected the ripples of the Russian Revolution of 1905. Yet Barnett was no revolutionary then – any more than he had been earlier. In 1905, when Balfour was still Prime Minister, Barnett had invited Ramsay Macdonald, a regular visitor to Toynbee Hall, to a small meeting in his study in 1906 'to see whether some attempt' could be made 'to unite the progressive forces in view of the growing unpopularity of the Tory government and the reaction against them'.

He was not concerned, as were many of the other people present, with 'organisation and negotiations', the subject of 'secret negotiations and manipulations'. What he wanted to find out was how far leading men in both groups could agree in principle. And he was impressed, as was Lord Ponsonby who was also present, by Macdonald's lucid exposition of the impossibility of open alliances for Labour which was 'just beginning to find its feet'.[144] After the election, when Labour won twenty-nine seats, he wrote enthusiastically, 'What a week! Has not the rising sun of Labour dispelled all wanting thoughts and made you feel young.'[145] Convinced that Labour was 'the coming power', he turned his energies to organising the growing campaign for university reform, and between 1906 and his death in 1913 he campaigned ceaselessly for the establishment of a Royal Commission on the University.

> 'What? [he wrote in 1906], people ask themselves at the establishment of a new Government. What is the most pressing need of legislation? . . . There is one for which I would gain a hearing. . . . It is that a way may be opened for an alliance between knowledge and understanding, between the Universities and the Labour Party. Knowledge without industry, slightly altering some words of Ruskin, is selfishness. Industry without knowledge is brutality.[146]

Barnett harboured no romantic illusions about the actuality of Oxford life. 'At present they [the Universities] are expensive schools and more and more tend to become like schools with school-boy ideals', he complained.

> The public school-boy rules colleges and dons. He is 'the finest product of the times' and because he is strong and rich, looks down upon the other boys . . . patronises his 'clever smug' from the elementary school. There is no-one to check this spirit. Jowett [former Master of Balliol], who was in with the great, could do so, but no-one had succeeded him.[147]

The 1902 Education Act had begun to extend secondary education and widen opportunities for university entrance but Barnett envisaged a much more extensive and demanding role for the universities than the mere creation of a meritocracy. Like Ruskin, he believed that the main aim of education ought not to be to enable the exceptionally brilliant or exceptionally industrious 'to climb into the positions usually thought higher than that of the workmen', but to raise the general level of society and to humanise the life of industry.

> What he desired to see was not merely the creation of greater opportunities of higher education for working-class children but the establishment of a system under which education of a University character would be easily accessible to working men and women. In his view such a system was not merely a temporary expedient, a pis aller necessitated by the backwardness of secondary education, but a permanent and indispensable part of the educational edifice. . . . What was needed was not merely selection, but universal provision; the Universities ought to provide education, not merely for the boys and girls who had been at school full-time up to eighteen, but also for the young men and women who had entered the workshop at fourteen and

to whom a liberal education was the condition both of personal culture and of intelligent citizenship.[148]

It was because of Barnett's stress on 'personal culture' as well as 'intelligent citizenship' that he wanted Toynbee Hall to be a centre of the arts as well as of social action; and in this development he had far more successes to record than disappointments. The most important expression of this interest was the annual Easter exhibition, backed by other exhibitions – of photographs (and of artefacts) as well as pictures – and the *Annual Report* for 1886 already spoke in characteristic language of the 'great dumb teachers, the artists, of which those who care can learn as they turn over the portfolios, look at the photograph books or study the gift pictures on the walls'.[149]

It was not only Barnett – or his artist friends – who preached this popular message. The politicians who opened the exhibition proclaimed it also. Likewise, the artists, who included William Morris and Holman Hunt, stressed, as Barnett did, the importance of social access and of art that 'everyman' would appreciate. There was no gulf in artistic tastes and attitudes between Barnett and his contemporaries. He was ahead, however, of some of his narrow-minded ecclesiastical colleagues who objected to Sunday opening and had to defend himself both to the Lord's Day Observance Society, which picketed the Exhibition, and to his Bishop. 'The preaching of a Puritan Sunday,' he did not hesitate to write to his Bishop, 'will not touch them [the East Enders] of God, while it may make them think that the clergy interfere with innocent pleasures for the sake of their own opinion.[150]

For Barnett and his wife beauty had to be brought to the East End if only as a counter to 'the paralysing and degrading sights of our streets'. Yet there was a deeper reason too. 'The sight of pictures, helped by the descriptions of those who try to interpret the artist' touched the memories and awoke the hopes of the people.

> Never in my intercourse with my neighbours have I been so conscious of their souls and their souls' needs as when they have hung around me listening to what I had to say of Watts's picture, 'Time, Death and Judgement'.[151]

Social access to the exhibitions meant access by children as well as by adults, and Barnett was also well ahead of his contemporaries in seeking to ensure (with Plato's blessing) that they would take advantage of the exhibitions. It was due partly to him that Gorst included an enlightened clause in his Board of Education code which 'allowed any time occupied by visits paid during school hours to places of educational value or interest, if accompanied by a teacher, to be reckoned for grant'.[152]

The success of the exhibitions, which brought down prominent West Enders to the East End, too, often for the first time – and Barnett shrewdly organised private viewings – led to the demand for bigger premises. In 1886, therefore, three additional rooms were added at a cost of £2,300. Eleven years later, there was a challenge to raise far more appeal money, when there were difficulties in continuing to use 'the ill adapted school rooms', 'small and badly lighted'; and Barnett turned hopefully to the public for £20,000 to augment £7,000, including a generous gift from Passmore Edwards which he had already at his disposal. The Press warmly supported the plan for a permanent gallery. 'We do not open our free libraries once a year, but every day' wrote the *Chronicle*, for example, 'and we imagine that everyone will sympathise with Canon Barnett's desire for making good pictures not less accessible than good literature.'[153]

The most interesting immediate letter of support came from Watts. 'A permanent gallery in Whitechapel,' the artist maintained in a letter to *The Times*, 'could be a very great boon to the dwellers in the over-worked and over-crowded district, shut out by the necessity of anxious and unceasing endeavour to make both ends meet.' Yet, like Barnett, Watts passed from social to both aesthetic and moral judgment, testifying to

> the humanizing and even encouraging effects works of art can have upon those whose lives are a round of dullness. . . . It is no wonder the weary and joyless should too often seek and find relief in gambling and drunken-ness. Art and music, which I should like to see enter into the gallery scheme, would be found possible auxiliaries of the pulpit, which cannot now give the weight possessed by the Hebrew Prophets or the Church of the Middle Ages.

Technical education would never be enough: 'no acquirement can be of the highest value that does not work for the development of those qualities which, not shared by the lower, are the distinguishing gifts of humanity.'[154]

Punch took up the same theme, noting that Barnett's appeal came in a year of royal jubilee:

> So charge this Canon, loud to the muzzle, all ye great Jubilee guns,
> Pictures as good as sermons? Any, much better than some poor ones.
> Where Whitechapel's darkness the weary eyes of the dreary workers dims,
> It may be found that Watts's pictures do better than Watts's hymns.[155]

A site was forthcoming in 1897 next to the Whitechapel Library. It cost £6,000 and Barnett raised the necessary money in a fortnight.[156] In 1898 Lord Peel, who very briefly succeeded Gell as Chairman of the Toynbee Hall Council, laid the foundation stone, and in March 1901 the building was completed. The gallery had a Director, Charles Aitken, and seventeen trustees, among them both Barnett and Henrietta. Another trustee was the Press proprietor Henry Lawson, later Lord Burnham, who himself was to serve briefly as Chairman of the Toynbee Council. Once again the Press was enthusiastic.

> At the moment when Burlington House and the New Gallery are given up exclusively to modern work not in all cases of the first order, [wrote the *Manchester Guardian*], the fine pictures of Whitechapel by the earlier English masters and the pre-Raphaelites may remind some of Sidney Smith's saying that the farther he went to the West the more convinced he became that the wise men came from the East.[157]

Two years later, moreover, the same paper was suggesting that 'if an art connoisseur today wishes to see the most representative exhibition of contemporary British painting that we have had in London for years he must run down to Whitechapel.'[158] According to the *Evening News*, however, there was 'a wider idea at the back of the Whitechapel Art Gallery than the mere exhibition of pictures'. Copies of pictures were to be lent out to be shown in homes, lantern slides were to be offered on loan to schools, and exhibitions first of local amateur work (including that of children) and of 'objects illustrative of teaching or painting' were to be arranged.[159] One of the most able students in the Toynbee Art Club, Samuel Hancock, a postman, had some of his pictures shown in the Royal Academy.

It was the view of Aitken, as of Barnett, not only that East Enders were just as capable of appreciating good pictures as West Enders, but that in some respects they were better able. 'Drab streets, dark rooms and the litter of a crowded life' had made people less, not more, colour blind.[160] And posters, which he displayed in 1903, were as likely to appeal as portraits or landscapes.[161] When Aitken moved to the Tate Gallery in 1910 as Director, to be succeeded at Whitechapel by Gilbert Ramsay, he carried these ideas with him.

Although there were no musical activities at Toynbee which were as well-known as the exhibitions – or the singing competitions at the People's Palace and the Choral Society at Oxford House – a series of Saturday afternoon concerts was started by J. M. Dent in 1897 and carried on by Mrs Aves and later by the Watson sisters. There was an average attendance of 250. Some of the gentlemen in the audience, wrote a *Daily News* reporter,

> were innocent of shirt collars, some even wore their bowler hats. . . . There were old men who had been very little bothered in the battle of life; and young boys, whose natural restlessness was subdued by the beauties of Mendelssohn's pianoforte variations in E flat. . . . Some of the customers looked rather tough, probably from Petticoat Lane round the corner.[162]

These remained Toynbee Hall's neighbours throughout the whole long period of Barnett's Wardenship which came to an end in 1906 when after twenty-two years he changed his title from Warden to President on being appointed a Canon of Westminster. Experience, he explicitly recognised then, had 'chastened' some of the hopes he had had when the Settlement was founded. 'Settlements had been inclined to become,' he wrote in 1905, 'too much like the "missionary" they were designed to supplement.' They had come to stand for 'work among the poor' rather than for 'the being of a body of educated people'. There was need now for the imagination as well as the energies of a new generation. 'Every age,' he claimed, 'is, I believe, inspired by the spirit in the age. The older generation may offer guidance, but the driving force comes from the young.'[163]

Already three years earlier a forceful representative of the new generation, William Beveridge, had arrived at Toynbee Hall, and a somewhat different pattern of activities – and range of motives – became apparent. For this reason alone, Beveridge, who had already been invited by Barnett to write the annual report, deserves a chapter to himself. Yet Barnett was to survive Beveridge's departure and to remain the key figure until his death in 1913.

Clemenceau is said to have related that he had met only three great men in England and one was a 'little pale clergyman' in Whitechapel.[164] The judgment sticks. Barnett had laid down instructions that there should be only one memorial service – at St Jude's – and this was held there, with two ex-curates officiating, four days after his death at Hove on 17 June 1913. He never saw the 'Great War', therefore, which was to establish Clemenceau's reputation.

There was only one memorial service, but there were many memorials. A Barnett Fellowship was set up in 1914 with Milner, who had become Chairman of the Toynbee Hall Council in 1912, as Chairman of the sponsoring Committee and Lord Haldane, Sir

Herbert Samuel and J. M. Keynes among the members. If they were already aware of the difficulty of recapturing 'the first fine careless rapture' of the Universities' Settlement movement, they were none the less conscious of Barnett's place in history. His 'greatness lay in his sense of direction', they claimed, 'so that those who knew him well felt that they could steer by him as if he were a spiritual instrument'.[165] Funds were collected from many countries, and the Fellowships were open to men and women of all nationalities. Some of their reports were later published as *Barnett House Papers*.

In Oxford itself Barnett House was opened by Lord Bryce in June 1914 only two months before war was declared. It was in Beaumont Street,[166] not far from Balliol, which had always been a centre of initiative as well as support in Barnett's life. It was designed to provide a centre for the advancement of knowledge of modern social and economic problems, both urban and rural. Yet it was part of its duties also to study 'the scope and progress of Settlements and securing contacts between them'. Oxford was not to be left to itself.

III
Beveridge and After, 1903–1919

When William Beveridge, who was to figure so prominently in twentieth-century history, was appointed Sub-Warden of Toynbee Hall in 1903, he wrote enthusiastically to his father that he had 'a vision of Toynbee [Hall] speaking one day with a voice of thunder' and of himself, 'if I prove capable of it', among others, 'directing that voice's utterance'.[1]

It was Barnett who picked out young Beveridge after hearing about him from the Balliol College Chaplain, E. J. Palmer. Beveridge had graduated in Greats with a First in 1901 and already by then he had more contact with Toynbee Hall which he first visited in 1900. 'I wish to go [to Toynbee Hall]' Beveridge himself wrote in 1903, because 'I view [social] problems in a scientific way – a hindrance to the future prosperity of the State.'[2] T. H. Huxley, the scientist, was his mentor, and it was not as a 'philanthropist' but as a scientist that he turned to the East End: he was as distrustful of 'the saving power of culture and of missions and of isolated good feelings,' he remarked, 'as a surgeon who distrusts "Christian Science" '.[3]

No-one could have gone to Toynbee Hall more purposefully. Yet Beveridge's purpose, as set out in two enormously long letters to his father and mother, who were uneasy about his going there, show how far removed were his motives from those of Barnett who invited him. Beveridge disliked all talk about 'soup kitchens and genial smiles for the proletariat'. Instead, he was seeking, in his own words, 'to make of Toynbee and kindred institutions . . . centres for the development of authoritative opinion on the problems of city life'.[4]

Barnett would not have used the phrase 'authoritative opinion' in this context; and he would not have talked about the language of power in such sentences as 'I suppose power is the thing everyone desires to exercise.'[5] Nor would he have refused, as Beveridge did, to use the phrase 'social problems' because it 'always' suggested 'slumming and drink'.[6] 'If anyone ever thought that colossal evils could be remedied by small doses of culture and amiability,' Beveridge went on, 'I for one do not think so now.'[7] Yet there was more than a touch of Barnett, who offered him £200 a year to serve as Sub-Warden, in a further Beveridge remark that

> such places [as Toynbee Hall] represent simply a protest against the sin of taking things for granted, in particular taking one's own social position or conditions for granted. No man can really be a good citizen who goes through life in a watertight compartment of his own class.[8]

Beveridge approached the problems of city and class from above, not from below – with sin, if not religion, prominent in the picture. And this did not disturb Barnett who understood his new Sub-Warden's character well enough. 'He is very able,' he wrote in 1903, 'a whale for work – with definite views of filling up his life in social service, but not very patient with his tools, nor a lover of the man in the fool.'[9] And Cosmo Lang, then the Bishop of Stepney, echoed the judgment to Beveridge himself. 'You snub people whose interests are not your own. . . . You are narrow in your view of life which is not purely intellectual.'[10]

Beveridge faced more difficulties in communicating face to face, therefore, than Barnett did – or even Lang, who counted the Labour leaders Will Crooks and George Lansbury among his friends and who responded cheerfully to the 'gaiety' of the East End.[11] Yet Barnett himself was interested by now in a different kind of communication – that to a bigger and more distant audience – a kind of communication in which Beveridge was to excel. The time was now more important than the place. 'The moment seems one of crisis,' he wrote at the end of 1903. 'Old things are passing away; there is a sound in the air as if a better time was coming, but as yet its character is hidden.'[12]

If society was to move into a 'better time', what it needed first and foremost, he felt, was a more accurate knowledge of social conditions. Beveridge, therefore, was perfectly qualified to respond to the challenge.

> Society needs facts and not sensational stories [Barnett wrote in 1902], facts as to children's underfed and ill-fed bodies, facts as to the workmen's use of their leisure, facts as to infant mortality, as to the necessity for casual employment, as to the damage to homes from women's trades. Society, in a word, needs the knowledge necessary for scientific treatment by philanthropists and public bodies. There is no more room for a policy of headlines. The East End demands well thought-out schemes of relief and of government.[13]

'If a new party gathered about you,' he suggested persuasively to Beveridge in 1903, 'a new life might begin just as the first thirteen men made the life which has gone on for the last nineteen hundred years.'[14]

Beveridge at that time looked younger than his 24 years, being lightly built and boyish in appearance, with lank fair hair and sharp features. His unwavering expression hinted at a certain, 'apartness'. Even then he was obviously a highly individual character. 'He is not an ordinary man, either in ability or character,' one of his Oxford tutors, Sir William Markby, wrote at this time to Beveridge's mother.[15] Markby was Treasurer of the University General Committee in Oxford which maintained the links with Toynbee Hall and which were always referred to in its annual reports.

Supremely confident in his own intellectual ability, Beveridge was anxious to make his mark through Toynbee Hall. Booth had revealed the 'true state' of the poor in society: Beveridge was determined to seek an explanation of, and a solution for, that state. And he was willing enough to use the State to do so. Old Liberals had trusted in the market: 'new' Liberals, like J. A. Hobson, felt that market mechanisms were not always calculated to meet pressing national needs.[16] What those needs were, Beveridge believed, could be ascertained in the East End, not among the soup kitchens but at the dock gates and in the hundreds of small premises housing 'home industries'.

Thus, while Beveridge's fond parents envisaged quite a different future for their beloved William, urging him to continue with his legal studies in order to be not a 'mere practising lawyer, but a jurist . . . or a Professor of Law'.[17] Beveridge already appreciated that making laws might be more useful than interpreting old laws. There were many lawyers, like A. V. Dicey, who feared the growth of 'collectivism' and the increased power of the State. Yet 'new Liberals', not a homogeneous group, professed themselves more interested in the beneficial effects of legislation to promote 'full citizenship' – inevitably social legislation – than in the dangers of too powerful a State, and they were to be given an opportunity directly to influence legislation after the resignation of A. J. Balfour, the Conservative Prime Minister, in 1905, and the General Election of 1906 which returned a huge Liberal majority to the House of Commons.

Beveridge was to stay in Toynbee Hall for a relatively short period from September 1903 to November 1905, so that he left it on the eve of the great Liberal return to power. Yet, during the years of Liberal reforms designed, never without controversy, to make Britain 'less of a pleasure ground for the few' and more of a 'treasure house for the nation',[18] he was to remain in close touch with Toynbee. Later in life, he was to write not only that his decision to go to Toynbee had proved 'from a worldly point of view' to be 'the best choice of occupation that I could have made' – it was the stepping stone to other things – but that he owed all his later jobs to the 'special knowledge' he had 'gained in Whitechapel'.[19]

Since human relations were never to be Beveridge's strongest point even after he had become a man of power, it is revealing that Barnett advised him from the start in private not 'to use up your time [at Toynbee] in taking classes yourself' but to become involved in organisational duties 'in connection with some public body'.[20] None the less, in public Beveridge was introduced to the Hall as someone 'not unfamiliar with the ways of the place' and old friends were asked 'to rally around him'.[21] And he, for his part, responded at once to the friendship of some of the Residents whom he met at Toynbee Hall, staying on close terms with them for the rest of their lives. He was proud of the fact also that at the very start there were more new Residents in his first year at Toynbee than there had been in any year since 1889.

The historian R. H. (Harry) Tawney was one of his closest friends: he, too, had arrived at Toynbee from Balliol and was serving at that time as Secretary of the Children's Holiday Fund. H. S. Lewis and Henry Ward were other friends. There were former Residents too, who visited the Hall frequently and from whom Beveridge was able to collect the kind of 'scientific' evidence about social conditions that he felt he needed. Among them were Hubert Llewellyn Smith of the Board of Trade, with whom he was to work later at Whitehall, G. L. Bruce and C. Jackson of the London School Board, T. H. Nunn, closely involved with the Charity Organisation Society, and the barrister R. W. Kittle, who had given up legal practice and devoted all his time to the children and schools of East London. Beveridge had thought at one time of following in the footsteps of Morant and going into educational administration, but he had been put off by the thought of having first to teach in a school, an activity which he feared. Now, however, he was able to learn, particularly from Kittle, just what it was actually like to meet and talk to children. He also served as School Manager for a school in Old Montagu Street and helped to choose a headmistress from 'three ladies' each 'old enough to be my mother'.[22] Interviewing old or young was to remain one of his favourite pastimes.

As Sub-Warden, Beveridge reminisced years later, he was at Toynbee Hall 'day and night'. In Barnett's absence (for example, on trips abroad with the 'Toynbee Pilgrims') he was in charge, and even when Barnett was there, he often had to serve as his 'mouthpiece'. He was drawn inevitably also into the grass roots politics of the East End, claiming later, for example, how by 'gigantic efforts' he got 'a Curate' elected to the Stepney Borough Council as an Independent, defeating by ten votes the weakest of three Moderates – a Jewish publican. In his own words Beveridge 'canvassed laboriously many times and learned the nature of our electorate', and, trying to learn even more, along with Tawney, he actually joined a Workmen's Club in Bethnal Green.[23]

Almost at once after his appointment, he had become 'municipal secretary' of the Stepney Committee of Public Welfare, a body which had been created by Barnett in 1903 in order to co-ordinate philanthropic efforts and to counteract the excessive influence of the Charity Organisation Society, and he was also launched on his first journalistic venture when he was given the editorship of the *Toynbee Record*. 'I shall practise the art of self-expression,' he informed his still anxious mother, adding that, as editor, he would eliminate 'gush' and dispense with 'the chaos of notes all too short to convey any information or any impression than of general good'. Instead, he would substitute 'specialist articles of some scientific value'.[24]

There was another Toynbee activity which interested him. The 'Poor Man's Lawyer' scheme at Toynbee Hall had become a well-known and much-trusted agency for many of Toynbee's neighbours – in particular, 'for Jews with little knowledge of English life . . . constantly seeking information and guidance on problems connected with the education of their children, difficulty with landlord or employer, or other domestic troubles'; and through the network thereby established, it was possible at 'moments of stress and social crisis' for Toynbee Hall to serve as 'a rallying point for the forces which may forward goodwill and social progress'.[25]

Such a moment came in 1906 when there was a strike among the tailoring workers of the East End, most of whose 'masters' were also Jews. It was a strike therefore, when 'Jew met Jew'.[26] And Beveridge watched with care not only what was happening but how participants and onlookers perceived what was happening. He had recognised in 1904 that the industrial conditions under which a large number of aliens worked in the East End fell well below 'the standard which ought, alike in the interests of the workmen and the community at large, to be maintained,' and he concluded that what was wanted was 'to strengthen and execute relentlessly the laws governing factories and workshops (domestic or other) so as to deprive the immigrant of any disastrous advantage he may reap by a lower standard of life and work'.[27]

When in 1906, therefore, the tailors 'brought their case to Toynbee Hall', he and other people closely associated with the Hall were entirely on their side. The tailors were

> working for incredibly long hours (ordinarily fifteen hours a day and not infrequently thirty hours at a stretch) in indescribably bad conditions (in the 'master's' backroom or kitchen, sometimes even in the cellar) on piecework, for miserable pay (in some

cases not more than 8s. a week) and some of the women were driven, by sheer want, into the streets, in order to keep themselves and those dependent on them alive.

'A mass meeting of the workers in the open air and a mass meeting in the hall were addressed by Toynbee men,' it was reported, and it was also reported that 'all parties found common ground in Toynbee Hall, for all knew that none was for a party and all were for a commonwealth.' Yet after what was euphemistically termed 'a compromise' had been reached, with the support of Toynbee men, the employers were deeply disturbed; and it was only after a 'long and stormy meeting' that the men gained their point. Even then the settlement proved difficult to enforce, as is obvious from a footnote to the Toynbee Hall *Annual Report* for 1906 which reported that 'in the smaller workshops the rules agreed upon have already been broken'.[28] Such experience predisposed Beveridge, who needed little prompting, to turn not to agitation but to legislation.

All this was good training for the journalistic job which Beveridge was to do immediately after resigning his Sub-Wardenship – a leader-writing post offered him (at the suggestion not of Barnett, but of Edward Caird, the Master of Balliol) on the Tory daily newspaper, the *Morning Post*. It was more than good training, however, for Beveridge came to appreciate through such work the complexity of those 'social problems' which at first he had been reluctant to identify as such. In dealing with the Whitechapel Charity Organisation Society, for example – with Miss M. E. Marshall as its 'admirable secretary' – he soon came to the conclusion, more intelligible in the late twentieth-century context than in the late-nineteenth,

> that the C.O.S. and the S.O.C. (i.e. the Socialists) were the front and back of the same coin. They ought to agree instead of quarrelling, because they were both against the half measures whether of casual employment or of casual charity that fostered sub-human forms of life.[29]

It was 'unemployment' rather than 'charity', however, that Beveridge came to identify as the major economic and social problem of the time, although the two remained interconnected so long as there were still rich and influential people who believed that charity was the best way of dealing with unemployment. While at Toynbee, Beveridge had already written a number of leaders on unemployment for Fabian Ware, 'a friend of Toynbee', who edited the *Morning Post*, and who did not object when, before taking him on for a full-time post, Beveridge described himself as 'in speculative politics . . . a bit of a Socialist'.[30]

There was, in fact, less speculation in the early Beveridge articles than distillation of Toynbee Hall experience, an experience which was reflected in many of the articles by other Toynbee residents in the *Toynbee Record*. There were criticisms in April 1903, for example, before Beveridge arrived at the Hall, of processions of unemployed demanding charity as an answer to their problems, and in 1905 there were articles on the attempts of Walter Long, the Conservative MP to introduce legislation to deal specifically with unemployment in London.[31] The young Beveridge, not very different from the old Beveridge, quickly learnt through the Toynbee experience to be 'authoritative' in the way that he had hoped to be, and within a few years it was his book *Unemployment, A Problem of Industry* which turned him almost overnight into an acknowledged authority.[32] When he sent a copy of it to

Beatrice Webb, she responded in a thank-you letter which included the memorable phrase 'We will break up, once for all, that nasty old poor law.'[33] Beveridge's name was to be associated with a different approach to social policy – not through the poor law, but through national insurance. There was a line of continuity when, following in Barnett's wake, Beveridge offered in the first instance not so much a scheme as a theory to explain unemployment.

Barnett himself argued from the start that the unemployed would have to be separated as a category from the unemployable, if only because labour was 'one of the most perishable commodities' and nothing rotted it so quickly as want of work. Nor, in Barnett's opinion, was there any reason for permanently maintaining 'an unemployed class' in order that there might be 'a reservoir of labour ready to meet exceptional demands'. It would never be a reservoir, he suggested, but rather 'a Dead Sea of labour'.[34] For Barnett, who used his eyes as well as his mind and heart, casual labour, commonly viewed as an unavoidable fact of industrial life in London, was not only morally degrading and therefore unacceptable, but economically wasteful. Yet the scheme which he himself suggested for dealing with it was itself totally inadequate. 'Colonies', he urged, should be set up in the country to offer employment for the able unemployed, and their wives should be paid an allowance while they received board and lodgings.[35]

When, in 1903, at Barnett's instigation, a Mansion House Committee, dormant since 1895, was revived to deal with pressing 'distress' in London, it set out to deal with the unemployed on these lines, employing a number of them outside the city limits. Beveridge was given the key role in its operation, with H. R. Maynard, another Resident, as a partner; and Tawney and many other Toynbee Residents and Associates offered voluntary assistance. Indeed, during this busy period at Toynbee, the scheme, in Beveridge's words, absorbed 'the time and thoughts of several residents and all visitors who could be pressed into service, to receive applications, verify the facts as to the family, visit or write to employers or references, select and finally despatch cases'. Yet only £4,000 was raised, and after two months Beveridge was to withdraw from the scheme (to Barnett's regret) because of what he thought was 'a misuse of funds'.

None the less, he learnt much directly from the experience.

> I was set to learn about the main economic problem of those days [he wrote in retrospect], not from books, but by interviewing unemployed applicants for relief, taking up references from former employers, selecting the men to be helped, and organising the relief work.[36]

Moreover, as he worked, more important still – for himself and for the country – was the fact that he began to ask himself persistently 'what had gone wrong with economic laws in East London?'[37]

It was not only that Beveridge came to appreciate for himself the grounds of Barnett's distaste, which he had first learnt from the Charity Organisation Society, for 'philanthropic sentiment in London – which loves to give doles no matter how injurious', but that he felt that he had to explain more clearly than Barnett had done why the distaste was economically as well as morally justified. As he put together a theory which he hoped would point to a new policy, Beveridge came to the conclusion that effective social action depended not on local action but on the State, guided by 'a department of industrial intelligence'.[38] Unemployment was a problem of industrial organisation, and as such demanded State machinery to deal with it. It was the duty of the State, he maintained, to

> meet an evil inherent in our industrial system, not less ruinous than the dangers at the factories [dealt with in the Factory Acts] and quite as far beyond the strength of private organisation as philanthropic. . . . The problem presented by recurring periods of unemployment is beyond the powers of charity and is wholly outside the scope of a Poor Law dealing with destitution in general.[39]

A new central body to grapple with unemployment was a necessary first step.

The way Beveridge worked in 1903, 1904 and 1905 forecast much of his later work, when he was to become renowned as a Committee Chairman. And in this also he was strongly influenced by Barnett. Thus, on 5 November 1903 – the date seems appropriate – he informed his mother that he was 'getting together a joint committee of Toynbee, Balliol House and Wadham House Residents, which is to sit in the manner of a Royal Commission on the Unemployed, examining in particular the various schemes proposed in the past',[40] and in the *Toynbee Record* of January 1904, he was promising his members that

> a report of practical suggestions for dealing with the question in future years, based on a complete review both of past schemes and of the events of the present years, would be forthcoming as a result of the Committee's labours.[41]

His Committee included Maynard, Tawney, E. J. Urwick, D. M. MacGregor, later to become Henry Drummond Professor of Political Economy at Oxford, and Ernest Aves, who had worked closely with Charles Booth; and at their first meeting on 12 November, it was decided that Beveridge himself would deal with the wide range of proposed schemes for dealing with the unemployed. He started with a Charles Booth scheme on dock labour, compiled at Toynbee Hall, while his colleagues were asked 'to compile a bibliography on the subject', 'to enquire into the state of employment, past and present', and to survey all other existing and past schemes of relief'.[42] Booth had proposed to the Royal Commission on Labour in 1893 the establishment of some form of labour exchange as a means of tackling the problem of casual riverside labour, and Beveridge, who was always willing to learn from others, now began to envisage the more general application of this idea to the whole of industry. He was gratified, therefore, when at the third meeting of his Committee on 15 December, he was able to report that sixteen firms had expressed willingness to take men recommended from a register of unemployed compiled in Toynbee Hall.[43]

As Beveridge and his Committee monitored closely the operation of the activities of the Mansion House Committee throughout the winter of 1903/4 and the results of its intervention during the following spring and summer, they rejected any possibility of depending on the provision of temporary relief to 'help the poor' during winter months or in 'cold snaps'. The winter of 1903/4, they pointed out, had not, in fact, been 'a period of exceptional distress due to seasonal causes'; it had been characterised rather by

> the acceleration of a general downward trend begun at the end of 1900, delayed (perhaps by the [Boer] War) during 1901 and 1902, landing us by the end of 1903

in a period of stagnation and prolonged distress which we have no reason to regard as the lowest stage.

As a result, only a very small proportion of the men who had gone to Barnett's labour 'colonies' had had anything like regular work between leaving the colonies (January to March) and the end of July. They were still suffering from 'enforced idleness and demoralising poverty beyond hope of return'.[44]

Given this evidence, Beveridge was now prepared to generalise.

> One may compare the course of industry with its cyclical variations to that of a point on the rim of a wheel [he wrote]. At the top of its course, when employment is brisk, even the weakest cling on and find a place. As it swings round and downwards the pull on all holding to the wheel becomes even greater; the stronger, losing little or no employment, or by membership of an expensive trade union get through somehow; the weaker, before or after the very lowest point drop off. The point whence they fell moves on and up. Trade revives, but they, degenerating through idleness and poverty, lost in the great trough of the non-industrial classes are in no position to profit thereby; their place another – migrating probably from the country – takes; by charity and chance employment, by the drudgery of their wives and the exploitation of their children's labour, at the dock gates, and in shelters, they live and linger and die.
>   It may be that this periodical extrusion of the weaker at times of stress is an essential part of the machinery of modern industry or of industry however organised. . . . Let it only be remembered that it is a tragedy – let us rather call it a process – to which two things are quite irrelevant; first, the giving of relief according to the state of the weather and the coldness of the charitable public's nose; second, the preaching of thrift, or sobriety. To take the second point first, it is not possible seriously to advocate thrift or sobriety to persons earning 24s. a week for six persons, as a complete solution of any little difficulty occasioned by four or eight or twelve months' enforced idleness.[45]

Given such firm conclusions, which left C. S. Loch and the Charity Organisation Society far behind and which pointed towards government intervention as not so much desirable as necessary, both Beveridge and Barnett now felt that it was essential to turn from Whitechapel to Westminster. And the way this turn was achieved was characteristic, like the investigation itself, of much of Beveridge's later mode of operation. In the beginning, there was careful preparation.

> Supper at Barnetts with Maynard and Aves [he reported to his father]. We discussed at great length what Maynard was to suggest to Long [Walter Long – President of Local Government Board and as such in control of the London Unemployed Fund]. It really is rather interesting being behind a person like Canon Barnett who (through Maynard) will instil wisdom into Long. On the other side is Herbert Samuel (MP for Whitechapel) coming down next Monday specially to be coached by him (and me) as to what he is to say in the House when the question comes up![46]

Such careful preparations having been made in advance, Barnett and Beveridge addressed a large meeting of Liberal MPs on 4 March 1905, on the need for legislation to provide machinery to tackle the problem of unemployment. 'Canon Barnett and I,' he wrote at the time – and it is the kind of writing which figures prominently in all his private papers then, and later –

> proceeded thither on Thursday and gradually the Liberal members – to the number of 60 or 70 assembled. I must say they had been summoned by a most important looking document, signed by ten or eleven people – John Burns and Sidney Buxton and I know not how many more. Asquith was in the Chair, with Canon Barnett on his right, and I modestly hiding behind the Canon, facing an audience of – 150,000 to 200,000 electors (assuming 5000 electors per member). The Canon opened with a very short speech, explaining two proposed bills; one was to establish Labour Organisation Committees (of the Town and County Councils) all over England, whose business it would be 1) to open Labour Registries and Labour Exchanges and really know when work was wanted 2) to manage (if they wished) farm colonies for testing and training men to emigrate or to migrate from the towns to the land 3) to arrange (in cases of exceptional distress) for emergency relief schemes. . . . Of course we really want them to do 1) and perhaps 2) so well that 3) won't be necessary.[47]

Barnett, having spoken, was questioned respectfully, turning some of the questions over to Beveridge, much to the latter's delight, 'Even I,' Beveridge wrote to his parents, 'addressed that magnificent audience.' Yet his own respect for his audience was strictly limited. 'With one or two exceptions they hadn't thought much about the subject and Trevelyan, who was one of the exceptions to this, apologised to me afterwards for the lack of intelligence shown.' John Burns, of Dock Strike fame (and future Liberal minister), 'who had rather a wild idea of his own' was the most pertinacious questioner, 'most anxious' to find out from Beveridge when he proposed to publish his *Record* articles 'on Unemployment as a whole'.[48]

When Long and Gerald Balfour, with Liberal support, succeeded in securing the passing of the Unemployed Workmen Act in 1905, and a Central (Unemployed) Body was set up to co-ordinate policy and manage relief schemes for dealing with the unemployed in London, a team of Toynbee Residents and Past Residents helped to administer it. Indeed, without this support, it was claimed, it would have been impossible to have carried out any complete and satisfactory test of the machinery created by the Act.[49] Beveridge was co-opted as a member in November 1905. 'I was put forward I believe both by the C.O.S. and the Socialists,' he reported gleefully to his mother.[50] It was, indeed, a landmark in his life. He was now recognised as an authority on the question of unemployment.

Although the Act was limited in its effects and conferred power to establish a connected system of employment exchanges only in the metropolis, Beveridge was fully aware of the national significance of what had happened. So, too, was H. Lawson, xenophobic MP for Mile End, who complained of State intrusion into the affairs of private enterprise.[51] 'Labour Exchanges,' Beveridge stressed, 'are pieces of industrial organisation and will only achieve success if they are given their proper standing in connection with a Government department of national scope and connected with industry rather than poverty.' Labour was

> the only commodity in the world which only, or as a rule, finds a buyer by being hawked from door to door. There must surely be a good reason for avoiding the economic wastfulness of this method in regard to labour as in regard to everything

else. A proposal for labour exchanges would be approached with the question, 'Why not?' rather than with the question, 'Why?'[52]

Beveridge had now won a wider audience to which he could expound his views, and it was doubtless in the light of this that Fabian Ware, who was in close touch with Walter Long, invited him to join the editorial staff of the *Morning Post*. And Barnett urged him to accept. Indeed, Beveridge believed wrongly that Barnett might have suggested his name.

Having secured his new job, Beveridge now decided to leave Toynbee Hall, although he was under no obligation to do so. He continued, however, to draw on the network of relationships centred on Toynbee Hall, and viewed his new position as a means of furthering the influence of Toynbee Hall: 'Just think of the people I should see and the wisdom I, and the Canon through me, should pump into the comfortable public about Poor Law, Trade Union Law, Unemployed, Garden Cities and Decentralisation.'[53] This was a longer list of social topics than he would have produced two years before, but even as far as the narrower subject of labour exchanges was concerned, he continued to find Toynbee Hall particularly useful. 'The Employment Exchanges,' he wrote in 1906, 'are in a critical position between being accepted and violently opposed by Trade Unions' and the Unions would need 'the most careful handling if they are not to come down on us'.[54] In such circumstances, trade-union links provided by Toynbee Hall mattered to him, as they did later when he became involved in the development of a system of national insurance.

Trade-union representatives frequently gathered at Toynbee Hall, where conferences were held in Edwardian England on health insurance, old age pensions and housing, all of which were issues which were passing on to the general agenda of government. In these circumstances Beveridge, like Tawney, saw the main function of the Hall as 'the provision of a neutral platform where different classes may meet to thresh out common problems, and submit to being permeated with each other's ideas'. It was a centre 'where difficult, and often conflicting idealisms can grind each other into some practicable shape'.[55] For these reasons Beveridge regularly attended the meetings of the Enquirers' Club and became President in 1911. The fact that Toynbee Hall was located in the East End now seemed to him less relevant than the hope that it would help to shape new national policies.

Once, while at Toynbee Beveridge delivered a paper at the London School of Economics on 'The Influence of University Settlements', a paper which, in his own words, he did not dare to show to Barnett. In it he 'chose perversely' (also in his own words of the time) to dwell on the influence of the Settlement on the Settlers and not on the inhabitants of the East End. And although he did not dare to show the paper to Barnett, then and later he stuck by its conclusion that 'a University Settlement is or shall be less a place of permanent residence than a college to pass through; it shall be a school of post-graduate education in humanity.'[56]

There was something of the same attitude in R. H. Tawney, who, after Rugby and Balliol, went down from Oxford to Toynbee Hall in 1903. This was the same year as Beveridge and the year of the foundation of the Workers' Educational Association, the body with which Tawney was to be so closely associated, although their interests and politics were eventually to diverge. It is illuminating to contemplate, however, that in 1903 Tawney might well have become an officer of the Charity Organisation Society.[57] The nineteenth and twentieth centuries seem to meet at this point. Tawney was saved when he was offered and accepted the almost, in retrospect, equally unlikely post of Secretary, at double the salary, of the Children's Country Holiday Fund, and he went on to spend three years in this position living as a Resident at Toynbee from October 1903 until 1906.

Unlike Beveridge, whose sister he married in 1909, Tawney lived in the Hall again for most of 1908 until the spring of 1913. And from the start he developed a strong sense of the East End. One of his most interesting reviews in the *Toynbee Record* was of Jack London's *People of the Abyss* where he accused London of going to the East End and spending eight weeks there only to discover 'painful things' and put them into a book.

> No-one would paint Whitechapel as a paradise of good living [he added], or even of good intentions. But behind both distress and the efforts to relieve it there is something which this author never touches – the humanity whose name he so often takes in vain.[58]

It was this insistence on 'humanity' which was to permeate Tawney's philosophy for the rest of his life, and he learned much from children as well as from East Enders. 'There is no touchstone, except the treatment of childhood,' he was to write, 'which reveals the true character of a social philosophy more closely than the spirit in which it regards the misfortunes of them, of its members who fall by the way.'[59] Barnett seems to have been as sensitive to Tawney's outlook and character as he was to Beveridge's. Tawney's view that 'a locality is not satisfied by a club of the cultural' was not likely to keep him forever in the East End. When in 1906, therefore, he contemplated moving to a university job, Barnett told him 'after saying several things' about his 'character' that only if he were 'satisfied with his life in Toynbee Hall' and the Children's Country Holiday Fund would he advise him to stay on. 'But, as you are not, I am inclined to advise you to try for Cardiff,' the university Tawney then had in mind.[60]

Tawney was to go to Glasgow University, not Cardiff, for a short spell before he went to the WEA, and he was not to abandon Toynbee Hall at any point in the transition. He lectured there frequently before becoming a WEA tutor, and on the eve of his move to Glasgow was giving weekly courses in the Hall on subjects as different as 'Trade Unions (Principles)', 'Co-operative Trading', 'Some Nineteenth Century Writers' (he was to write little about the nineteenth century later), and 'Belief and Criticism'.

In fact, Toynbee Hall seems to have strongly influenced Tawney's views on 'belief'. He always had stronger religious convictions than Beveridge – and they were to remain with him – yet he noted when at Toynbee Hall how religion, 'one of the great social forces of history', was 'gradually and reluctantly drifting out of the lives of no inconsiderable part of society'. We shall not go far wrong,' he also noted, 'in stating that all over London Church attendance varies roughly in proportion to the poverty of the district under consideration.' Tawney added, however, that 'Church attendance' was 'after all, but a narrow and misleading test of the Churches' influence'. Statistics were never enough. He looked for 'the encouragement of a human voice' amid 'a wilderness of diagrams'[61] and accepted the Church as 'the centre of social activity'.

Two young men:
(*above left*) William Beveridge
and (*above*) R. H. Tawney

(*left*) James Joseph ('Jimmy')
Mallon at the time of his
arrival in London, 1906

(*below*) T. E. Harvey
(*centre*), Barnett's successor
as Warden with some
Residents

The entrance to Toynbee Hall from Commercial
Street with the Warden's lodging on the upper
floors

TOYNBEE HALL,

28, COMMERCIAL STREET,
WHITECHAPEL, E.

University Extension Lectures on LABOUR QUESTIONS.

"Labour and the Law."
W. H. BEVERIDGE, M.A., B.C.L.
Tuesdays at 8 p.m., beginning Oct. 10th.

1. The Labour Contract.
2. State Regulation in the Past.
3. The Claim to Combine.
4. The Claim to Combine (*cont.*)
5. The Claim to Personal Safety.
6. The Claim to Compensation.
7. The Claim to Live.
8. The Claim to Live and the Claim to Work.
9. The Interests of the community and Compulsory Arbitration.
10. The State and Labour.

"Social Aspects of Industry."
R. H. TAWNEY, B.A.
Fridays at 8 p.m., beginning Oct. 13th.

1. Before the Factory.
2. The Factory System: Division of Labour.
3. The Factory System: Machinery.
4. The Factory System: Concentration of Capital.
5. Trade Unionism.
6. The Factory Acts.
7. Profit Sharing.
8. Home Industries.
9. The Factory and the Citizen.
10. The Factory and the Citizen (*cont.*).

FEE for the two courses (20 lectures) 1s. Inclusive Fee for these two courses and a course on "CITIZENSHIP," by Graham Wallas, on Fridays, beginning January (30 lectures altogether) 1s. 6d

The first lecture of each course may be attended without fee. Each lecture will be followed by a discussion class.

PRELIMINARY MEETING, FRIDAY, OCTOBER 6,
AT 8 P.M.

Mr. GRAHAM WALLAS will deliver an address on "Francis Place, the liberator of Trade Unionism from the Combination Laws."

The curriculum

Men's Evening Classes

AT

TOYNBEE HALL,

28 COMMERCIAL STREET, E.

SESSION 1905-6.

MONDAYS, TUESDAYS, WEDNESDAYS & THURSDAYS.

Enrolment Night, Wednesday, Sept. 13.

Classes commence Monday, Sept. 18.

Admission Fee, 1/- This fee entitles a Student to attend all Classes **EXCEPT SHORTHAND**, for which an additional fee of 2/- is charged, returnable under certain conditions.

DAY.	8 TO 9.	9 TO 10.
Monday . .	**Shorthand** (*Pitman's*) **English Literature** **Arithmetic** (*Intermediate*) **Arithmetic***	**Shorthand** **Geometry** **Composition** **Singing***
Tuesday . .	**Vocal Music**	**Vocal Music**
Wednesday	**Shorthand** (*Pitman's*) **Reading*** **Arithmetic** **Grammar** (*Intermediate*)	**Shorthand** **Composition*** **Arithmetic** **Grammar*** **Theoretical Mechanics**
Thursday .	**Book-keeping** (*Elem.*) **Book-keeping** (*Adv.*) **European History**	**Book-keeping** (*Elem.*) **Book-keeping** (*Adv.*) **Chemistry** **Composition**

Classes marked * are intended for beginners.

There is a Club Room, supplied with papers, magazines, games, etc., for use of students, open on Friday and Saturday evenings from 8 to 10, and on Class Nights from 7.15.

Responsible Teacher - Mr. H. O. BARKER, L.C.P.

Printed by PENNY & HULL, Leman Street, E.

The curriculum continued

THE LITTLE THEATRE,

TOYNBEE HALL.

Sole Lessee and Manager - - - - T. Hall.

SATURDAY, DECEMBER 18, 1909.

TOYNBEE HALL

PRESENTS

A NEW AND ORIGINAL FAIRY PANTOMIME IN THREE ACTS, ENTITLED,

ALI BABA

AND THE

FORTY BOROUGH COUNCILLORS.

By F. J. HARVEY DARTON.

❋ ❋ ❋

THE TABLE OF PERSONS

(IN THE ORDER OF THEIR APPEARANCE).

Morgiana (Slave of Ali Baba : in love with Hoki Poki).. Mr. T. S. Lukis
Ali Baba (a poor but liberal and free trader of Bagdad) Mr. E. F. Wise
Cogia Hassan (Chairman of the Forty Borough Coun-
    cillors) .. .. Mr. M. Birley
Chop-chop (Cook to Cogia Hassan) .. .. Mr. R. C. Woodhead
Guava Djelli (a leading Borough Councillor) .. .. *Mr. C. R. Attler
Rahat Lakhoum ⎫ Mr. J. S. Nicholson
Curri Chutnee ⎬ (Borough Councillors) .. Mr. L. Paterson
Tutti Frutti ⎭ Mr. C. B. Hawkins
Cassim Baba (Brother of Ali Baba) .. .. Mr. A. Sorensen
Bhar-el-Obir (Host of "The Whole Hog") .. Mr. G. A. Ramsay
Hoki-Poki (Son of Ali Baba, of no settled convictions;
    a Boy Scout) .. .. Mr. T. R. Castle

A programme for the annual Christmas pantomime with Clement Attlee in the unlikely role of Guava Djelli

Henrietta Barnett continued to take a close interest in Toynbee's affairs until Mallon's appointment in 1919. Thereafter she was an honoured guest

The Toynbee Scout Troop - one of the earliest in London

Working-class education was to provide Tawney with the encouragement of many a human voice. Yet, there is no account of his first meeting with Albert Mansbridge, the 'wild-looking young man' who produced a 'scheme for the Higher Education of Workmen'. This was the man who was to draw Tawney from the East End to industrial Rochdale. It was Beveridge who recorded his impression of his first meeting with Mansbridge, much approved of by Barnett who called him the 'young man with fire in his belly'.[62] Mansbridge, then in his late twenties, had launched the 'Association to Promote the Higher Education of Working Men' in 1903, a title changed two years later to the more manageable Workers' Educational Association.

In the beginning Mansbridge was the WEA, just as afterwards there were to be many people who were to think that it was Tawney. And there were early links with Toynbee. Mansbridge's mother had attended meetings of the Women's Co-operative Guild at Toynbee Hall, and Mansbridge himself had attended Extension Classes there. He also shared Barnett's conviction that proper education rested on spiritual objectives. An active churchman, who had been befriended by Charles Gore, then Canon of Westminster, he had been a Sunday School Superintendant and a Band of Hope leader before he turned to the WEA.[63] 'I hate cleverness,' Mansbridge once wrote. 'Knowledge and skill without wisdom are no more than bricks on mortar. You can use them for building devils' houses. Christianity must keep knowledge pure. It must save knowledge from materialism.'[64]

Barnett, who shared this approach, approved of Mansbridge the man, but seems to have been as sceptical initially about the new Association as he had been about Booth's statistical investigation of London poverty. He said that it would need a lot of money – £50,000 perhaps.[65] Yet in public he backed Mansbridge wholeheartedly and behind the scenes gave him invaluable advice, telling him not to dissipate his energies and to be sure that through his new Association he offered direction and organisation as well as spiritual guidance. Moreover, it was Barnett who ensured that through the Oxford connection of Toynbee Hall, and the links which it had forged with working-class movements the new Association would immediately find a place on the map of higher education. Indeed, an initiating meeting held in Toynbee Hall to launch the Association played the same part in the history of the WEA as the initiating meeting of 1883 as St John's College had played in the history of the Hall itself.

It was in F. E. Douglas's room at Toynbee Hall on 14 July 1903 – Bastille Day – that the small provisional association of what was to eventually to become the WEA first met, and at that meeting two members of the TUC Parliamentary Committee, completely at home in the Toynbee Hall setting, agreed to back the new venture. Soon afterwards, further trade-union support was forthcoming – with the enthusiastic help of David Shackleton, MP, who was to become the President of the TUC in 1908–9. Progress thereafter was rapid, although the first funds amounted not to £50,000 but to 2s. 6d., and in December 1903, 'a large and representative conference' was held at the Hall to promote the new 'University for Working Men', a designation used not in London but in Yorkshire, a sign that Toynbee's publicity network was wide outside as well as inside the metropolis.[66]

Mansbridge learnt much from the Toynbee Hall experience not only in University Extension, which was languishing in the late-nineteenth century, but in debates and conferences, and his philosophy was very similar to Barnett's. 'Education unites and does not divide,' Mansbridge claimed. The new Association should 'unite in one body, without conscious difference, men of all experiences – the peer's son rejoices in the fellowship of the miner's son, and the casual labourer in the friendship of the don'.[67] 'The desire for education' was a desire for 'a way of life', not just 'a means of livelihood or a mere intellectual exercise'.[68] And that 'way of life' was more than a political way. From the start, the Association was, like Toynbee Hall, 'non-political and non-sectarian', and from the start it was determined to provide 'the best', not an inferior product. There was realism as well as idealism in this. If the WEA had not been non-political and non-sectarian and if it had not stressed high standards, it would never have secured a government grant for its first tutorial classes in the provinces at Rochdale and Longton.[69] The possibility of securing such a grant-in-aid was enhanced, of course, by reason of the fact that Morant, then Permanent Secretary of the Board of Education, remained very much a Toynbee man. 'We believe it is to small classes and solid, earnest work,' he wrote, 'that we can give increasingly of the golden stream.'[70]

In the years before the grant, Barnett stressed that it was essential to win publicity and support for the new Association – not only in the industrial areas, but in Oxford, the birthplace of his own institution. London University might be helpful – Mansbridge was to write later that it was 'able to support experiments more easily than either Oxford or Cambridge'[71] – but to Barnett, Oxford, as always, was still the great national influence to cultivate. Indeed, he judged rightly or wrongly that if the WEA were to secure not only academic support but to win the necessary working-class support to establish itself and to grow, Oxford University must be seen to embrace the cause of workers' higher education. 'Nothing but the best will do.' It was in Oxford, therefore, that 'a varied crowd of men and women . . . representing two hundred organisations of working people in England – plus Morant – thronged the Examination Schools' on 10 August 1907 to launch the WEA nationally. 'Barriers of creed have been thrown down,' the Secretary to the Oxford University Extension Delegacy, a future Conservative MP, J. A. R. Marriott of Worcester College, exclaimed. 'We hope it will become more national, not by the exclusion of the rich, but by the inclusion of the poor.' 'I would rather have better education given to the masses of the working classes than the best for a few,' the Labour MP, Philip Snowdon, remarked on rather different lines as the Conference closed, 'Oh God, make no more giants; elevate the race.'[72] They were lines which were to become more familiar in the doctrines of a later generation.

Between 1903 and 1907 Toynbee Hall had played an important role in pressing for the kind of change in outlook in Oxford which was a prerequisite of the action contemplated at the 1907 Conference, and Barnett, Beveridge and Tawney – always in close touch with Sidney Ball – were all key figures in the struggle for university reform. Soon after the 1906 election, therefore, Beveridge was reporting to his father how Barnett had launched a campaign for university reform with an article in the *Tribune* entitled 'Labour and Culture'.[73] It was difficult for any one to challenge its idealism, but a passing allusion in it to the endowments of Oxford and Cambridge 'roused quite a storm in Oxford'. Nor was this the only article to raise a storm. 'The outraged University is blaspheming, horribly,' wrote

Beveridge to his father after another Tawney article in the *Westminster Review* caused 'great excitement'.[74] Clearly there had to be influential voices inside Oxford who favoured reform if the WEA was to win full recognition – and here Barnett's – and Mansbridge's – contacts were indispensible. Other key figures included not only Alfred Zimmern, a young New College tutor, H. H. Turner, the Savilian Professor of Astronomy, and William Temple, son of an Archbishop of Canterbury and later to become Archbishop of Canterbury himself – and President of the WEA – but Sir William Anson, the Warden of All Souls' and a Unionist MP.

Barnett, Beveridge and Tawney together secured the publication in *The Times* in 1907 of an important series of lectures on 'Oxford and the Nation' and together – with the invaluable support of the Chancellor of the University, Lord Curzon – they inspired a remarkable report of a Committee set up after the Examination Schools Conference, *Oxford and Working-Class Education*. 'An Oxford education,' the Report stated, should be

> accessible to every class, not merely in the formal sense that it admits every applicant of good character who satisfies its educational requirements, but in the practical sense of making it certain that no-one will be excluded merely upon the ground of poverty.[75]

Oxford went on to set up a Joint Tutorial Classes Committee on which there was full WEA representation, and this was the body which sent Tawney to Rochdale. Moreover, although the first hopes of establishing the closest of all links between the tutorial classes and the university were not realised, the system had come to stay, and in 1910 was given the full blessing of the Board of Education after J. W. Headlam, a Board Inspector, and L. T. Hobhouse had reported favourably upon it. 'Its efforts,' they claimed on Barnett-like lines, would be 'likely to be permanent and to spread from the actual members of the [tutorial] class to those who came into contact with them.'[76] Barnett did not wish to place too much emphasis on the system. 'The WEA has life,' he wrote in 1910, 'but how to give it the organisation which will extend and not fill the life is the difficulty.'[77]

Meanwhile, Barnett had arranged WEA lectures in Westminster Abbey in 1907 – on 'The Story of the Abbey in Relation to the History of the English People' – and Toynbee Hall put on its own first WEA tutorial class, rather late, in 1911, with a second one to follow a year later. Finally, in 1911, arrangements were made whereby the Toynbee Hall Library could serve as a central library for WEA students in all parts of the country.

There was one other new line of development before 1914. Already in the 1890s, there had been increasing interest in what would now be called youth work. Now in 1908, the year of the Children's Act – and of the Prevention of Crime Act – boy scouting arrived at Toynbee Hall, and the 1st Stepney Toynbee Troop was inaugurated on 27 May 1908 'at a meeting characterised by the greatest enthusiasm'. Dr T. S. Lukis, a new Toynbee Resident, was the scouting enthusiast who was responsible. He had read Baden-Powell's *Scouting for Boys* published in that same month and he was determined to act at once. Later in the year, J. Landsberg organised a further troop, and soon many of the Residents were involved. They contributed both to the practice and to the philosophy of scouting, noting that Baden-Powell in his *Yarns for Boy Scouts* had quoted Gorst's statement that the university

Settlements had succeeded in training and civilising some of the most difficult boys in every city. Perhaps not surprisingly, Baden-Powell selected the Toynbee troop at the Earls Court Rally of 1909 as the most efficient troop present.[78]

Lukis has left an account of the first disastrous camping expedition in Epping Forest, which scarcely pointed to such a commendation. Of his troop of six, half, he said, deserted, 'one because he was bitten by mosquitoes, another because he did not wish to miss his Sunday dinner, and a third, who had never shown great keenness, out of sympathy for the other two'. And other meetings in the East End also met with initial difficulties:

> After our second Sunday in town, being the first time we had practised in the neighbourhood of Finsbury Circus [Lukis reported], there was considerable disaffection among the boys, because so many of their friends frequented that neighbourhood and were inclined to jeer at them.

In such circumstances it is difficult to know whether to admire more the imaginative faith of the scoutmaster or the pluck of the first scouts. For Lukis there was something in common between Epping Forest, a favourite haunt, and the East End, although in the forest the animals were sometimes, he thought, less wild than the boys.

In 1911 Lukis had to give up scoutmastering temporarily when he began living and working in a hospital, but E. C. Blight, who had been helping him, and L. B. Bluett, who joined Blight in 1913, continued to develop the talents of the Toynbee Troop, which was soon followed by a separate Jewish Troop. Lukis himself always dwelt on the civic role of scouting – the way in which it could 'bring all classes into touch with each other' and 'break down the existing barriers, which are only artificial after all' – and he was critical of much of the 'paraphernalia' of the movement and 'the lurid and impossible yarns' in the *Scout*.[79] Yet after war had broken out in 1914 he was to summon a meeting of the older scouts of East London and lead eighty of them to the nearest recruiting office.

There were some Residents of Toynbee Hall who were uneasy about the emphasis placed on such activities in the years before 1914, although of the two Quaker Wardens Harvey, if not Birley, was a keen supporter, both of scouting and of the old boys' clubs. It was he, indeed, who wrote with enthusiasm in 1906 that an increasing number of Residents were taking part in the management of the latter both in the East End and at camps 'where even more than in the club-room, everything depended on discipline'.[80]

It is significant that such new activity carried with it a further slackening of the old activity. Thus, Extension lectures were in decline, the Toynbee Workmen's Travelling Club was in difficulties in 1912, and the Toynbee Travellers' Club amended its constitution in the same year in the light of recognising that 'the average age of members made it more undesirable than formerly to undertake Expeditions involving chance discomfort in travelling and hotel accommodation'. There was the further problem of 'forming parties sufficiently large for economical travel'. It might be 'a matter of congratulation' that 'many members are now capable of arranging their own Continental tours', but there could be no cause for congratulation in the fact that 'very few members were now students of Toynbee Hall, and there was no Resident representation'.[81]

The last point was the most serious of all. The *Annual Report* for 1913, which included an obituary article on 'the late Canon Barnett', also included a melancholy sentence in the Warden's Report that 'perhaps to a larger extent than usual during the year there has been a lack of Residents who have been able to give their whole time, and, in consequence, there has been less individual work in the neighbourhood undertaken.'[82]

The Warden who wrote these lines – Maurice Birley, a Toynbee Resident since November 1904 – was the second of Toynbee's Wardens after Canon Barnett's retirement in 1906, and in Henrietta Barnett's formidable opinion 'ought never to have been appointed'. 'He is a nice man,' she said, 'and people are fond of him, I believe; but he is a poor creature, without power of organising or attracting, or keeping men.'[83] Many people did not agree, as a laudatory article in the *Toynbee Record* made clear.[84]

Henrietta was doubtless comparing Birley not only with her husband but with Birley's predecessor, T. E. Harvey, who had been chosen by Barnett as Deputy Warden in July 1904, who had become Warden in 1906, and who had resigned not when he became a Liberal MP in 1910 but when he married in 1911. Harvey was very much Barnett's choice and fitted into the same mould.

> The Canon was a wise old bird [Beveridge wrote years later about Harvey's appointment]. He knew that men should be used for what they can do best, not for what they cannot do well if at all. He realised almost at once that I was not the stuff of which a Warden could be made.[85]

Harvey, a Quaker from Leeds, seemed to have all the right qualifications. He had taken an active part in the Toynbee campaign to grapple with unemployment, and he was to become Treasurer of the WEA and a London County Councillor. Barnett, as first Warden, lived long enough to enjoy what he called the 'crowning blessing' of living through what he called 'the reign of his successor' and was 'satisfied'.[86] Unfortunately, however, he also had to face the difficulties associated with Birley's succession as a kind of caretaker Warden who had never asked for the job. Henrietta felt that worry about the implications of the change darkened the last months of her husband's life. She was particularly annoyed that when Barnett tried to complement – or in her word 'supplement' – Birley 'by a go-ahead forcible sub-Warden', Birley 'quarrelled with him and the two did not speak, while living in the same house'.[87]

Personalities have always counted for much in the history of Toynbee Hall – to such an extent, indeed, that its history is best written around them. Yet the problems of Toynbee Hall between 1906 and 1914 were more than problems of personalities. Under Harvey as well as under Birley they began to loom large – problems of finance; problems of ageing; problems of maintaining a balance between old and new activities; and, most important of all, problems of maintaining the drive behind the daily operations of the institution.

There seemed to be little wrong in 1906, when the introductory notes to the *Toynbee Record* for July – September 1906, price one penny, expressed the 'happiness' felt by all connected with Toynbee on receiving the news of Barnett's appointment as Canon of Westminster, adding that there was 'no sense of separation'.[88] That year there had been ample evidence of lively group activity, ranging from the choral class to the Art Students' Club and from the Toynbee Nursing Guild to the Sunday evening discussions, including one introduced by Barnett himself on 'Luxury'. There had been well-attended debates — one of them on 'free medical aid', another on 'the Tramp' — a production of *Twelfth Night* and a highly successful series of Sunday afternoon concerts.

The lecture programmes had included a series by the gifted Fabian socialist, Graham Wallas, who was working on his post-Victorian book *Human Nature in Politics* and who had offered ten lectures on 'The Government of an English City'. Such a series looked ahead, but in a second series by Dr A. Rickett, 'Personal Forces in Modern Thought', which had just been published in book form, the forces described were all Victorian or pre-Victorian, and were all English, with Newman, Huxley and Dickens prominent in the list. There was a Victorian flavour, too, to the invitation cards, two of which survive from this year — the first inviting 'all members of the Committee which, in 1884, helped to lay the foundation' to a party 'at the end of the 21st year' and the second, for Founders' Day, inviting guests to a dinner 'to help make old and new Residents feel the unity of Toynbee Hall'. During the year, eighty-four people from the Hall had visited Trinity, Exeter, Corpus Christi and Balliol colleges, when the message proclaimed was exactly the same as that of 1884, 'Luncheon was served at Oriel, and at the conclusion of the meal Canon Barnett spoke of the lessons that Oxford might teach Whitechapel and Whitechapel Oxford.'[89]

Nevertheless, there were many signs in the *Record* of the changing social context, and the same number of the *Record* described Kiralfy's plans for improving the Mile End Road, Spitalfields and Shadwell in the East End: 'old and narrow streets would be replaced by gardens and terraces, with trees and fountains.' There was much talk, too, of social conflict in the world as it was so that alongside notes on unemployment there were descriptions of the strike of Jewish tailors and tailoresses in May 1906, 'the spontaneous and irresistible revolt of over ten thousand men and women in despair'.[90] On the wall of a neighbouring street the words 'Death to the Strikers' had been chalked. This was a time, too, when anti-alien agitation tapped the prejudices, never far from the surface, of old East Enders. They shocked Barnett — and they shocked Harvey too. 'Is England on the brink of a revolution infinitely more profound and disturbing than the French Revolution?' S.D.S. began an article in the *Toynbee Record* in November 1911, when every kind of discontent had snowballed.[91]

In the same year Barnett argued that 'Strikes accompanied by violence hinder more than they help' and 'support the illusion that force is a remedy'[92] and Milner expressed his detestation of 'any form of social cleavage' on the very different grounds that 'it weakens my country'.[93]

> Among civilised peoples of more or less equal size [he went on], that one will be, as it will deserve to be, the strongest, which is the most successful in removing the causes of class antagonism in its midst. It will be the least vulnerable to external aggression, the most capable of influencing the future development of the world.[94]

There had been sharp difference of opinion at Toynbee Hall during the Boer War, sometimes described as Milner's War, when sixteen Residents were pro-War and four, along with Barnett, against; and there were to be similar differences of outlook in 1914.[95]

Harvey's philosophy was well expressed in his introduction to the *Annual Report* for 1910, a year when the Hall attracted a particularly interesting group of Residents — among them Walter Layton, later to become newspaper proprietor, Editor of *The Economist* and Liberal politician; Henry Clay, economist, at the end of his career to become Warden of Nuffield College, Oxford (and to marry the daughter of A. L. Smith, Master of Balliol); Gilbert Ramsey, subsequently Director of the Whitechapel Art Gallery; and Clement Attlee, Toynbee's only Prime Minister. Even in this vintage year – although it was not immediately recognised as such – Harvey insisted that the Settlement was 'the work of many lives, and not only of those who have actually lived within the precincts of its quiet quadrangle'. 'The tired workers who found refreshment in the Sunday concerts' contributed to 'the many-coloured web of intermingling activities'. So, too, did the large numbers of people who attended the Sunday evening 'discussions on religious subjects' which he inaugurated and which were condemned by critics as anti-religious discussions.

'Nearly twenty-seven years have passed since the founding of Toynbee Hall,' Harvey wrote. 'In many ways it has altered, as a living thing should, but while the needs which called it into being are with us, will the spirit its founders brought to their work have cause to die?' East London and the old universities had 'changed for the better' as education became 'widely shared', but it was still not 'deep' enough, not sufficiently 'humane'.

> Too many men are content to replace the Bible by the last edition but one of the *Encyclopaedia Britannica* and to think it a good substitution. Others of us shrug our shoulders at moral failure in our own lives and in society and fancy we can cure it all by means of a formula derived from Karl Marx.

> Until we have awakened alike in East London and in the homes of wealth and comfort a divine discomfort with our own ignorance and selfishness, with our laziness and lack of courage [he concluded] we shall not have begun that civic education which must accompany all enduring social reform.[96]

Harvey insisted that Britain was still 'far from a real democracy', that London needed 'civic volunteers', that in the East End there were signs everywhere of 'the very failure of our civilisation'. What was needed, he suggested, was a common approach to the issues. 'None of us share quite the same outlook on politics, but all may be said to unite in the aim of the [Stepney] Council of Public Welfare,' which during the past year has met frequently at Toynbee Hall, 'serving as a focus to draw together social workers, clergymen and local administrators, to promote the public health and moral welfare of the Borough'. Nationally, too, there had been a wide recognition of the need to deal with the problem of the poor in a different way from those of the past.

Following the Reports of the Poor Law Commission, which had been commissioned by Balfour's Conservative Government in the very different conditions of 1905, Beveridge gave an introductory paper on the subject at the fifty-third meeting of the Enquirers' Club on 9 March 1909. After describing the content of the Majority and Minority Requests, he complained of 'the rooted distrust of democracy' shown in both of them – in the Majority Report, openly and in the Minority Report, drafted by Mrs Webb, 'cleverly concealed'. He was already thinking on different lines. Yet on 7 May 1909, Mrs Webb had had the opportunity to present *her* case at Toynbee, taking as her subject 'Rival Principles of Poor Law Reform' and describing how 'light had broken in upon the Commission and how she herself had first been converted'. For her, Toynbee Hall was not so much neutral ground as a possible constituency, for in conclusion, 'she invited the members and visitors of the Club to join the new society she was forming for the break up of the Poor Law.'[97]

On 21 May, Dr Bernard Bosanquet, a distinguished philosopher and supporter of the Majority Report, schooled in the traditions of the Charity Organisation Society, spoke on 'Difficulties in the Minority Report'. (One wonders if Beatrice Webb was present.) He expressed the opinion that while the charge of 'socialism' commonly brought against the Minority Report was hardly justified, the charge of its pretentiousness was, and he concluded by comparing the Minority Report with the obsolete journal *Logic* which, he said, was wholly divorced from life.[98]

At a later meeting of the Enquirers' Club, the Secretary of the Poor Law Unions, W. Davey, spoke in defence of the existing Poor Law system, instancing amongst the good work done by the Poor Law Guardians the advance in institutional classification of the poor. He denied that what had been called 'heterogeneous herding' any longer existed and, obviously aware of his vulnerable position, maintained that 'the Guardians would welcome any criticism and co-operation from outside provided that it did not involve their own extinction as a necessary preliminary.' To his mind, all that was necessary was a 'continuance of the present state of affairs' with somewhat stricter control by the Local Government Board.[99] Davey's views were less congenial to most members of the Enquirers' Club than those of the other two speakers. Yet the Guardians were to continue in existence for another twenty years until Neville Chamberlain finally changed the poor law structure in 1929.

Meanwhile, the young civil servant from Oxford, W. J. Braithwaite, a Resident from 1898 to 1903, played a major part behind the scenes in developing the insurance system which was to secure governmental priority over the 'break-up of the Poor Law'; and his memoirs, *Lloyd George's Ambulance Wagon*, not published until 1957, set out the best record of what happened. They reveal *inter alia* his dispute with another ex-Toynbee man, Morant, described by Beatrice Webb as 'the one man of genius in the Civil Service', and there is the occasional glimpse of Beveridge whom Braithwaite had known well 'off and on, for years'.[100] There was a series of discussions at Toynbee Hall on the National Insurance Act of 1911 with Professor L. T. Hobhouse introducing 'some matters of principle' and Dr Fothergill complaining that it was 'regrettable that the medical profession had not been consulted in the framing of the Act' and doubting whether 'in its present form it would prove beneficial to public health'.[101]

Other Toynbee Hall speakers in 1909 had dealt with 'School Clinics' (Margaret MacMillan), 'The Future of Hospitals', 'The Boilermakers' Dispute' and 'Disputes in the Cotton Trade' (S. G. Chapman) and with the railways, while Ernest Aves turned more generally to 'The Causes of Trade Disputes and Methods of Settling them'. Richard Pell emphasised how in any dispute

> the men were at a disadvantage in the statement of their case, since they served in
> humble capacities only, and were not a match for the Companies' officials. . . .
> Even when the award of an arbitrator was issued, it was often difficult to interpret
> and the Companies were able to enforce their interpretation and the men were
> not.[102]

The independence of Toynbee Hall as a forum was demonstrated when W. Collinson, Secretary and General Manager of the National Free Labour Association, spoke in the same year on 'Labour Disputes' and the means of settling them from 'the free labour standpoint'. He argued forcefully that trade unions 'with their socialism and their misrepresentation' were 'the cause of the present discontent', a discontent which was to grow in 1913 and 1914 on the eve of the First World War and which led one Toynbee speaker to prophecy the possibility of civil war. At a time when the Labour Party was small and powerless, Collinson anticipated arguments of the future when he complained that 'legislators bowed down to the Labour Party and gave its members Government jobs.' 'Curse your charity, make us officials,' was the new motto of the Labour Party. Strikes could only be ended quickly if the Board of Trade held aloof.[103]

This was controversial stuff – and would have been outside the East End. So, too, was the argument presented by Mary Macarthur, then Secretary of the Women's Trade Union League, when at the height of the suffragette agitation she spoke on the subject of 'Women's Trade Unions'. After she had proudly proclaimed that there were then 'over 200,000 women organised', the debate turned on the problem of whether or not it was right that women should have the same wages as men for doing the same work. Miss Macarthur thought it logically unanswerable, of course, that they should, but Toynbee Hall then, as almost always, was not of one accord.[104] Nor was the East End. It is interesting that the first speakers on the subject of women's suffrage at Toynbee Hall in 1910/11 were both from outside East End society – Isobel Sterling and the Honourable Mrs Richard Grosvenor. There were other lectures with highly interesting titles in that year – including E. F. Wise on 'A Minimum Wage' and J. J. Scott and J. E. King on 'The House of Lords' Veto'. Yet it was in the following year that the most interesting speakers took part in the Thursday evening Smoking Debates – among them Erskine Childers on 'Home Rule', A. M. Carr Saunders, a Resident and future Director of the London School of Economics on 'The Value of War', Wilson Harris, future Editor of the *Spectator* on 'Railway Nationalisation' and J. J. Mallon, future Warden of Toynbee Hall, on 'The Present Labour Unrest'. Neither Harvey nor Birley was entirely in favour of these Thursday sessions, on the grounds that there seemed to be more smoke than debate, and there were other critics who described Toynbee Hall on these occasions as an indoor Tower Hill. Yet the need for genuine debate was always stressed, not least for debate amongst the Residents. One influential Toynbee Resident who was not in accord either with the majority view which usually prevailed there nor with the views of most of the speakers was E. J. Urwick, Sub-Warden before Beveridge. He opposed state-provided old-age pensions on the grounds that they were a form of socialism and objected to relief schemes for the unemployed on the grounds that those offered work under them did not work. Once looking out of his window, when four unemployed men were engaged in such a scheme, he wrote sarcastically, 'They work for a time – never more; and the rest looking on expectorating vigorously the while. I won't sit in judgement on them; put it rather that they are economising effort.'[105]

Urwick, surprisingly, was a sociologist, whose considered views were stated at greater length in his book, *A Philosophy of Social Progress*, published in 1912, a book which should be set alongside *Social Evolution in Political Theory* by Hobhouse, a writer to whom he acknowledged his debt. For all his prejudices, Urwick dwelt, like Hobhouse – whose name is commemorated in London School of Economics lectures as Sidney Ball's name is in Oxford – on social harmony and progress. There were no obvious signs of the influence of Toynbee Hall experience in his highly abstract analysis which culminated in his conclusion – that 'what is of importance is not the reform but the will that prompts it'[106] – yet he may well have been thinking of Barnett when he drew it. Hobhouse, however, might have been thinking of Barnett, too, when he wrote that 'the social ideal is not to be reached by logical processes alone, but must stand in close relation to experience.'[107]

A review of Urwick's book in the *Toynbee Record* shows that there was diversity without enmity in Toynbee Hall during the exciting years between 1910 and 1914, when there were more signs of internal conflict in Britain, much of it socially generated, than there had been since the 1880s when the Hall was founded. 'We cannot agree,' the reviewer wrote, 'that the results of reform are not to be counted, but only the will to reform; rather we should have said that to the reformer who has realised the purpose of reform, results are everything.' Yet he praised 'excellent passages in the book', among them the most contentious which provided 'a relief from what is otherwise commonplace and no matter of dispute'.[108] The reviewer may have been E. F. Wise, Sub-Warden between 1911 and 1912: he was a vigorous advocate of new social legislation.

One of the problems of Birley's Wardenship was that he seemed less interested in these big national themes than in the daily routines of Toynbee Hall. He attached great importance to informal contacts. 'It is in opportunities for social intercourse which gives our work its unique position,' he maintained, giving priority to 'making friends'.[109] He would have found particular pleasure in a comment of Werner Picht, the German observer who lived at Toynbee for a time and wrote one of the first general books on Settlements – 'sometimes I think I feel more at home in these rooms (at Toynbee Hall) than anywhere else in the world.'[110]

Far from appreciating this approach, critics felt that too much of the activity at the Hall had become routine. Many of the societies which met there were still meeting there, it was claimed, either because of past association and because they could 'have the use of good rooms and lanterns free of cost', and new members were only being welcomed by those who managed their affairs 'from among their own friends and class'.[111] In 1913, therefore, a group of 'rebellious critics' drafted a new plan of action which required a different kind of leadership from Birley's. Toynbee Hall, they urged, should seek to become 'the centre for Tutorial classes in the East End of London' and to work more actively with the WEA, 'one of the living movements of the time which captures precisely the type of men whom we wish to have in connection with Toynbee Hall'.[112] It should abandon 'activities which can as well or better be pursued elsewhere' and turn instead to Friendly Societies and trade unions, the latter 'a most important feature in the social organisation of this and every other civilised country' which formed 'the chief centre of interest for very much of what is best among the working classes'.

> At the present time there is a great gulf fixed between the Trades Unionists and the so-called upper classes of society [the critics went on]. On both sides there is gross ignorance and unjust suspicion. Toynbee Hall should bridge the gulf. The Councils

and Executives of the Unions often meet in London, though the strength of their membership lies elsewhere. Toynbee Hall also possesses the great advantage that Trade Unionists are not suspicious of the Settlement.[113]

The Enquirers' Club, they complained, had recently ceased to exist, and in the opinion of the petitioners there were 'few things more to be desired than its revival'; the Club had made Toynbee Hall 'a meeting place of the very men whom we most desire to see there'.[114]

Unfortunately for Birley, this memorandum reached the redoubtable Henrietta, who did not hesitate to apportion blame in a typically forthright manner. Mr Birley she felt, had to go. And she had already identified a successor who she felt could restore confidence – Canon J. H. Masterman, who had given the series of WEA lectures in the nave of Westminster Abbey: 'He is not a great *deep* man like Canon Barnett,' she conceded, 'but he cares for all good causes and is "in" with people of every sort.' Perhaps, more important still, he seemed willing to accept Henrietta's direction. She had offered

> to go again and live in the Lodge and put the House right and on an economical basis and give that confidence to the habitués . . . which I cannot but know that my presence would create. This offer I have made to Canon Masterman and I find he considers it most valuable – especially to begin with. I, therefore, will write it to you, and if it commends itself, I will make it to the Committee.[115]

Perhaps foreseeing an adverse reaction to her proposal, Henrietta promised to be humble and unobtrusive.

> I do not mean that I plan to return with an outrider and a flourish of trumpets. I just propose to furnish my old lodge upper room and a cupboard to sleep in and slip back to be an out of sight general servant.

She was aware that she could not assume such a pose for long, but she was, she went on to assure Milner, 'the one person who can link up the old and new and bridge the gulf which now exists'.[116]

Henrietta's offer was not taken up. Instead, J. St George Heath, aged 31, was appointed the new Warden of Toynbee Hall in March 1914. Like Harvey, he was a Quaker – though a Quaker by conversion – who had been a Resident for a brief period ten years before. Since then he had been Warden of the Neighbour Guilds Settlement at Sheffield, had spent six months in Germany studying social questions, and had been a Lecturer on Social Questions at Woodbrooke Settlement, Birmingham. He had also worked with the WEA and with Seebohm Rowntree on the preparation of the Land Enquiry Committee, chaired by A. H. D. Acland, which Lloyd George believed offered the key to Liberal political success in the future.[117] As Secretary he had been responsible for schedules which, in Rowntree's phrase, might have been answered in twenty years if Lloyd George had placed the whole Civil Service at the disposal of the Enquiry.[118]

Heath had little chance to impose his personality on Toynbee Hall before war broke out, a war which threatened not only all existing political strategies, but all institutional continuities. Indeed, once war began, 'it seemed for a time,' in his words, 'as if we should have to suspend our activities altogether through lack of Residents.' (Some had enlisted, some had been drafted to administration.) By the end of the war, 'Toynbee men' were in key positions – among them Morant, Llewellyn Smith, Beveridge, Wise, and J. R. Brooke at the Ministry of Food, Arthur Salter at the Ministry of Shipping, J. A. Dale at the War Office, Layton at the Ministry of Munitions, H. D. Henderson at the Cotton Control Board, Hitchcock at the War Office, Heath himself at the Ministry of Labour.[119] Meanwhile, Oxford and Cambridge had long been 'empty' of undergraduates and 'many links had been snapped', including the all important Balliol link, which it would be difficult to restore. There were many Toynbee deaths too, thirteen of which are recorded in the Roll of Honour in the Dining Hall. T. S. Lukis was killed at Neuve Chapelle in March 1915, to be followed by G. A. Ramsay in the Dardanelles. And it was two former Toynbee Scouts who had carried Lukis's dead body from the battlefield.

In such circumstances, Heath decided in July 1915 on drastic action – a move east to Poplar. Volunteers were now drilling in the Toynbee Hall Quad, recruiting meetings were being held in the Lecture Hall, and Balliol House was to be turned into a camp for the Royal Field Artillery. There had been talk of a general move east even before the war began and already five Residents, including Birley and Carr Saunders, had moved out of Whitechapel to live further out. Now, Heath urged, the residential part of Toynbee Hall should be moved from Whitechapel to Poplar, leaving the Whitechapel building as 'a centre for educational and institutional activities'. Such a move he argued, would revive 'a spirit of adventure' akin to that which had been so conspicuous during the early pioneering days of Toynbee Hall:

> There is always a danger in old-established institutions that they become too proud of their traditions, too timorous to apply the pruning knife, too apt to let the free spirit be choked by the accumulation of the past. And it may be that Toynbee Hall had suffered somewhat from the same cause, that it has been tempted to rely too much upon its reputation.[120]

The move to Poplar was also justified, Heath claimed, because of changes which had been taking place in the neighbourhood – 'undreamed of when Canon Barnett first planned Toynbee Hall'.

> The City, with its warehouses, had been pushing itself almost up to our doors, slums have been swept away, and an immigrant population has covered nearly the whole of the neighbourhood – a population very well looked after by those of the Jewish faith, with its own Jewish Board of Guardians. Slowly and steadily the conviction has been deepening that Whitechapel no longer secured for young men fresh from the Universities that living experience of the need and outlook of a normal British working class population which they wished to obtain.[121]

Heath had the courage of his convictions, and in October 1915 he, his wife and a few Residents moved to two early Victorian houses, 4 and 5 Montague Place in Poplar. And, as further evidence of change, in two nearby houses in High Street, Poplar, a Women's Settlement for Women from the Universities, which like Montague Place could accommodate up to eight persons, was opened. What the Suffragettes – or the Toynbee Hall Council – had not been able to achieve before 1914 was now being accomplished. The houses had previously belonged to a philanthropic old lady who offered hospitality to troops on the sole condition that they should say the Lord's Prayer before they went to bed.

There is no doubt that Heath was a man of high principle, convinced that small-scale endeavour rather than large-scale planning was the most fruitful activity for those who hoped to promote social justice:

> The ten years that preceded the War [he argued] were marked by a great outburst of national legislation. The younger generation began to think on a heroic scale and were impatient of anything that seemed small and humble. . . . And yet it is impossible to live in a poor district without realising all the legislation which has been passed has only touched on the fringe of the question and that much of it has tended to be out of touch with the real needs of the people. There is a greater need than ever in Social Reform for mystics who can not only be practical but content to labour away at humble things. All social organisations need to be perpetually reinterpreted in terms of social beings.[122]

There was a more obvious link with Birley than with Barnett in such an analysis. There was a more serious element still in Heath's thinking and feeling, however, which was bound to create increasing difficulties. He was a pacifist, as was his wife, and at a time when conscientious objectors were subject not only to derision but to violent hostility, they found it difficult to carry out either new or old activities (with the exception of a Eurythmics School which attracted two dozen girls between the ages of 13 and 15 and a social club for factory girls working on the Isle of Dogs). Public feeling against the Heaths was at its height when a local infant school just off the East India Dock Road was bombed and seventeen children were killed, and after taking up a post (with Milner's help) in the Ministry of Labour, Heath resigned the Wardenship in October 1917. (He was to die of pneumonia soon after the war ended in November 1918.)

> It seems to be a disastrous thing [Heath wrote] that, after having been led into such a big enterprise as starting a second Toynbee in Poplar, we should now have to abandon it; but if this is inevitable, there is certainly a great deal to be said for trying to revive the residential character of the old Toynbee, which, personally, I never intended to get rid of altogether. At one time I thought I saw my way to keeping both as live and mutually supporting institutions.[123]

In fact, only Toynbee remained alive, for even the Women's Settlement in Poplar went too, dismissed tersely by Henrietta as 'alien to Toynbee subscribers'.[124]

Not everyone at Toynbee had shared Heath's enthusiasm for the move to Poplar, and E. F. Hitchcock, the Toynbee Hall Secretary, had elected to remain behind at Whitechapel in the Warden's Lodgings, ostensibly to oversee the societies and classes, some of which were very popular, like a course on *Modern Jewish History from Mendelssohn to Herzl*, the largest extension course in London. And lectures could have their dramatic moments too. For example, once when Gilbert Slater, the Principal of Ruskin College, Oxford, from 1909 to 1915, was giving a popular University Extension Lecture on English Local Government, 'so absorbed and short-sighted was he that he failed to notice an abrupt tenseness of silence, followed by a sudden and unusual roar.' Nor according to Hitchcock, who told the story, did he notice how rapidly one by one the members of his class ceased interest in his lecture and departed to the outside quadrangle. It needed repeated 'admonitions from his chairman . . . by the usual expedient of pulling his coat tails' before Slater at last woke up to the situation and the two of them went out into the quad 'to see the horizon above the long low roof of the drawing room a blaze of flashing redness from the Tower Guns and from all angles converging of searchlights focusing on a tiny and beautiful silver cigarshaped object', a Zeppelin, 'which hovered and then disappeared in the high clouds. Shrapnel was splattering on the ground and against the walls.' Having seen what was happening, Slater 'imperturbably walked back to the Lecture Hall to continue his Lecture'.[125]

Since Hitchcock with equal imperturbability carried on the old Toynbee Hall traditions throughout the most difficult years of the war on the spot, he it was who was asked to serve as Acting Warden for the duration of the war when Heath resigned, although he was working in the daytime as Deputy Director of Wool Textiles at the War Office. The combination of jobs was curiously appropriate for the East End remained a textile centre throughout the war, and after an early, shortlived slump, which led the Mayors of Bethnal Green, Hackney, Poplar, Stepney and Shoreditch to appeal for relief, there was a boom which brought more prosperity to the East End than it had known since Barnett's arrival there. By the end of the war tailoring stood out among London industries as the one which had absorbed 'by far the largest number of fresh workpeople, and which had much the largest percentage (nearly two-thirds) working overtime'. In the docks, too, there was an 'abnormally brisk demand for labour'.[126] Not surprisingly, therefore, the name 'Poor Man's Lawyer' was changed to 'Working Man's Lawyer'. There was little time to discuss the future, although there were many ex-Toynbee Hall men in the Reconstruction Committee of which Vaughan Nash was Secretary and the subsequent Ministry of Reconstruction which he also served. There was now a closer link between Toynbee Hall and Whitehall than between Toynbee Hall and Oxford University.

When Poplar closed, Hitchcock and the Toynbee Council none the less had to appeal for funds to Oxford and elsewhere 'to share in considering the great works of reconstruction in our social and civic life to repair the ravages of the War'; and as soon as it began to be feasible new Residents from the universities were discovered with the help of old Residents. There were twenty of them by the end of 1918, more this time from Cambridge. Austin Robinson and Gerald F. Shove had arrived in 1916, Claud William Guillebaud arrived in 1915, and Alexander Loveday in 1916. Now in 1918 there were nine new names in one year, and another sixteen new names in 1919 – with some old names restored, including that of Attlee, who lived at the Hall from March to October.

'It is about a year since Toynbee Hall was opened,' a memorandum on future policy had stated in January 1919. 'The main object of reestablishing a community of men with, in the main, similar interests and ideals, has therefore been achieved.'

> It is felt that Toynbee Hall shall continue to differ from the usual type of settlement in that it will regard social work not only as an attempt to deal with the actual difficulties with which it comes in contact but as a means of throwing light on national problems. Social work as ordinarily understood would be by no means excluded, but if possible should be given a national obligation?[127]

Two months later a reunion dinner was held over which Bryce presided and which Henrietta Barnett attended. So also did Beveridge. Another guest was Arnold Toynbee's first pupil at

Balliol. There was a backward look in all this, but Toynbee Hall was, in fact, on the eve of another new period in its history.

Army cadets at work leather-stitching in Balliol House which, according to Mallon, they treated as 'a fortress which had not surrendered'

IV
The Mallon Years,
1919–1954

The new Warden appointed in 1919, James Joseph Mallon, despite his long association with Toynbee Hall, was viewed in some quarters with a tinge of disquiet. The *Daily Express* described him uneasily as a 'blue-blooded Labourite'.

> He is witty [it went on], he believes in the public house becoming the pub, he invents trade boards, he is a member of the Whitley Committee. But will the Oxford undergraduates flock to Toynbee in the future or will it become a nursery of Labour M.P.s?[1]

The *Evening Standard* echoed the question. Would not the 'witty conversationalist' with 'solid sympathies' turn Toynbee Hall into 'the happy hunting ground of the crank and doctrinaire socialist'?[2]

Mallon's appointment as Warden was announced without any such questions in the Toynbee *Report* of 1916–19:

> The Council of Toynbee Hall, of which Lord Milner is Chairman, has appointed Mr. J. J. Mallon to be Warden of Toynbee Hall on the retirement of Mr. E. F. Hitchcock. As is generally known, Mr. Mallon has taken for a long time past a prominent part in industrial and social movements and possesses an intimate knowledge of settlement work. . . He is a treasurer of the Workers' Educational Association and lectures at London School of Economics. For many years he has been in close touch with measures for the improvement of social conditions in the East End of London. Mr. Mallon's many friends among past and present residents and adherents of Toynbee Hall will heartily welcome his appointment.[3]

The timing of Mallon's appointment was as interesting as the timing of Barnett's appointment in 1883. The year 1919 was a year of industrial unrest, when the groups of people with power, those who could rightly be described as 'the Establishment', were very nervous about the influence of 'doctrinaire' socialists.[4] They knew also that only one year earlier the Labour Party, which was to have its first taste of government in 1924, had acquired the new constitution on which its future growth was to be based.[5] Yet Mallon, while influential within the Labour movement and on close terms with many 'doctrinaire socialists' – he actually stood as a Labour candidate in 1922 – had the exceptional gift of getting on well with everybody, not least with members of 'the Establishment', some of whom wanted to reach 'an accommodation' with Labour. He was the perfect Warden for the times, just as Barnett, the founder, had been. It has rightly been said, indeed, that from 1919 to 1954 Mallon was Toynbee Hall, and many historians (and Residents) judge this period as the most successful in the Settlement's history.

In background and in experience, 'Jimmy', as he was known to all, was different from each of the previous Wardens. The son of Irish Roman Catholic parents, who had moved to the North of England, Mallon was born in Chorlton, Manchester, on Christmas Eve, 1874. His father died when he was 4, and he was offered no possible opportunity for prolonged education. When he left school, he did not find a job in textiles or engineering as might have been expected, but was apprenticed to a jeweller; and it was through this apprenticeship – and not through industry – that he secured a practical education in trade unionism as well as his craft. As a boy, he joined the Shop Assistants' Union, to which he felt committed for the rest of his life, and through this union he learned at first hand about others.

Mallon soon became interested, too, in social politics outside the workplace, and after taking part in debates, in which he excelled, he joined the staff of the University Settlement in Ancoats, located in one of the poorest parts of Manchester, in Mallon's own words, 'a place where misery was profound'. Later in life, he recalled trying to rouse a street-corner audience there by telling them that whereas the average expectation of life in England was fifty years, in Ancoats it was only thirty-three. 'Thirty three years of life in Ancoats,' a voice called out in reply, 'it's a damned sight too long.'[6]

Mallon flourished at the Ancoats Settlement, the origins of which paralleled those of Toynbee Hall. Charles Rowley had founded a Brotherhood there in 1877, and the Settlement, which was influenced by Barnett, had acquired an Art Museum, too, established by T. C. Horsfall.[7] It was one of twelve other settlements in England, and Barnett's connection with it was close.[8] It was Barnett, indeed, who had addressed the first Manchester meeting on the subject of Settlements in 1895 on the invitation of the Principal of Owen's College, the mid-Victorian institution which was to provide the nucleus of the University of Manchester. Within a few months of Barnett's address, an even shorter space of time than the interval between the St John's meeting in Oxford and establishment of Toynbee Hall, the new Ancoats Settlement had formally come into existence.

People who knew Mallon at Ancoats recall him as 'the life and soul of every activity, bubbling over with fun, and breaking into jokes on every occasion'. Slightly built, with dark curly hair and twinkling blue eyes, already at that time he was enthusiastic, convivial, bursting with energy, and brilliant in his use of – or play with – words: he was so mentally and physically agile, indeed, that he was often compared with Puck. Yet Mallon was no mere entertainer. There was a deeply compassionate side to his nature, and a compelling interest in all kinds of social reform. He was to write later that at Ancoats 'even education and recreation mattered less to us than reform'.

It was from that base, therefore, that Manchester unemployment and slum housing were carefully studied, and campaigns pursued for improvement in both working and in living conditions. Nor was Mallon content with study.

Under a non-party banner [he recalled] we went into local politics and in the conflict, which seemed to us to make history, carried T. R. Marr, our housing candidate to the City Council. We formulated a municipal programme and explained it at local street corners. We demonstrated – we were always demonstrating.[9]

Mallon was soon drawn from Ancoats as his first base into national demonstrating and politics – away from the industrial North towards Whitehall, Westminster – and Fleet Street. In 1906 he was appointed Secretary to the National League to Establish a Minimum Wage, the first of many such national appointments through which he met fellow reformers. In particular, he worked in close partnership with the outstanding woman trade unionist Mary Macarthur, who had become Secretary of the Women's Trade Union League in 1903 and three years later founded the National Federation of Women Workers. It was an inspiring partnership of common motives and contrasting talents, which cast the spotlight on the exploitation not only of shop workers but of 'home workers' engaged in the 'sweated trades', the kind of workers familiar to Toynbee Hall and its Residents. Indeed, workers who were too weak to organise were more familiar in the East End than they were in Lancashire.

Mallon and Mary Macarthur spent much of their time lobbying behind the scenes, getting to know MPs and members of the House of Lords, some of whom needed no persuasion to press for legislation.[10] Yet it was essential for the reformers to win publicity if they were to be successful, and it was with publicity in mind that Mallon turned hopefully to the Press. His initial victory came when A. G. Gardiner, the intelligent and energetic editor of the *Daily News*, who claimed to know everyone in power, offered to put the full weight of his newspaper behind the campaign.[11] It was through Mallon's secretaryship of the National Anti-Sweating League that he was first drawn towards Toynbee Hall; and ten years later, soon after he became Warden, he was to marry Gardiner's eldest daughter, Stella Katherine.

Toynbee Hall, guided by Ernest Aves and E. F. Wise, had been closely associated with the largely forgotten anti-sweated labour agitation even before Mallon. Indeed, it was so quickly forgotten that Tawney, who himself wrote on the plight of the chainmakers and home tailors[12] was surprised and amused later in his life when a lady doctor asked him just what was wrong with sweating and why he had been so opposed to it.[13] In Edwardian England, few people could have failed to understand sweating was news. Not everyone at Toynbee Hall, however, was pleased with Gardiner's Sweated Industries Exhibition in June 1906: it seemed to be lacking in relevant statistics and even in a good catalogue. It was 'one of those things,' the author of an article in the *Toynbee Record* claimed, 'in which good intentions have not done everything that was hoped.'[14]

None the less, the Exhibition pointed the way to the legislation of 1909, the Trade Boards Act, introduced by Winston Churchill and described by one of its vociferous opponents as 'a complete surrender to the socialist party'.[15] Mallon led a deputation of the Anti-Sweating League to meet Winston Churchill, who had moved to the Board of Trade in 1908, and was carrying out an intensive programme of social reform there – not without irony, since he had refused the Local Government Board on the grounds that he did not want to be 'shut up in a soup-kitchen with Mrs. Sidney Webb'.[16] And that was only the first stage in Mallon's public commitment. After the passing of the 1909 Act fixing minimum wages in a number of specified 'sweated' trades, he became Honorary Secretary of the Trades Boards Advisory Council as well as a member of thirteen of the first of the new Trade Boards. And in 1913, as an Associate of Toynbee Hall, where he met Clement Attlee, he organised a conference there which led to the establishment of a new voluntary body, the 'Home Workers' League for the Care and Protection of Homemakers'.[17]

By then, Mallon was already as well known a figure in the East End as he had been in Manchester, and was sharing in a partnership with Ernest Aves, who himself presided over eight Trade Boards in England and five in Ireland. When Aves died in 1917 he was rightly described in the *Toynbee Record* as 'as true a knight as ever tilted spear, redressing human grievances'.[18] Mallon was on the eve of a change in his own prospects, for the War of 1914–18 radically changed the agenda and timetable of British social politics and brought about major changes in the structure and management of the 'labour force' which had always interested him so profoundly. Mallon now discerned new opportunities for himself and for the success of 'the social struggle' in the long and wearing conflict in the trenches of France. He was keenly interested both in mobilising labour in support of the war – munitions were as important as soldiers – and in 'reconstruction schemes' once the war was over. Indeed, he saw the two as directly related.

With the Labour leader, J. R. Clynes, he took part, therefore, in an official study of workers' committees in 1916, and, like him, came to believe in what was usually called 'Whitleyism', a system of Joint Industrial Councils, named after the Speaker of the House of Commons, John Whitley. The message behind such a system was thought at that time to be universal. In the words of Harry Gosling, the Chairman of the Trades Union Congress in 1916, a Congress which Mallon attended, 'We are tired of War in the industrial field (but)...we shall never get any lasting industrial peace except on the lines of industrial democracy.'[19]

Like the Liberal J. L. Hammond and the Socialist G. D. H. Cole, Mallon joined the small 'Romney Street Group', founded in 1917 by Joseph Thorp, the drama critic of *Punch* which included several people with Labour sympathies who met regularly at a weekly lunch in Dean's Close, the workplace of the Ministry of Reconstruction.[20] The group also included Thomas Jones, until 1917 Secretary of the Welsh National Insurance Commission and later (until 1930) Deputy Secretary of the Cabinet under four successive Prime Ministers. And soon it was Jones, who had been introduced to London life by Mallon, who was reversing roles, and describing Mallon to Lloyd George as a man who 'would bring some red blood into the rather anaemic arteries' of the Ministry of Reconstruction. Jones had an eye for people and used his influence behind the scenes to help the people he liked get on. He added in his note to the Prime Minister that Mallon was 'persona grata' with Vaughan Nash, Secretary of the Ministry, who had been a Toynbee Hall Resident from 1887 to 1889.[21]

Mallon, who never required much of this kind of promoting, served as a Commissioner on Industrial Unrest for Lloyd George and paid two clandestine visits to France – on one occasion meeting R. H. Tawney, then an infantry sergeant and securing a draft statement from soldiers in the front designed to influence discontented munitions factory workers in Britain. The move was welcomed, if not initiated by Lloyd George, but not surprisingly General Haig vetoed the transmission of the statement.[22] Mallon was by then Treasurer of the Workers' Educational Association which brought him into touch with a group of trade unionists and educationists with whom he was to remain in close contact throughout his life.

Politics inevitably came into the picture. Indeed Jones and Mallon met frequently during the war, lunching or dining together, meeting with trade unionists (and with Tawney, when he was on leave), and discussing post-war strategies. On one occasion for example, they were plotting together for Mallon to interview Gardiner quietly to discover whether the *Daily News* would support the Labour Party at the post-war General Election.[23] There was a sense of 'malleability' at that time, as Lloyd George himself once put it, in the London political scene, with some of the people who met so frequently at this time to discuss future social politics, remaining civil servants, as Nash did, and others going into party politics. Moreover, of the latter, some were to remain Liberals and others were to join the new-style Labour Party.[24] It is within this context that the concern of the *Daily Express* when Mallon's appointment as Warden was announced must be examined. He was on familiar terms with leading Liberals, but he had served also on a number of Labour Party committees after the reorganisation of the Party in 1918. Gardiner's *Daily News* described him enthusiastically as 'an old head on young shoulders.'

It was after Mallon had moved to Toynbee Hall, however, that he fought an election at Watford (unsuccessfully) in 1922 in a campaign which Hammond claimed 'signalled the end of liberalism'.[25] Characteristically, his election manifesto, which had the support of the veteran Liberal Editor of the *Guardian*, C. P. Scott, who told the electors that Mallon would be of 'great value' in parliament, referred less to the official Labour programme than to the fact that the candidate had been 'one of the authors of the famous Whitley Report' and had served as 'a member of every important committee appointed during and after the war to consider industrial affairs'. 'He had worked tirelessly,' the manifesto went on, 'for the extension of the Trades Boards Act,' which had led to over a hundred boards being brought into existence. And it concluded with a testimonial to Mallon from H. J. Tennant, who had been Under-Secretary of State for War in the Asquith Government and who was described as one of Lord Kitchener's colleagues at the War Office:

> The War Office was indebted to you in the severe crisis at the beginning of the war for services, which your special knowledge enabled you to render, particularly in regard to supplies of clothing to the men who responded to Lord Kitchener's appeal. To those men your help was invaluable. These services were only a small part of the total services you rendered with disinterested devotion to the State throughout the War.[26]

Mallon was asked to stand again as a Labour candidate – in the special circumstances of the Second World War – and though he remained interested in the possibility he was too effervescent for party selection committees and lacked the singlemindedness of party purpose which made acceptable backbencher MPs. Instead, he devoted the rest of his life to Toynbee Hall much to the advantage of the institution, and he was to draw in people of every kind of political complexion to help him. In the process, he came to know the East End, it was said, as an actor comes to know Charing Cross Road. In fact, while there was a touch of the actor in him, his knowledge of the area was greater than theirs was of their own locale. He met people in their homes and got to know their families.

In the first instance, however, it required a considerable act of faith on Mallon's part to accept the Wardenship. Hitchcock as Acting Warden had struggled heroically to prevent the closure of the settlement, but morale was at a low ebb, and the financial difficulties were considerable. Indeed, the Chairman of the Finance Committee reported on 11 October 1919 that 'the present bank balance' was 'practically nil and realizable assets come to about the same'.[27] And as late as January 1923, J. A. Dale, Resident from 1913 to 1915 and from 1918 to 1921 and then Honorary Secretary though living in Northern Ireland, reported sadly that he was 'making very poor progress in raising the Warden's salary fund'.

> I have asked the Council [he went on] to have an emergency meeting to deal with the matter. The first quarterly payment is due at the end of this month, and the fund at present consists of at the very most £65, whereas £100 is due then. I am loath to trouble you but it would be disastrous if we could not raise Mallon's salary, and I think that if it has to be paid from the general fund, we shall place Mallon in a very disagreeable position of having to raise his own salary.[28]

It was fortunate for Toynbee Hall and the Settlement movement as a whole that Mallon had little interest in pecuniary rewards and accepted with equanimity his uncertain financial position for the rest of his Wardenship.

The Council of Toynbee Hall recognised that Mallon would continue to be much in demand as an industrial arbitrator, speaker and campaigner. A new Sub-Warden was appointed at the same time as he was, therefore, a Quaker, E. St John Catchpool, who had already spent some time at Toynbee Hall between August 1914 and May 1915. Solemn and conscientious, Catchpool provided the perfect foil for Mallon, while efficiently and affectionately supporting his Warden for almost ten years before leaving in 1928 to become Secretary of the Welwyn Garden City Association and later National Secretary of the Youth Hostels Association, an increasingly important organisation which had its origins at Toynbee Hall.

Meanwhile, Mallon remained convinced that Residents constituted the heart of the successful Settlement, 'the link that binds them to the University, the Civil Service and the professions'.

> The Resident in the Settlement [he maintained] is a member of the family who without ceremony can be asked to lend a hand or to undertake a role for which there is an occasion. When he moves away from the Settlement, he is still on the outer fringe of the family circle. He can remain helper and consult, and embody active or passive goodwill.[29]

It was with this conviction that Mallon brought back into the affairs of Toynbee Hall old Residents, like Frank Wise, Clement Attlee, Maurice Birley and Edward Blight.

Room for the accommodation of additional Residents was found in the premises formerly known as Balliol House, 'which suffered rough usage at the hands of the cadets who were allowed to occupy them during the war', but were now renovated thanks to the generosity of G. M. Booth, the son of Charles Booth. In acknowledgment, the Council of Toynbee Hall changed the name of the reclaimed premises from Balliol House to Charles Booth House and the lecture room on the ground floor was renamed the Aves Room, after

Booth's collaborator Ernest Aves, who had become known at Toynbee Hall as 'Pater'. Booth House was formally reopened on 1 December 1920 by Lord Bryce who saluted with equal enthusiasm and with characteristic grace 'the old and the new Toynbee'.[30]

A year later, in order to maintain close contact with the Universities of Oxford and Cambridge, a Universities Week was held at Toynbee Hall 'to further the study of industrial questions' and participants were invited to meet experts in these questions and leading employers and Trade Unionists, and to look over industrial plants and establishments. Sixty people attended and listened to morning lectures in Toynbee Hall, inspected factories, slum areas and building schemes in the afternoons, and in the evenings met representatives of local industries.[31] The project was so successful that the University Week thereafter became an annual event. A study week at Easter for London university students was introduced later and attracted even larger numbers of undergraduates.

Mallon himself thought of this early post-war as 'a prelude to adventure'.

Educational and other activities have proceeded as in recent years [he wrote in 1920] but special attention has been given to the questions of the functions of the Settlements in the world which the War has made, the relationship of the individual Settlements to one another and to the Universities, and to strengthening the connections of Toynbee Hall with the vital forces in East London life and to making new connections.

And it was with this in mind that in 1920 he summoned a weekend meeting at Balliol College, Oxford, to reformulate the Settlement ideal.

At the Balliol meetings addresses included 'Early Days in Toynbee Hall' by one of the most active of the first Residents, Bolton King, 'Settlements in America' by Walter Clark and 'The New Task of Settlements' by Mallon.[32] An even more important meeting was organised at Toynbee Hall itself in April 1920 – the first representative conference of the sixty-one Residential Settlements of Great Britain. It was at this conference that an Association of Residential Settlements was created with Mallon as President and Dame Henrietta Barnett as Deputy President. One of the objects of the Association was 'to seek the close association and co-operation of Universities, local Education Authorities and Voluntary Bodies engaged in adult education', and it was because of this orientation that the new body was given the task of organising the Universities Week.

In 1922 a World Association of Settlements was set up on Toynbee Hall initiative following a meeting of the Hall attended by 300 delegates from twenty-one different countries. Different slogans were heard, like the German 'first do, then preach,' but there was a strong sense of a uniting bond. The Settlements philosophy knew no frontiers. Nor did the philosophy of the Workers' Travel Association which had been founded at Toynbee Hall a year earlier under the inspiration of T. N. Rogerson, who had been brought to Toynbee Hall by Mallon. It secured the help of Harry Gosling and of the young Ernest Bevin, who as a future Foreign Secretary was to dream of a Europe where passports would not be necessary. It was a financially successful venture and in its first year of operations was able to provide milk for starving children in Germany and Austria. Two years later it become too big for Toynbee Hall and had to move to Transport House. Its success was all the more remarkable in that throughout the 1920s there were large numbers of workers in

England who had no paid holiday. Indeed, legislation to secure this was not passed until 1936. It is interesting that Pimlott, who wrote the jubilee history of Toynbee Hall, went on to write a scholarly study on English holidaymakers.[33]

In 1921, there was a further sign of increasing international involvement at Toynbee Hall when Mallon launched an annual American seminar to bring American politicians, academics and social workers to Toynbee Hall – first, to study the British political and social system and, second, as the international situation darkened during the 1920s, to promote American understanding of European affairs.[34]

Already by the mid-1920s, some 150 Americans were attending the American Seminar in Toynbee Hall, and by 1930, the figure was over 1,000. The participants were selected by an American Committee headed by Dr Sherwood Eddy, and they were chosen because of their interest in international matters and because as editors, educationists, and heads of institutions they were persons of influence in their own communities.[35] They usually followed up their visit to Toynbee Hall with a short visit to the Continent. In 1931 they planned to visit Moscow, and Lady Astor and Bernard Shaw decided to join the party. Even Mallon's sense of the possible must have been challenged when Frank Wise warned him that though the Russians would be delighted to receive a visit from Bernard Shaw, and would certainly fête him and make him a centre of attention, real embarrassment would be caused by the presence of Lady Astor. (In his column for 'Action to be taken' Mallon wisely made no comment!).[36]

Henrietta Barnett, never given to unnecessary praise, welcomed 'the quiet but potent influence' that Toynbee Hall seemed to be wielding in international relationships, not only through the seminars but as a conference centre.

> Every year [she wrote] hundreds of people of many nations are entertained in the Settlement; large parties of Americans stay for weeks and leave with extended hearts, kinder feelings and a more subtle comprehension of British difficulties. Without claiming credit, T. H. might be counted as an active partner in the League of Nations.[37]

The atmosphere of the 1930s was to be far more difficult, of course, although the seminars survived until the Second World War began and 2,000 visitors had been brought over. After the First World War Toynbee Hall had been the first adult education agency in the country to resume teaching of the German language – and to bring British and German universities together.[38] Now, it was spotlighting the plight of the Jews and the need to 'fight Fascism'.

There was no sense of sharp breaks, however, and even in 1939 Mallon would have defined the function of Toynbee Hall in much the same way as in 1919. It was to be a 'laboratory' for social study and a 'social force' – the latter always required amplification – but it was also to be a 'common friend', and no amplification was needed here.

Its renown as a place of help brought appeals from people of all types in distress, 'too numerous and dissimilar to classify', but including many men of 'the ex-prisoner type' and other men, who for one of several reasons, could not hope without aid of some kind to find employment or surmount the difficulties in which they found themselves. The treatment of these special cases was the personal responsibility of the Warden.[39] He was the 'common friend' *par excellence*.

Meanwhile, the Hall, on the invitation of a group of prison chaplains, regularly arranged lectures in London prisons, collected books for prisoners at Pentonville and other gaols and encouraged Residents to enrol as Prison Visitors. Equally important, the 'common friend' element in the 'Poor Man's Lawyer' scheme was now known inside and outside East London and was highly recommended inside as well as outside the Courts. 'Have you never heard of Toynbee Hall?' a judge of the Shoreditch County Court asked a workman who pleaded that he had sinned in ignorance of the law. 'The lawyers there would give you the soundest advice obtainable, and it will cost you nothing.'[40]

'The tribute is not undeserved,' was Mallon's comment. The senior poor man's lawyers at Toynbee Hall were eminent in their profession and had given free legal advice in war and peace for a generation; and they were aided by several 'young lawyers in residence' so that they could handle 'thousands of cases every year.' Their 'patience, interest and energy' were he added, 'unfailing', and the work which they carried out covered the widest possible range of family grievance. Awaiting them on every Tuesday evening were husbands and wives seeking redress or escape from their partners; tenants and wage-earners at variance with their landlords or employers; and workers – or employers – troubled by difficult Workmen's Compensation or pensions cases.[41]

The expanding hire purchase system created even more problems than well established pawnshops and the money lending associated with them. Yet resort to the law was never recommended without careful thought, and it was often noted that visits to the Toynbee Hall lawyers were not usually followed by litigation. 'Where it was clear that the claimant would burn his fingers by taking proceedings, the P. M. L. firmly advised "don't".' The lawyers thought of themselves primarily as dissuaders or as peacemakers, bringing common sense and friendliness to bearers of the stories submitted to them. They were always jealous custodians of the legal interests of the local poor, however, and where an issue for legal or other reasons was deemed important, they not only would counsel action but would find money, if need be, to ensure that it was fought.[42]

The Toynbee Hall Legal Aid Service became so widely known at this time that written applications for legal aid were often received from all over Great Britain, and the Prince of Wales, always warmly welcomed to Toynbee Hall by Mallon, came unannounced on many occasions to see what it was doing. Hopes were expressed that the system could be extended with greater financial support, as in Sweden, from the State.[43] 'Voluntarism' was never advocated as an ideology.

The President of the Committee administering the scheme in 1939 was a Judge, Justice Talbot, and the Secretary was Patrick Browne, who also became a Judge. Robert (later Sir Robert) Turton, MP (now Lord Tranmire), who was to become 'Father of the House of Commons' before moving to the Lords, was associated with the scheme, as were Lords Roskill and Birkett, Sir Frank Milton, the Chief Stipendiary Magistrate, Norman Bentwich, and many others equally distinguished. Turton played an important part in seeing through to the Statute Book the Poor Prisoners' Defence Act of 1930 and the Summary Jurisdiction

Appeals Act of 1933. He also won considerable publicity for his efforts in the popular weekly periodical *John Bull*.

Friendship and help were extended to young people as a whole as well as to young offenders, with four agencies at Toynbee Hall providing care and direction, the still active Children's Country Holiday Fund, the Stepney Branch of the Invalid Children's Aid Association, founded in 1939, the Toynbee Branch of the Apprenticeship and Skilled Aid Employment Committee, and the Association for the Care of Young Girls. There was still a role, too, for the Metropolitan Association for Befriending Young Servants.

Toynbee Hall was also a centre of leisure activities for children and adults. The Brownies and Cubs survived the war, and a new Toynbee Guide Company was formed in 1926. As for the Scouts, the oldest troop consisting of thirty Scouts sent two of their troop to the World Jamboree in 1937, a new troop of sea scouts, the 'Lukis' Sea Rovers, was formed in 1938, and the six-patrol Jewish Troop flourished in the late 1930s, receiving special commendation in *The Scouter*.[44] It was a commentary on the times, however, that half the members of the First Stepney Troop could not afford to buy their uniforms in the early 1930s, and that the whole impact of the organisation on the life of the neighbourhood remained seriously limited. Boys in the East End seemed to a Toynbee Hall reporter, to be 'everywhere', 'on the pavement tumbling over one another, chasing round lamp posts or having a friendly fight in some dark corner'.[45]

One club for girls at Toynbee Hall continued to provide exceptional service. The Girls' Dinner Club, dating from a time 'when women earned less than ten shillings a week' and 'sweated labour was the rule rather than the exception', ensured that local female factory employees, who frequently resided at some distance from their workplace, were able to obtain cheap and sustaining midday meals. The small factories in the East End, it was pointed out in 1926, had, with few exceptions, no dining rooms or canteens, nor, because of the limitation of building space, could they hope to acquire them. 'Restaurants and tea rooms abounded', but they were crowded in the dinner hours; and 'many work girls cannot pay their prices except at the cost of sacrificing clothes or amusements, which many of them value more than food'. 'Left to themselves, the girls would obtain somewhere a cup of tea and a morsel of bread and butter and somehow, no doubt, with injury to their health, hold up until the time for their evening meal'. The Hall did not choose to leave them to themselves, however, and the Club had 200 members, who, in the same dated language of the period, during 'their dinner hour' could eat cheaply and after eating 'the exuberant spirits dance or sing, the quieter ones converse, or read or knit'. On two evenings in the week the girls were encouraged to return to Toynbee Hall for one night of singing and one for dancing. 'To the second of these evenings, the girls might, and did, bring their young men.'[46]

It was a society as removed from that of the 1980s as it was from that of the 1880s, as can be seen too in the detailed record of the Boys' Clubs.

> The lot of the East End Boy [Mallon himself wrote] is not a happy one. He is meant to be vigorous, he possesses a genius for adventurous play, but is denied opportunities. His district is not furnished with playing grounds; he is too poor to provide apparatus for games; he is cut off from the country and natural things. In

these circumstances much of what is healthy and fine in him decays or is deflected into wrong channels. He takes to the streets, he makes evil friends and imitates bad models. He loses any ambition he may have cherished and finally may have only one: the ambition to possess money without working for it. At this stage the boy is in great danger and what may have been an inherently strong and healthy character is marred.[47]

Apart from the Toynbee Scout Troops, two of the Old Boys' Clubs founded before 1900 flourished in the 1920s, – those of Northey Street and Pell Street – and they continued to be run by Toynbee Residents and Associates. The Northey Street Club, the particular concern of W. J. Braithwaite until his sudden death in 1938, had many adult members who had grown up with the Club; and thanks to Braithwaite's unstinting efforts funds were raised to buy extensive playing fields at Hainault, 'a door into the country'. Meanwhile, back in the East End, Braithwaite ran a savings club and a co-operative bank. Again, the language of the *Toynbee Annual Reports* is dated but evocative. 'There was no room for slackness at the club, in camp, or on the playing fields,' we read in 1938. One year before Braithwaite's death T. W. Barrett, a Toynbee Resident, took over and began a reorganisation both of Club activities and premises, the latter 'renovated by the men themselves'. When the Second World War broke out, membership was increasing.[48]

The Pell Street Club, for long the special interest of Maurice Birley and two young Toynbee Residents John Oldfield and James Forest, was situated 'in a dark alley, in the neighbourhood of which the population was one of the poorest' and was reopened in 1925. A year later it had one hundred teenaged members who packed the school premises every week night, as well as a following of younger boys who occupied them at an earlier hour.[49] But the Club was not mentioned in the *Reports* of the late 1930s.

This dated picture of youth activities would not be complete if Stepney Juvenile Court were left out of it, incongruous though the association may seem, even given the emphasis on discipline which was so evident in many of Toynbee Hall youth activities. Indeed, there were at least some children in the East End who felt that it was incongruous. 'Please, miss, is this a prison?,' enquired a small boy in 1937, 'regarding Toynbee Hall with disfavour'. Nor did the comment on this question in the *Toynbee Annual Report* entirely dispose of the matter.

> If some of the children of Stepney think of us in this way we can nevertheless feel sure that those of them who come here to stand before the Magistrates in the Court are thankful for the kindliness, understanding and informality with which they are treated.[50]

It is more easy to appreciate why Toynbee Hall was so closely connected with the long established Stepney Skilled Employment Committee, which linked schools and firms, and with the Stepney Juvenile Advisory Committee, which among other activities visited juveniles with problems in their homes. It was also the District Headquarters of the Insurance Department of the Ministry of Health, which administered the Unemployment and Health Insurance scheme, and of the Ministry of Labour Juvenile Employment Exchange, which placed thousands of juveniles annually. And they were official enough. A court, however, is a different matter. Yet the first children's tribunal to be held in a place other than a police court in London was Toynbee Hall, and when it became one of the first eight London Juvenile Courts, Mallon was appointed one of the Justices. The first Chairman, Clark Hall, was grateful 'for the atmosphere of the Settlement' and the co-operation of its Residents,[51] and his successor, Basil Henriques, who succeeded him in 1931, was an old Resident himself. One of his fellow Justices was Lady Cynthia Colville, a Lady in Waiting to Queen Mary, who brought the Queen to the Court on many occasions.

There were two further elements in the picture. The first was John Benn Hostel and Milner Hall for homeless boys, which sometimes accommodated boys on remand, although their names were not divulged. The second, for a time, was a London Council for Voluntary Occupation, set up, with Mallon as Chairman, and with two members of the Toynbee Hall Council, to promote local action, to offer limited finance – for example, for camps, and at the height of the depression, day classes for the unemployed. It benefitted from a Prince of Wales Appeal in 1931. The Prince, indeed, seemed as interested in Toynbee Hall as Queen Mary herself. One night in 1934, for example, just before Christmas, unannounced, he accompanied Mallon into 'the high ways and by ways'. 'In some mysterious way,' wrote a reporter, 'his visit suddenly became known and Wapping (one of the places he visited) simply stood on its head.'[52] The timing of the visit was certainly not unpremeditated, for at that particular Christmas Toynbee was celebrating its fiftieth anniversary.

To introduce *new* friends to Toynbee Hall, Mallon, who was naturally gregarious, organised 'at homes' on Tuesday evenings on rather different lines from Barnett's parties but with the same objects in view, and from the start they were a great success. Politicians, trade unionists, groups of employers, local school teachers, welfare workers, leaders of the Scout Movement, and many similar groups attended them by invitation, and there were streams of other visitors to the Hall, too, among them the Prince of Wales, who got to know the Hall well, and the Crown Prince and Princess of Japan, who knew of the Settlement movement in Japan. Perhaps 'the most unusual and unexpected visitor' was Amelia Earheart, who flew the Atlantic alone in 1932 and came straight to Toynbee. 'She headed off enquiries about her historic flight,' Catchpool recalled, 'and sweeping aside the strain of her lonely journey, she plied me with questions concerning Toynbee and its manifold activities.'[53] Those were 'big names', but there was always an accepted place also at Toynbee Hall for neighbours from adjoining tenements who were encouraged to feel free to 'drop in' when they liked.[54]

A sign of the new vigour at Toynbee was the revival of the Enquirers' Club, and weekly debates at Toynbee Hall once again drew large audiences. 'Whatever the subject', the Hall was said to be 'congested', and 'the supply of speakers in excess of the demand'. 'These debates,' Mallon maintained, were 'much more than a source of instruction and entertainment to a wide circle of men and women.' They were 'a safety valve for thoughts and feelings which, if suppressed, turn into bitterness and morbidity', an expression of the 'Englishman's way' of 'getting things off his chest'. They took place in an atmosphere of 'toleration and good humour, to which all contribute and which are seldom if ever arrested'.[55]

Mallon was impressed by the 'fine native capactiy' of many of the local speakers, a few of whom seemed to him 'erudite'. 'It is amazing,' he wrote, 'that so many poor men should have found time for wide reading and thought. . . . Their proper category is that of the intellectuals, but their poverty has held them back.'[56] There could be repartee at Toynbee Hall too. Thus, one night after Lord Astor had spoken on the perils of the liquor trade, an East End carter, 'looking as jolly as the elder weller', interposed, 'Very good to pitch into the working man but what about the old saying, "drunk as a lord"?'

There was still plenty of smoke inside Toynbee, but during the summer, the Lecture Hall was deserted and debates were held in the coolness and spaciousness of the quad. Some of them were addressed by Americans, Germans, Italians and even by Chinese. 'The open forum is open indeed,' Mallon wrote.[57]

As far as research for action was concerned, Mallon continued to address the problem which had become his particular area of interest – the condition of the home-workers, and he watched with deep concern what happened to them before and after the brief post-war boom. He also supported the scheme of the Enquirers' Club to devote the whole of the session of 1920–1 to unemployment – with Beveridge as a key figure and the socialist G. D. H. Cole as another of the participants.[58] In consequence, a new inquiry was launched in 1921 into the extent and effect of unemployment in London. It was carried out by a committee of Residents and representatives of voluntary bodies in Bethnal Green, Poplar, Shoreditch, and Stepney and its conclusions were twice referred to by Lloyd George in the House of Commons.[59]

Meanwhile George Lavin, a Balliol student, researched from Toynbee Hall the implications of unemployment insurance. Four years later, Kenneth Lindsay, the first holder of the Barnett Fellowship, a young Worcester College graduate who was to become a junior minister and a founder of Political and Economic Planning, completed an enquiry of his own into 'The Scholarship and Free Places System' which was published later in a book *Social Progress and Educational Waste*.[60] Finally, in 1930, one of the oldest former Residents, Llewellyn Smith, knighted in 1908, completed – in the Charles Booth tradition – the first volume of a *New Survey of London Life and Labour* – the beginning of a seven-year task of direction in a field of obvious national importance.[61] The survey suggested too optimistically that 'the appalling squalor of the Spitalfields area' in Booth's time had been 'well nigh swept away by the wholesale demolitions and rebuilding and (it is fair to add) by the replacement of gentiles by Jews'. Yet it recognised that 'certain streets' retained 'the ancient forms of poverty and degradation'.

Llewellyn Smith kept all his Toynbee Hall interests. As long ago as 1898 he had published with another ex-Resident, E. H. Spender, a book *Through the Pyrenees* which was illustrated with his own drawings, and in 1924 he published a fascinating short study on *The Economic Laws of Art Production*. He retired from the Board of Trade in 1927 at the age of 63, and wrote a monograph about it in 1928. Between 1935 and 1943 he was Chairman of the National Association of Boys' Clubs, and in 1939 he completed a *History of East London*.

Llewellyn Smith appreciated how the old established Toynbee Societies, such as the Shakespeare Society, presided over by Otto Sallmann, the Natural History Society, the Art Club, 'without rival among amateur art clubs', the Dramatic Society, the Gardening Society and the St John Ambulance Brigade continued to draw members, both local and from all parts of London, during the 1920s and 1930s. Like other old Residents, too, he observed the care being taken to try to ensure that such societies did not become exclusive preserves but were an integrated part of the life of the Settlement and the neighbourhood. Thus the Toynbee Gardening Society, with its slogan 'Brighter balconies', enrolled residents in the adjacent tenements who through the Society were able to obtain plants and bulbs and window boxes at cheap rates.

Toynbee Hall set out too to continue its function as 'the Popular University', concentrating, as it had done in its beginnings, on higher education of a non-vocational kind. 'As vocational and technical training is provided abundantly in other institutions,' Mallon wrote in the same tradition as the WEA, 'Toynbee is able to concentrate on the "humanities". It is in this respect alone among London institutions.'[62] By 1926, 700 to 800 men and women were enrolling in Toynbee classes, 'They appeal,' it was said – and this time it was the language of Barnett – 'to the best minds among the local inhabitants and especially attract the younger Trade Unionists.'[63]

Of the classes on offer that year, five were three-year tutorial classes, the members of which pledged themselves to join and attend the class regularly for three successive winters. 'The standards of these classes are high,' the Hall reported on the lines of all WEA District Reports, 'the student must read widely; he must also submit written work at regular intervals to his tutor.' Though there were some students who found the requirements of such a class beyond their capacity and the weaker ones fell out before the concluding year,

> in most cases a dozen or more of the original students will hold on to the end and the keenest spirits not be satisfied even then. The survivors of certain classes started at Toynbee four or five years ago still meet informally and voluntarily to continue their studies. . . . It is hard to overpraise the efforts of such students whose leisure time is limited and whose reading perhaps may be carried on in congested houses or rooms and amidst innumerable distractions. . . . Bear in mind too that these studies are not intended to increase a salary or advance a career. The object of them is generally self-development or a desire to participate effectively in social or other public work.[64]

It was perhaps because Toynbee Hall was the place where such a philosophy had always been articulated, that it remained a popular venue for adult education. An added attraction, however, which contributed greatly to the success of the educational activities at Toynbee was the social back-up provided for the students. Through the Toynbee Students' Association members of every kind of class, society and group were encouraged to feel part of the Settlement, to make their own contribution to its life, and to add to its amenities. Weekly meetings of the Students' Association were addressed by speakers of distinction, as they had been before the First World War. Nor, it was insisted, did the Association confine itself to meetings.

> It will persuade Professor Rothenstein to guide it through the National Gallery or Mr. Aitken to devote to it a Saturday afternoon at the Tate. It is keen on theatres, especially when the play is by Shaw or Galsworthy or Barry or a great Continental. In summer too, it penetrates into the adjoining counties and makes the most of Saturday afternoons or occasional weekends. Lastly the Association recognises that it should give as well as receive and is always ready to help any Toynbee project or activity. Recently it raised £10 to help the work of the Skilled Employment

Committee. Now it is about to provide a magic lantern to be used in illustrating lectures at Pentonville Prison.[65]

Toynbee students had their own reputation too. As one of the lecturers there, Sir Wyndham Deedes, put it, 'whereas one had to "talk down" to most audiences one had to "talk up" to the Toynbee Students' Association.'[66] There was obviously a marked distinction, however, between the students and most of their neighbours, not least when from 1925 onwards summer reunions of members of Toynbee classes and groups, 'vast revels', were held on the tennis courts, 'ushered in by Maypole and country dancing, by Greek dancing, by displays by the Toynbee Troop of Scouts, by the Toynbee division of the St John Ambulance Brigade'.[67] Nevertheless, according to the Reports, 'the frolic was not confined to the tennis courts; it spread to the balconies of the surrounding tenements,' and towards midnight, when the revel ended, 'the figures of hundreds of our dancing neighbours silhouetted against the summer moon, lent a touch of strangeness to a beautiful spectacle.'[68]

One of the students on an Oxford and Cambridge study week in December 1928 described what it was like to discover Toynbee Hall from the outside.

On Monday I went to Toynbee Hall in the East End, which was to be my home for the week. I found the days of great interest [he wrote]. Generally, in the mornings, we had lectures from employers and employed in various trades, for example, building, printing and clothing. The evident desire to understand each other's point of view was impressive. The Trade Union representatives, men and women, seemed people of intelligence and good economic sense. Our afternoons were spent variously, one in the docks as guests of the Port of London Authority (they gave us a splendid lunch), one at the Trade Schools in Southampton Row, one to Welwyn Garden City, and one at the Varsity Rugby Match. One night we had a 'Dockers' At Home', during which I sang a song from the *Pirates*.

The Hall became his 'home', but from it he discovered London too.

The last night [at Toynbee] was an all-night tour of London. We split into groups, and my group visited the *Daily Express* office first. Here we were very courteously shown round and spent an engrossed two hours. Then, in a free hour or so, three girls and I walked along the Embankment and had some food at Lyons' Strand Corner House. Then to the Gas Light and Coke Factory where the heat of the furnaces was very welcome in the frost of the night. The raking out of the numerous ovens was an inferno-like sight. They gave us a very handsome meal at 3.30 a.m. Then, to St. Martin's-in-the-Fields where we sat for half an hour amid the stertorous snorings of the tramps. From there, in batches, to Covent Garden, which did not impress me, and to Billingsgate, which did. It was an amazing sight. Icy cold morning, hundreds of queerly hatted porters, balancing heavy fish boxes on their heads, surprisingly cheerful, with plenty of backchat, but no blasphemy that I heard. But most remarkable of all, white, pallid, fleshy bloodless faces, just like the fish they spent their life amongst. We had coffee and a delicious ham sandwich at a porters' eating house, after a long wait and a big squash. Then back to Toynbee to pack and pay my bill (22 shillings and 6 pence for the week). It had been a thoroughly enjoyable week of many new spectacles and experiences.[69]

An unexpected means of linking university students with workers in the East End came in 1926, with the outbreak of the General Strike. Yet most of them, whether they set out to support the strikers or not, found their inspiration outside Toynbee Hall. Mallon believed even before the strike began that Herbert Smith, the miners' leader, would not be able to deal with Baldwin. Smith, though a charming old man, was simply too honest, he felt, to be a good bargainer. Not everyone felt Smith's charm: most people were impressed by his Yorkshire grit. Mallon knew A. J. Cook, too, but he did not share Cook's militancy. When the strike began, he called it a catastrophe and stated unequivocally that

> the obvious and only goal of peacemakers was to assist to keep tempers sweet. . . . There was a unanimity at Toynbee Hall [he went on] that while Residents should be free as individuals to act as they thought desirable, the Settlement as such should maintain its cordial relationship with the local Trade Unionists, and in the interests of order and good feeling, render them any services within its power.[7]

Following this familiar policy, well established in the 1880s, dockers, transport workers and railway men were allowed to 'sign on' each day at Toynbee Hall before their own officials and on Saturday to collect their strike pay there, and concerts for the men and their wives, 'a powerful influence in the presentation of local good humour',[71] were held in the afternoons on Mallon's initiation. (Gladys Cooper was one of the performers.)

> The behaviour of the men was exemplary [Mallon wrote]. Considerable numbers of them lived miles away from Toynbee Hall. These left home in the early morning and after a good interlude in picket duty returned somehow on weary feet. The men were tried too by the exiguous character of their strike pay (15 shillings in most cases, though 20 shillings had been expected), and the length of time, perhaps four or five hours, during which in interminable queues, they had to wait for it. Yet there was never any manifestation of exasperation or ill-feeling and the on-looking policemen, whose common sense and tact were also admirable, had never any cause to interfere.[72]

A glimpse of Mallon's own life during the strike can be caught in a thirteen-page handwritten account of the strike (not his) in the Toynbee Archive and in an article he himself wrote in the Toynbee Hall *Annual Report* for 1926. 'No buses go further East than Liverpool Street,' the chronicler was writing on 4 May, and all of them had two special constables on board, and the following day he was attending a crowded meeting in St George's Town Hall, Stepney, where about a thousand strikers were listening to 'rather poor speeches urging them to stand firm, not to blackleg, and above all to give the police no cause for using violence or calling in the military'.[73] Mallon preferred, however, to talk to individual strikers, like the one who came into the quad with his child, 'a handsome boy of some four years, who had seen me on our concert platforms and promptly pointed me out to his father as "the concert man",' and who told Mallon that 'he did not like strikes and knew they were seldom any good, but that the present strike, however regrettable, was necessary to protect the wage earners.'[74]

May 7 and 8 were 'uneasy days' when one of the chronicler's friends was told at Bishopsgate Police Station that had it been known how weak the City Police Force was 'every place in the City could have been looted'. Yet a walk down Wapping High Street and Shadwell High Street revealed 'not the slightest sign of disorder' and round the docks there was 'absolutely no movement'.[75]

When the strike was over Mallon brought together Cambridge undergraduates who had been serving as Special Constables and twenty dockers.[76] This the chronicler, a Toynbee Resident, who was favourable to the strikers, felt would 'do a lot to relieve the situation of the aggressive Specials and aggrieved dockers'. 'Both sides – the government and the Trade Union movement – seem to have emerged without loss of prestige,' he concluded after a visit to Eccleston Square, headquarters of the TUC, 'the TUC were surprised at the strength and unity of the strike.'[77]

The general strike was separated by only three years from the Great Depression, and although there was far less of a contrast between the 1920s and the 1930s in Britain than there was in the United States, there was a new sense of uneasiness as unemployment rates mounted; and at what Mallon called 'a trying moment in the history of the nation', he felt that Toynbee Hall enjoyed 'special opportunities of exploring and illuminating some of the social and industrial problems which perplex our generation'.[78]

Among these problems unemployment was an even more pressing local and national issue during the late 1920s and 1930s than it had been when Beveridge had turned his attention to it a quarter of a century before, or in 1921, when he acted as an adviser to the Toynbee Hall Committee which produced a report on the subject. The intensity of the world depression which followed the collapse of Wall Street in 1929 was not matched by the attempts to deal with it. Socialists predicted that it would lead to the imminent downfall of capitalism, those Liberals who followed Lloyd George believed that 'we can conquer unemployment', and J. M. Keynes was recasting his economic theories to prove that this was possible. Yet at Toynbee Hall there was more emphasis in this new situation on dealing with the human aspects of unemployment than on probing its causes.

Mallon was a member of the London Council for Voluntary Occupation which was established with the co-operation of the National Council of Social Service to provide occupation and education for the unemployed, and the Stepney Council for Voluntary Occupation in the neighbourhood had its headquarters at the Hall. Mallon was Vice-Chairman and Jo Hodgkinson, the Sub-Warden, was the Secretary, and funds were collected and facilities supplied for classes in physical training and in carpentry, tailoring and motor engineering, in various centres throughout the borough.

At one time, over 300 men were attending the physical training classes, and there was a steady and keen demand for classes in other subjects, with tutors paid for by the LCC. The Council made the most of small successes that were obviously welcomed at least as small mercies by the local unemployed. For example, following the agreement of the Stepney Baths Committee to permit the unemployed to use the baths without charge there were many expressions of thanks, while a letter was addressed to the editor of the *East London Advertiser*, signed 'Unemployed', expressing appreciation for the carpentry classes. It is an illuminating document for the social historian of the period.

> When the scheme was explained to me by Mr. Young [the writer began], I was inclined to treat the whole thing as a joke, but I found a bright cheerful hall with benches and first class tools under a highly skilled carpenter. Though I had done no woodwork since leaving school, I was soon put at ease and in a very short time I made a cot for our baby, a kitchen table and a cupboard for our clothes.

OXFORD AND CAMBRIDGE STUDY WEEK.

December, 1925.

Subject: "A PERSONAL APPROACH TO SOCIAL PROBLEMS."

FRIDAY, December 11th.

6.30 p.m. Assemble at Toynbee Hall.
7.0 p.m. Dinner.
8.30 p.m. Address by
The Rev. The Hon. EDWARD LYTTELTON,
M.A., D.D., D.C.L.

Chairman: W. McG. EAGAR (President).

SATURDAY, December 12th.

"Housing."

(a) "My work as a School Medical Officer."
10.0 a.m.   Dr. L. HADEN GUEST, M.P.
to   (b) "My work as a Sanitary Inspector."
1.0 p.m.   T. H. H. HANCOCK.
(c) "My work as a Settlement Resident in
connection with Housing."
Miss CATHERINE TOWERS
(Canning Town Women's Settlement).

Afternoon. Visits to bad areas in Limehouse and new
schemes at Beacontree, etc.

SUNDAY, December 13th.

8.30 a.m. Corporate Communion at All Hallows Church
(Toc H.) and Breakfast.   (By special
request).
Morning. Visits to Petticoat Lane, Club Row (Dog and
Livestock Fair) etc.

MONDAY, December 14th.

"Education."

(a) "My work under the Education Authority."
G. SAMPSON (Late Hon. Sec. English
10.0 a.m.   Association).
to   (b) "My work in Adult Education."
1.0 p.m.   H. FLEMING (World's Institute of
Adult Education).
(c) "My work as a Settlement Resident in
connection with Education."
B. HENRIQUES (Warden St. George's
Jewish Settlement).

Afternoon. Visits to Elementary, Secondary, Central and
Day Continuation Schools, etc.
4.30 p.m. Tea at I.C.F. Headquarters, Fellowship
House, (By special request).

TUESDAY, December 15th.

"Drink."

(a) "My work as a Licensing Justice."
10.0 a.m.   Alderman W. GROVES.
to   (b) "My work as an Investigator into Public
1.0 p.m.   Houses."   E. SELLEY.
(c) "My work as a Settlement Resident in
connection with the Drink question."
J. J. MALLON (Warden Toynbee Hall).

Afternoon. Visits to "Charley Brown," West India Dock
Road, "Rose & Crown," Camberwell,
(Public Houses,) and to Whitbread's
and Barclay's Breweries, etc.
Evening. Visits to Newspaper Printing Offices, The
Embankment, Crypt St. Martin's Church,
Salvation Army Hostel, etc.

Oxford and Cambridge study weeks were inaugurated by Mallon to encourage students to live at Toynbee Hall

American seminars led by Sherwood Eddy played an important part in the Toynbee Calendar during the 1920s and 1930s. Eddy is in the middle of the second row with his arm on Mallon's shoulder

PROGRAMME

The Meetings will be at Toynbee Hall except where otherwise stated.

JULY

Monday, 2nd
10 a.m. J. J. Mallon,
11.30 Arthur Greenwood, M.P.

Tuesday, 3rd
10 a.m. E. D. Simon,
11.30 H. N. Brailsford,
2.30 Norman Angell.

Wednesday, 4th
10 a.m. Viscount Astor,
11.30 B. S. Rowntree.

Thursday, 5th
10 a.m. Major Elliott, M.P.
Tea at Lady Astor's to meet Mr. G. Bernard Shaw.
3.15 H. D. Henderson.

Friday, 6th
10 a.m. Dr. A. H. Gray.
Visit to Welwyn Garden City and to Hatfield House. Capt. R. L. Reiss will speak on The Housing Problem in Great Britain.

Saturday, 7th

Sunday, 8th

Monday, 9th
10 a.m. Professor Philip Baker
11.30 Professor H. J. Laski.
Afternoon Reception by Mr. J. Ramsay MacDonald and Mr. Arthur Henderson at the House of Commons.

JULY

Tuesday, 10th
10 a.m. Canon T. W. Pym.
11.30 A. Duff-Cooper, M.P.

Wednesday, 11th
10 a.m. Wickham Steed.
11 a.m. Lord Cecil of Chelwood.

Thursday, 12th
10 a.m. The Earl of Lytton, (Late Governor of Bengal).
11.30 Rt. Hon. Philip Snowden.

Friday, 13th
11.30 Visit to Lambeth Palace.
2.30 Dean Inge.

Saturday, 14th
Visit to Oxford.
Meeting with the Master of Balliol, Dr. Selbie, G. D. H. Cole.

Sunday, 15th

Monday, 16th
10 a.m. W. L. Hichens.
12.00 Rev. G. A. Studdert Kennedy.

Tuesday, 17th
10 a.m. Philip Kerr.
11.30 J. A. Spender.
4.30 Reception by the Bishop of London at Fulham Palace.

Wednesday, 18th
2.30 G. P. Gooch.
3.45 E. F. Wise.

Thursday, 19th
11.30 S. K. Ratcliffe.

(*above*) Programme of the American seminar, July 1928

Midsummer dancing and drama festivals in the quadrangle attracted much local interest

Mallon's friends at Toynbee Hall in 1926: (*from the top, left to right*) Jimmy H. Thomas, Margaret Bondfield, Hugh Dalton, Philip Carr (Lord Lothian,) Harold Laski, Seebohm Rowntree, George Lansbury, G. D. H. Cole, Arthur Greenwood

Royal visitor: the Prince of Wales at the Pell Street Club, February 1927

(*below*) Riots near Aldgate East when thousands of people congregated in protest against a proposed march of Fascists

The New Building, opened in 1938

The Theatre, with murals by Clive Gardiner

The Music Room, which was also used as the Juvenile Court

The roof playground

Visit of King George VI and Queen Elizabeth to Toynbee Hall to the New Building, November 1938

(*above and left*) Toynbee Hall was bombed on 10 May 1941. The Warden's Lodgings and the Library were totally destroyed

(*above*) East End victims of the bombing recovering at Bottingdean

(*right*) Mallon rallying support. A meeting at Toynbee Hall to press for a new Education Act

Both Individual Citizens and Members of Local Groups
are invited to attend a

PUBLIC MEETING

at 7 p.m. on
THURSDAY, SEPTEMBER 17th, 1942,
at
TOYNBEE HALL,
Commercial Street, Aldgate, E. 1,
on

EDUCATIONAL RECONSTRUCTION

NATIONAL,   METROPOLITAN   & LOCAL

BUILDINGS GONE !	CHILDREN RETURNING
CHILDREN DISPERSED !	WHAT RE-BUILDING ?
SCHOOLS CONTINUE !	WHAT RE-GROUPING ?

WHAT EXTENSIONS ?   WHAT MODIFICATIONS ?   WHAT EXPANSIONS ?

Chairman :
Dr. J. J. MALLON, C.H., LL.D., M.A., J.P.
Speakers :
MONICA PEARSON
(Reynolds News)
RONALD GOULD
(National Union Teachers)

Please show this notice to all neighbours and colleagues. *Bring them along with you.*
Has East London any ideas for improving the educational facilities for its own children ?
Come and hear the suggestions. Be ready to get together to put forward the views of your
own Group, Club, Church, Party, Society or Association.

This meeting is convened by the EAST LONDON TEACHERS' ASSOCIATION
(The Local Association of the National Union of Teachers for the Boroughs of Poplar and
Stepney) in co-operation with the EAST LONDON EDUCATION COUNCIL (formed in
1938 to assemble local opinion on education). Further information about the East London
Education Council can be obtained from, and requests for invitations to its Council Meetings
should be sent to T. E. Newell, 21, Lyndworth Close, Headington, Oxford.

H. & H. G. Peterken, Printers (Reg. T.U.), 63, Three Colt Street, E.14

Mallon with Lord Waverley, the Chairman of Toynbee Hall, and Clement Attlee, the President in 1947

Attlee with some members of the Toynbee Veterans' Club. Attlee continued to give most valuable support to Toynbee Hall in the post-war years. It enabled him to retain his contact with the East End

Mallon at his retirement reception in front of the bust of him by Jacob Epstein.

And then he turned from experience to attitudes.

> When I entered the Centre, I was bitter and fed up. I now feel that life is as you
> make it. I am only one out of a thousand who have been attending daily. I get up
> each day at 5 a.m. and spend the whole morning in looking for work but in the
> afternoon, instead of lounging at the alley corner, I go to the Centre. Here there are
> no religious people or party politics to worry one. I was allowed to go to two classes
> and was given free admission to Stepney Men's Institute in the evening where I can
> take any subject I like. My pals and I, through your paper, wish to convey to Mr.
> Young our thanks.[79]

Toynbee Hall was a more friendly place than an office as it served as the district
headquarters of the Insurance Department of the Ministry of Health, which administered
Unemployment Health Insurance schemes, and of the Ministry of Labour's Juvenile Employment Exchange, which placed thousands of juveniles annually; and the work of the Juvenile
Employment Exchange was supplemented by that of the Stepney Skilled Employment
Committee, the largest and most active of six such committees in the London area which
tried to find jobs of the right kind for people with qualifications. In 1933 it 'placed' in
acceptable situations 593 learners or improvers and thirty apprentices.

The Grith Fyrd Camps also had their headquarters at Toynbee Hall. They dealt with
the special problems of people who had been unemployed for some time, 'offering scope
for individuality, resourcefulness, and initiative'. Selected unemployed men were able to
stay at camps in the New Forest and in Derbyshire for periods varying between six and
eighteen months, where they were encouraged 'to build for and maintain themselves in the
hope that in the struggle with nature, they will regain the confidence and skill which they
have lost'.[80]

Mallon believed also that new Settlements in depressed areas could achieve something
of the same result in an urban setting and secured funds from the Pilgrim Trust (£1,000)
to support the encouragement of new Settlements in two areas which had been heavily
stricken by unemployment – Durham and Lanarkshire. In 1932 Settlements were established
in Durham City, in Spennymoor, a mining village outside Durham, and Bells Hill, on the
Lanarkshire coal fields near Glasgow. 'It may fairly be claimed,' Mallon reported soon
afterwards, 'that many hundreds of miners and their wives attend the Settlements for
handicraft or educational classes, or for social gatherings,' while 'in Durham City, the
Settlement has aroused a new interest in social work' and was 'energetically attacking the
inertia that has fallen upon the discouraged inhabitants of the neighbouring villages'. 'The
stimulating effect of the Settlements in Durham and Lanarkshire has been such,' he added,
'that the founding of further Settlements in these areas and elsewhere may soon be
expected.'[81]

Mallon was convinced that the Settlement principle could help not only to revive
declining areas but to provide an identity and a sense of community for new housing areas.
He played a leading part, therefore, in the foundation and development of the New Estates
Committee (a Joint Committee of the National Council of Social Service and the Associations
of Residential and Educational Settlements) and secured a grant of £10,000 for 'the Carnegie
Trustees to carry out experiments on ten such estates, where social centres – some of them

in the nature of Settlements – could be set up'. It was not easy to find leaders, but successes were reported as 'residents who at first were out of touch with one another' were being brought together either at new centres or in 'one or other of the numerous societies and groups which were brought into existence'.[82]

Mallon was fortunate that in the middle of the Depression in 1930 he found a new Sub-Warden to succeed C. K. Rutter, who had himself succeeded St John Catchpool. Jo Hodgkinson, a young graduate of Liverpool University, had been recommended to him by George Haynes, the Warden of the Liverpool University Settlement, and Mallon took to him at once. Hodgkinson's enthusiasm, ability and dedication enabled Mallon to realise far more of his vision than he would have been able to alone. In particular, Hodgkinson involved himself with the steadily increasing numbers of young men and women for whom Toynbee Hall had become a centre of culture and recreation. He was keenly interested in the arts and he was able at the same time to supervise the classes. It was largely due to him, indeed, and to Eddie Rose, a London schoolteacher, that a Toynbee Musical Society was formed in 1932 and that with slender resources both an orchestra and choir and a 'Little Theatre' were built up. Among the most successful dramatic productions was Toller's *Masses and Man*, one production of which took place at Friends House before the author himself. The cast of another production, not uncharacteristic, produced by a Resident, A. J. Duggan, included an unemployed factory worker and a barrister-at-law. Meanwhile, another link between East End and West End was forged as a scheme was worked out whereby the Music Society arranged with other musical societies and organisations for special concessions for its members so that tickets could be purchased at special prices for concerts at the Queen's Hall and other places in the West End.

The educational work of the Hall was examined in 1933 by nine inspectors of the LCC, who noted that it afforded instruction 'of a kind and type' which was not available in any other institution in the East End of London and that the Warden was 'very ably assisted by a Sub-Warden whose methods follow closely those of his Principal'. There was praise for the teaching staff who were said to have been 'well selected', many of them possessing 'both high academic qualifications and enthusiasm'.

The personality of the Warden at Toynbee Hall

and his extensive contacts with national affairs and well-known personalities [the Report went on] have had a notable effect on the prestige, reputation and success of all the work of the Settlement. His ability to attract workers and students of the higher type, his extraordinary vitality in pressing forward his chances, and the good humour he shows in order to maintain sustained effort on the part of all who come in contact with him are the outstanding factors which have combined to make Toynbee Hall a place of unique importance to the social welfare and educational development of the people living in the East End of London.[83]

Yet the problems of Toynbee Hall were not minimised in the Report. 'Most of the present premises were built very many years ago,' it went on, 'and were designed to meet the needs of a far less ambitious programme than is at present in operation.' The point had often been made by the Toynbee Hall Council, which stressed that its rooms were 'inadequate and over used', but had concluded that 'in a time of widespread financial loss and depression it is idle to entertain projects of enlargement and reconstruction'. Now the inspectors themselves recognised that 'any marked development or extension of activities, social or educational, would be impossible in the present premises'.[84]

Special mention was made by the inspectors of the cultural activities at Toynbee Hall – both the excellence of the dramatic art course and the appeal of the Sunday evening concerts with performers of the highest distinction and of the musical appreciation classes held in the middle of the week. 'Young people in the neighbourhood have a strong natural interest in drama,' the inspectors wrote, 'and are not slow to take advantage of the class. They are lively and interested and are undoubtedly deriving much benefit from the course.' And there were students too who felt that music was an 'essential part of life'.[85]

Toynbee celebrated its Jubilee Year in 1934, and Mallon now felt able to report triumphantly that 'after fifty years of effort, the place of Toynbee Hall in the regard of its neighbourhood is established. It aims to be and is the Common Friend.' It was a common life above all else which Mallon longed to promote:

> East London is a piece of England in which it is possible to heighten and expand and, by experiment, to ascertain and measure the genius for co-operation of the race. Waving no party flag, attached to no religious denomination, caring for men as such and dedicated to their cause, in touch with all the elements of a diversified society, Toynbee Hall may be able, if assisted, to show for the general enlightenment how in East London social goodwill may be enlarged, and the forces of friendliness mobilised in aid of understanding, and toleration and the enrichment of the common life.[86]

Long before the Second World War there was a touch of the Dunkirk spirit in Mallon's message.

The fiftieth anniversary was celebrated on Christmas Eve, 1934, by a wireless interchange of speeches – interspersed with carols – between the English and American Settlements arranged jointly by the BBC and the National Broadcasting Company of America. The main speeches were delivered by Jane Addams (from Hull House in Chicago, which she founded), Helen Hall, President of the National Federation of Settlements (from the Henry Street Settlement in New York), Margaret Bondfield and Mallon himself. There were by then over 600 American Settlements 'all derived from Toynbee Hall', which Jane Addams described as a 'pathfinder'. For Miss Bondfield the fact that there were more Settlements in the United States than in England could be explained straightforwardly because in Britain more social work 'had been transferred from voluntary agencies to local or national government'. Mallon, however, avoided all explanation. Toynbee Hall, he said, was

> almost as much an American as a British Institution. . . . It was a happy circle in which Americans and British so much agreed that they wished it might be allowed to deal with all British-American differences. It would deal with them in the sense of abolishing them and would enable the two nations to go through the world as they ought to do – arm in arm.[87]

While much was made in 1934 of the fact that Toynbee Hall was 'the mother of settlements' and that what had been started in the East End had been copied by 'all America',[88] the *Morning Post*, the newspaper for which Beveridge and Tawney had written, struck a different and more domestic note. 'Economics touched with emotion' were the first words in the account given in it of the Jubilee. Toynbee Hall represented 'the reaction against the laissez-faire doctrines of the Manchester school'.[89] The *Morning Post* was soon to disappear and Toynbee Hall to go on, but no-one would have suspected that from this particular news item. The *Spectator* too recalled its first doubts about Toynbee Hall in 1884,[90] noting how much had been accomplished through its presence. Yet it drew a contrast between the 1880s and the 1930s.

> When Barnett founded Toynbee Hall, the educated men of the upper classes were still the effective rulers of the world. They initiated new ideas. They carried them out. . . . The reform movement at that time was pushed forward by volunteers who to influence the experts had themselves to become experts. . . . Since then there had been two great changes, due in no small degree to the efforts of these pioneers. Firstly, the government itself has armies of civil servants who are carrying out as officials the work of the social reformer.[91] Secondly, Labour and the Labour Party have grown up; they have their own organisations, their own experts, their own lecturers who have actually emerged from those strata of life which the Toynbee pioneers set themselves to explore. So successful was the University Settlement movement that, in its original form, it has ceased to be necessary.[92]

It was a judgment which was often to be made after 1934 – yet the speculation behind it was as limited as the speculation in the *Spectator* of 1884, as the author of the 1934 article half recognised when he wrote that 'the need for voluntary action is different from what it was fifty years ago, but it is not less.'[93] J. A. R. Pimlott, author of the specially commissioned Jubilee history, was more specific.

> The social problem is more serious and complicated than ever. Housing, unemployment, the entry of the school leavers into blind alley occupations, the provision of adequate and satisfactory facilities for the employment of leisure, and social investigation – these are questions to which Toynbee Hall so far as its resources will permit is directing its attention at the present time, and they are problems of immediate national importance.[94]

If the phrase 'so far as its resources will allow' stands out, the omission from Pimlott's list of intentional activities would have been picked out by Margaret Bondfield who referred in her broadcast to the famous 'Peace Ballot' of 1934. 'Peace was the greatest of all causes,' she told the Americans, and

> the ballot would show that this nation was set on peace. When the people of America received the amazing figures of the Ballot they would realise how little justification existed for the charge that Great Britain was imperialistic. Such a charge was sheer nonsense, the British were determined to love their neighbours.[95]

The Second World War was less than five years away. Between then and 1939, however, the Peace Ballot, important though it was politically at the time, was soon forgotten. Nor was the theme referred to at the Jubilee Dinner in the Merchant Taylors' Hall on 13 December 1935 at which the Archbishop of Canterbury, who presided, read a letter from the Prime Minister, Stanley Baldwin, regretting his inability to be present. His predecessor, Ramsay MacDonald, was among the speakers, however, along with Clement Attlee, Sir

John Simon, and the Master of Balliol, A. D. Lindsay, and the guests included Herbert Morrison, Walter Elliott, Sir Percy Harris, C. R. Ashbee, Sir William Beveridge, Albert Mansbridge, A. G. Gardiner, Sir Austen Chamberlain, Dame Elizabeth Cadbury, Lord Askwith, L. S. Amery, Arthur Creech-Jones, S. K. Ratcliffe, A. J. Toynbee, R. C. K. Ensor, Sir Ernest Barker, Sir Montague Burton, Lord Snell, Chairman of the LCC, the Mayor of Stepney, the Dean of St Paul's and the Rector of Whitechapel. The *Guardian*, the Church of England newspaper, noted that although the Vice-Chancellor of Cambridge had sent a congratulatory letter, those present were mainly 'Oxford men'.[96]

At the dinner, Baldwin's letter announced a gift of £10,000 from the Pilgrim Trust. And he offered moral as well as financial tribute. 'Toynbee Hall is a part and a distinguished part of the social history of this country, and not of this country alone,' was his message.

> It brought into our life an enlightened humanity and a new approach to the problem of correcting and ameliorating the inequalities of society – It recognised that pity was not enough and that charity was not enough; but that these things must be implemented by a new spirit of association between the classes and based upon continuous enquiry into social evils and the best means of eradicating them.[97]

With such encouragement an appeal for funds for the long overdue physical extension of Toynbee Hall was likely to be successful. The first extension, built for the Jubilee was very much in the style of the period with Alister Macdonald, son of Ramsay Macdonald, as architect and with murals designed by Clive Gardiner. Over the theatre, which seated four hundred, was a music room panelled with timber from the old Waterloo Bridge, which was to be used in the daytime as the Juvenile Court. On the second floor there were classrooms, a science laboratory and two art studios, and on the top floor a dining room and a recreation room were linked by removable partitions which, when taken down, left space for dancing. The sound of the Lambeth Walk was to be heard not only in Lambeth but in Whitechapel. There were now thirty-five regular members of the Neighbours' Club where darts flew at the double and chop and smash were 'practised at the Ping-Pong table'.

'The shadow of our new building already darkens the Quad,' wrote Mallon in 1937. 'To me, however, it is a point not of darkness but of light.'[98] In the process of reconstruction, some old buildings had been destroyed, notably the St Jude's School and the Exhibition Buildings, but the tennis court remained. So, too did the sense of history, for in the ground beneath the new building a jar was buried containing bread, coal and a threepenny piece, symbolising food, warmth and wealth, along with a lead casket in which were placed Dame Henrietta Barnett's biography of her husband, Pimlott's history, and Baldwin's congratulatory letter. The Mayor of Stepney laid a foundation stone in March 1938, and King George VI and Queen Elizabeth inspected the new buildings in November of that year, with police crouching so that East End children could stand on tiptoe and see them.[99] Finally, a few months later Mallon, linking two traditions, received Queen Mary at the People's Palace; he had recently been made Chairman (in 1935) of this old, popular institution, the history of which had run parallel to that of Toynbee Hall.

For Mallon, it was important not only to put up new buildings but to make his neighbours proud of them, and he was proud of other new East End buildings, too, including new blocks of flats constructed by the Shoreditch Housing Association over which his Sub-Warden presided and also inspected by the King and Queen. Yet Mallon himself became even better known than he already had been outside the East End between the Toynbee Jubilee and the outbreak of war in 1939. The arts played a large part in his life, and he brought to Toynbee Hall and the People's Palace many well-known actors, musicians, painters – and patrons. Val Gielgud, Tyrone Guthrie, Michel St Denis and Irene Vanbrugh were among the visitors to the theatre, where Hodgkinson's repertoire of plays included Yeats's *Countess Cathleen*, produced in the quad, and Jean Renoir was brought to see a performance of *Le Malade imaginaire*. A gala matinée to raise funds in 1938 had the Marchioness of Crewe, the Marchioness of Salisbury, the Countess of Lytton, Lady Diana Cooper, the Viscountess of Bearsted, Mrs Walter Elliott and Mrs Israel Sieff among its patrons, and was attended by Queen Mary. The matinée itself included songs by Heddle Nash and Ina Sowez, a ballet with Constant Lambert as conductor and Frederick Ashton as choreographer, and a short play by J. M. Barry, *Shall we Join the Ladies*? produced by Guthrie and with Rex Harrison, Gwen Ffrangcon-Davies, Leo Genn and Richard Goolden in the cast.

A new Musical Society had been founded in 1932, and a Music Department was created three years later as part of the educational network with John Tobin and Peter Gellhorn, a refugee from Germany, on the staff. There was an Opera Club, too, which brought in singers from Glyndebourne – Gellhorn's first opera was Gluck's *Orpheus* in January 1939 – and a year earlier there had been the first performance in London of *The Wandering Scholar* by Gustav Holst, who had been a young Director of Music at the Mary Ward Centre in Bloomsbury. Finally there was a symphony orchestra under the direction of Alec Sherman of the BBC.

In 1937 Mallon himself became a Governor of the BBC, and although his tenure was to be interrupted in 1939, when the total number of Governors was reduced by the Government, he was to resume his office from 1941 to 1946. He formed many new friendships through this connection, and in 1939 it was no surprise when he was made a Companion of Honour.

There was a touch of glamour in all this. Yet there was no glamour in Mallon's persistent and successful efforts to counter Fascist violence in the East End. 'We shall advance to power quicker than the Germans,' Sir Oswald Mosley had announced two months after Hitler achieved power in Germany in 1933; and although he was in no position to realise such an ambition, as Fascist strategies developed the East End almost inevitably became one of the chosen fronts for any advance to be made.[100] Indeed, it was in Bethnal Green, Shoreditch and Stepney that Mosley attracted his first mass following between 1936 and 1938. Anti-Semitism could be exploited blatantly: so, too, could the social conditions which fostered it. Yet the first Bethnal Green branch of the British Union of Fascists was not formed until the last months of 1934 and the first Shoreditch branch in the first months of 1935. Stepney and Limehouse followed in 1936. The mobilisation of opinion depended from the start on an appeal to prejudice. There was ample tinder around, too, for the Communist Party was another active force in the East End.

The climax came on Sunday 5 October 1936, just after Communists and Fascists were pitted against each other in the Spanish Civil War. It was a day when Mosley's Blackshirts planned a march through the East End with speeches at four points on the way. 'They shall not pass,' the Communists thundered: 'Stop Mosley' ran a headline in The *Star*.[101] The result was the so-called 'Battle of Cable Street', followed by the prohibition of the march by the police and the dispersion of the Fascists, but a week later there was a retaliatory Fascists pogrom in the Mile End Road, 'the most violent anti-Semitic outbreak the East End had ever seen'.[102]

Mallon, deeply shocked first by Fascism itself, then by the violent clashes, called a meeting at Toynbee Hall which appealed to the 'citizens of East London' to work against local forces conjured up by 'outsiders' who were seeking 'to destroy the commonsense and toleration and good humour on which we pride ourselves'. 'Communist sympathies in the East End would have been unlikely to cause disturbance,' he maintained, 'if Fascist propaganda had not driven members of the Jewish population into defensive alliance with the local Communists.'[103] 'The Communist Movement is not large,' he pointed out, 'though it makes a great deal of noise, especially on Sunday afternoons when other people want a quiet sleep.'[104] Toynbee Hall's reputation with the Jewish community, local and national, meant that it could command support when it demanded government action.[105]

The outcome of the Toynbee Hall meeting was the setting up of a Council of Citizens of East London 'to take such action as may be necessary to bring to an end the gross disorders which have recently disturbed the area'.[106] The Archbishop of Canterbury, Cosmo Lang, the old supporter of Toynbee, was elected President, the former General, Sir Frederick Maurice, was chosen as Chairman of the Executive Committee, and Mallon was appointed Secretary.

The situation remained dangerously tense, not least because a few days after the Battle of Cable Street Mosley went to Berlin for talks with Hitler; and an anxious deputation led by Herbert Morrison, Harold Clay, a trade unionist and future President of the WEA, and Mallon went to see the Home Secretary, Sir John Simon, to press for a Public Order Act. The Government announced that it accepted the need for such a measure in the King's Speech at the opening of Parliament, and a Bill was duly introduced banning the public meeting of political unions, forbidding the use of stewards at open air meetings, strengthening the law relating to insulting words likely to lead to a breach of the peace, and giving the police power to ban processions. The bill quickly became law on 1st January 1937.

It met with opposition from Communists, from many Socialists and from some Conservatives, but Mallon had no doubt about the necessity for it. 'The Public Order Act. . . brought about a transformation,' he claimed in 1938. 'There is now comparative quiet in East London, which it is hoped will continue.'[107] He regarded the Act, indeed, as one of those pieces of pre-war legislation which had been directly influenced by Toynbee Hall, and his own reputation, already high, was 'higher than ever' as a result of it.[108] The other two were the Education Act of 1936 and the Hire Purchase Act of 1937.

Since the Education Act of 1902, progress in the development of secondary education had been slow. Moreover, despite the clear and forceful recommendations in 1927 of the Hadow Committee on 'The Education of the Adolescent', of which Tawney was a member, no action had been taken to prolong compulsory school attendance to the age of 15. Mallon judged, therefore, that the time was ripe in 1935 – with a General Election pending – to set up a national body to press for action, and after a characteristic bout of consultation behind the scenes, he summoned a conference at which the decision was taken to found a School Age Council 'with the object of inducing the government to raise the school leaving age as rapidly as possible, and of making every effort to remove the remaining difficulties in the way of such actions'.[109]

The Council was fortunate to secure the novelist, John Buchan, later Baron Tweedsmuir, as its Chairman, and it attracted to its ranks no fewer than seventy-nine Chairmen of Education Committees and eighty-one Directors of Education. There was sufficient influence here, in the words of a historian of education, to carry 'the demand to the centre of government';[110] and a pledge to raise the age figured in the National Government's election manifesto of 1935.

The Education Act of 1936 which followed was designed to implement the pledge; and although it was described by its critics, including the Association of Education Committees and Mallon himself, as a 'travesty of reform', it was sharply attacked by people who felt that the proposal to raise the age was misconceived. Ironically, 1 September 1939 was set as the fixed date for implementation; and the outbreak of the Second World War meant that the Act was not put into effect. Mallon was disappointed throughout at the failure, as he saw it, to act quickly and decisively enough in relation to what he thought of as a major national issue.[111]

By contrast, the Hire Purchase Act of 1939, the third piece of legislation to be mooted in Toynbee Hall was highly successful. There had been an enormous increase in hire purchase during the years after the First World War, and there seemed to be many consequent abuses, particularly in districts like the East End.[112] Following a meeting at Toynbee Hall of the British Association of Residential Settlements, the Poor Man's Lawyers were consulted about how best to deal with the abuses, and E. S. Watkins, Honorary Legal Adviser to the Hall drafted a Hire Purchase Bill. It set out to ensure that the hirer in a hire purchase transaction should fully understand the terms and his own future obligations, to enable the hirer to terminate an agreement on terms favourable to himself and the owner, to prevent the owner from regaining possession of goods by force if an instalment had not been paid; and to lay down fair procedures in such ways which would be handled by the local County Courts[113]

It was fortunate for Toynbee Hall that the President and Secretary of the Hire Purchase Traders' Federation – Sir Harold Bellman and Cuthbert Grieg – were sympathetic to the idea of legislation, and that the legislation itself was taken up by one of the liveliest of all backbench MPs, 'Labour's red-haired, tousled' Ellen Wilkinson, who won a prominent position in the Private Members' ballot.[114] Yet it required much clarification of the legal issues and even more conciliation of interests before the Hire Purchase Bill became law, and Mallon made the most of the Hall's reputation for disinterested action as he worked through a group of MPs of all parties.[115]

The story of its passing became the subject of a much publicised film in 'The March of Time' series, dubbed the 'Never Never Film' by the *Daily Sketch*.[116] 'Twelve hundred cinemas will soon be showing a film which ought to be called "The Exploits of Ellen",' wrote the *Daily Herald*, 'or "How She Beat the Sharks".'[117] It recognised, however, as did the film, that what Ellen accomplished all began with 'Jimmy', who had been strongly supported by George Lansbury and in the House of Lords by Lord Amulree. There was one incident that could not be filmed. When the Bill successfully went through the Commons, the Attorney-General, Sir Donald Somervell, walked across the floor of the House and warmly shook Ellen Wilkinson's hand.[118]

While such incidents hit the headlines, there was much – and some would have said the most important part – which did not. It is necessary to turn to the *Annual Reports* for relevant information and to the *Toynbee Outlook*, a quarterly publication edited by Pimlott, which took the place of the old *Record* which had not survived the Depression. There are reminiscences too, like Alexander Hartog's *Born to Sing* which describes the singing lessons a young East Ender received at Toynbee Hall from Robert Kent Parker in 1938 and 1939. 'I always called him "Mr." and I very rarely call anybody "Mr.",' Hartog recalled. 'His classes were fun.'[119]

The last pre-war Report, which did not cover the year 1939, described, for example, 'the remarkable increase in the number of students attending evening classes in the last three years':[120] there were now eighty-three classes as against forty-five, eleven of them tutorial classes. The Toynbee Hall Branch of the WEA was now organising regular Wednesday evening lectures, which were attracting an average audience of a hundred. The Rotary Club of Stepney now met at the Hall for its weekly lunches, while the Co-operative Bass Dressers of Stepney still held their meetings there also. F. E. Douglas, an old Resident, had been President for a quarter of a century.

Yet there were ominous elements in the situation which did not figure in the Report. Jo Hodgkinson wrote letters to *The Times* about gas masks and air raid shelters, and Toynbee Hall was now a place of welcome for political refugees from Nazi Germany, Austria and Czechoslovakia, who brought with them terrifying news of the collapse of civilisation and the imminence of war. George Cadbury was one of the Residents who gave a warm welcome to men like Julius Deutsch and John Mars and has been remembered since: others helped to get them out. Almost half a century later Mars has recalled his months at Toynbee Hall in 1938 as 'one of the happiest periods of my life immediately after my perilous flight from capture by Austrian Fascists'.[121]

All such 'normal' activities briefly came to an end on 3 September 1939, and Toynbee Hall almost overnight underwent what was called at the time a sea-change as Jo Hodgkinson and most of the Residents moved away to other civil and military duties. The People's Palace fell into Government occupation and Hindustan House, which had been set up as a social centre for the first Indians to reach the East End, was required for Indian sailors. Ambulances were parked on the tennis court. Yet before the Blitz of 1940 came the 'phoney war'. 'For the first twelve months,' Mallon recalled, 'there was a blackout, but nothing seemed to happen.'[122] Indeed, of 734,883 children evacuated from the London area in September 1939, 43 per cent had returned by February. Some of them who stayed corresponded with the former Resident, W. C. Johnson, who before the war had distributed partially used tennis balls to East End children and now sent them out to their new country addresses. This is one of the letters of thanks which he received from Somerset: 'I could hardly understand what the people said, but after I had been here a month or two I began to speak the country talk.'[123]

On 7 September 1940 the Blitz began, and during the first half of that month over 2,000 civilians were killed by bombs in Britain and nearly 10,000 were badly wounded, four-fifths of them Londoners, the majority living in East London. Not only were houses and homes totally destroyed, but water mains, gas mains, electric cables, telephones and much else were put out of action. For fifty-seven nights 200 planes dropped their bombs. These were the months of the shelters, and the shelters not only had to protect: they had to provide the board and lodging. Sometimes as many as 200 people slept in the cellars of Toynbee Hall itself.

Two of the largest London shelters were within 500 yards of Toynbee Hall, and volunteers at first organised makeshift meals and provisions, and then investigated and petitioned until health, sanitation and bunking received more forceful attention. As result, Mallon added to his own burdens, for he was appointed Adviser to the Ministry of Food on shelter feeding for ninety boroughs in the London area. Aware that many people in Stepney were staying in underground tube stations, although moving in there was at first officially prohibited, he insisted that food must be provided there as well as in shelters.

Edith Ramsay was a volunteer at Toynbee during this period and has left direct evidence of events and atmosphere.

> At Toynbee Hall [she wrote] there were great activities under Dr Mallon ('Our Jimmy'), so ably assisted by his Secretary, Miss Bigland, who did magnificent work. Let me try to describe an incident on the night of October 21st 1940 at Toynbee Hall. Thanks to Dr Mallon, the work people who had special responsibilities there slept in a room, all on mattresses on the floor. On this night Winston Churchill was due to speak, and we assembled to hear him. Dr Mallon had an unrivalled memory for English verse and loved to quote at length, and what a joy it was to hear him. On this occasion he had just finished the closing passage of Shakespeare's *King John*, when the final words 'If England to itself do rest, but true.' were completely drowned by the noise of a nearby plane, and in seconds a bomb had exploded. The ceiling of our room partly collapsed, all the glass was broken; mortar and shrapnel hit us all and there was no electricity. Covered with debris, cut by glass, bruised by falling masonry, our hair matted with dirt, we stood silent for a minute. Then someone called: 'I'm all right; who is hurt?' The silence was broken and nobody in that room was seriously hurt. But curiously, as we waited, we all kissed each other – a strange occurrence for a group of highly undemonstrative people.[124]

In the last October raid of 1940, three people were killed, nearly a score injured, and hundreds of families became homeless overnight. 'For several hours,' it was tersely reported, 'the shelters and dining room became casualty clearing stations.'[125] Deservedly, however, the remarkable heroism of a middle-aged Jewish woman, Mrs Abrahams, and her husband was given special mention.

> The woman lost an eye in the raid and her leg was terribly injured. Her husband, who was patrolling a near-by shelter in his role as a Shelter Marshal, organised a rescue squad and came upon his wife buried in the debris of his sister's flat. He carried her to our shelter and at once went back to find other victims. First-aid

work was proceeding as fast as possible but this most seriously injured woman begged that others should be attended to first, and it was not until the Warden told her husband that he could do no more at Toynbee that he walked beside the stretcher and saw his wife safely into hospital. Later he developed heart trouble and for months both were in different hospitals.[126]

Survivors were provided with such shelter as could be found in the devastated area of Stepney, and arrangements were made for evacuation, billeting and rehousing. The Settlement appealed also for beds, blankets, clothing and help of every kind, and received it. Two Jewish Air Wardens ran a clothing depot for several weeks on the stage of the Toynbee Theatre, and the Jewish costers and small traders of Petticoat Lane sent to Toynbee Hall every day free of cost, bread, fruit, and vegetables for distribution to victims. Yet more than beds and blankets were provided. Money collected by Toynbee Hall started the first concerts in London shelters. A newly founded Veterans' Club thrived.

As well as ensuring overall co-ordination and surveillance many services on a more personal level were rendered. Thus, a small Air-Raid Distress Fund was collected, and later a donation was received from the Lord Mayor's Fund which provided fares for mothers and children and old people who had to be got out of London but for whom there was no official travel voucher. Many kinds of 'comforts' were distributed, ranging from folding chairs and cushions for old people who spent weary nights in Anderson shelters, to clothing for delicate children working in open-air schools. Two nearly blind old sisters who had lost their wireless set in a raid were given another set.[127]

The periodical *John Bull* drew national attention to these activities at Toynbee Hall,[128] and as a result letters poured in from its readers offering to provide hospitality for the homeless and elderly in East London. Toynbee became thereafter the headquarters of the Anglo-American Fund for London mothers and children, and Lady Gunston, a Toynbee volunteer, was authorised to proceed with a scheme for accommodating children from the bombed areas of London in eight large houses in Gloucestershire, Devonshire and Somerset. In all, nearly 3,000 London children benefitted from this initiative and grew up in beautiful country houses free from fear.

For those children who remained in East London and in the shelters Toynbee Hall provided a supply of cheap milk and shelter concerts. It opened its premises at weekends to young shelterers who wanted to rest and to listen to music, and it edited and distributed a shelter journal. Finally, in 1941 a 'Toynbee Restaurant' was opened with staff and equipment supplied by the LCC. Thereafter 600 hot meals were provided every day at an average cost of 1s. 3d.

When the raids were at their worst, Admiral Brodie lent Toynbee Hall his beautiful home and garden at Bottingdean near Midhurst in Sussex as a rest home for the injured, the aged, the convalescent and the distressed; and over a thousand men, women and young children stayed there for varying lengths of time. 'The spirit of the house, in which Jew and Gentile mingled,' it was claimed, 'was truly remarkable.' The Residents were of every type and condition; and

> under the admirable guidance of the Matron, the minds of the harried community were directed away from their own misfortunes to those of others and to the help

which even the bereaved and injured might bestow. Toynbee Hall and Stepney owe much to Admiral and Mrs. Brodie.[129]

In March 1941 a large bomb narrowly missed the New Buildings at Toynbee Hall. It broke doors and windows and wrecked the adjoining school. And there was worse still to come.

On May 10th 1941 in a very heavy raid on London, the Warden's lodge, the Library and several bedrooms were destroyed in a devastating fire as both incendiary and high explosive bombs rained down upon Commercial Street. The Toynbee Fire-fighters dealt swiftly and effectively with the bombs which fell on Toynbee premises, but unfortunately a warehouse adjoining Toynbee was full of inflammable merchandise and was soon ablaze from end to end.[130]

There was a lack of water, but miraculously, so it seemed, the main building of Toynbee Hall was saved, and the New Building and Booth House each escaped with only slight damage.

Mallon had spent the weekend of the raid in Liverpool at the behest of the Assistance Board in order to examine raid damage there, and deeply affected by the scenes of destruction, he wrote to Stella on 9 May of his 'sense of pain and loss; a sense of the unreality of life; a sense that the world which I knew and enjoyed had come to an end and that I too had ended suffused me'.[131] And it was in that mood that he returned home to find his own home a roofless shell.

I have been and still am in a sea of troubles, the greatest of which is the complete destruction of my house at Toynbee Hall and the loss of my possessions of every kind [he told a friend]. It was a complete consumption and included the destruction of every paper I had accumulated for thirty years,

including the manuscript of the autobiography which he had been writing.[132] His main distress, however, was his wife's loss of 'many lovely and cherished things, among them her beloved Bluthner piano. . . and all her personal treasures'.[133] Surprisingly, this was the last air raid of its kind, and except for the occasional advent of a 'Tip and Run' raid, no bombs fell on London for the next three years.

Mallon and his wife squeezed thereafter into a little room in Booth House, distinguished from all the other rooms by its window box of geraniums, and it was from there that he continued to carry on the job of directing the work of the settlement – and much else besides. Gloomy he might have been in May 1941, but he was indefatigable after disaster had struck, both in official business, much of it of national importance, and in dealing with the endless personal problems brought to him.

On what had been the floor of the Library, Mallon's housekeeper, Mrs Reardon, and her husband now grew tomatoes, lettuce and beans. A load of earth was brought from Victoria Park and carried bucket by bucket on to what had become a roof, and the dining room became a storehouse for coal and coke. Yet Mallon could write on 20 December 1941 to David Garley that he felt 'lucky to have any habitation at all. We have 34,000 separate dwellings in the Borough of Stepney and of these 32,000 have been damaged more or less seriously.'[134]

Toynbee Hall housed one of the largest of the Citizens' Advice Bureaux in East London, opened 'to advise and help people in the many difficulties that will arise because of the war'.[135] It was organised and run by the friends and Residents of the Settlement with help from the Friends Ambulance Unit, and at the peak of its labours it had 50,000 clients. Rents, rates, hire purchase, allowances, wage disputes, house repairs and compensation were old subjects for staff. Now, however, they were supplemented by new subjects, like soldiers' leave, evacuation, and alien rights.

> My husband is an alien [one old-style query began]. He is not sure of the date of his birth, but thinks he is nearly 65. Can he get the Old Age Pension? I am British born. If my husband can't get it, can I? I don't work, but my husband is a street trader on his own.

> We were bombed out the night before last, and the pawn tickets went [an entirely different kind of query began]. Now the pawnbroker says he can't give us our stuff back without them. It is blankets and our best clothes he has got of ours, and now we have lost our home we need them badly.

A third kind of query was well-suited to Toynbee Hall –

> My mate's in a bad way. . . . He is in Heavy Rescue and last night had to dig his Mum and Dad out. Is there anywhere he could go right away from here till he gets over it a bit? His wife's badly shaken up too; perhaps they could go away together, but of course he can't afford to pay very much.[136]

When a problem required legal redress, it was referred to the Poor Man's Lawyer service, which continued to function, although often under strain, during the war. The greatest difficulty was that the panels of advisers shrunk in size as a result of the calls of war service.

The East London Juvenile Court continued to sit at Toynbee Hall also – with an added volume of work. The blackout and 'Shelter life' did not promote improved individual behaviour. Nor did evacuation. Indeed many of the children appearing in court had had long absences from school, and some of them had been evacuated from London and brought back again several times. Toynbee Hall was now perfectly situated to help, and a Play Centre, clubs and classes were organised for in and out of the shelters. During air raids the Court itself was sometimes moved into a passage to avoid broken glass, but usually the proceedings went on until bombers were actually heard overhead. Meanwhile, six local Probation Officers moved into rooms which had been vacated by Residents and turned them into offices and interview rooms for the young people attending the court.

In the midst of such rough and tumble, a valiant attempt was made to maintain a fair semblance of normal activity. At first, the combination of blackout, conscription and longer working hours made it seem doubtful whether evening classes would be possible and some tutorial classes were arranged during the day while the rest were abandoned. In January 1940, however, the demand for classes resulted in evening work restarting on pre-war lines, and 1,050 students enrolled as compared with 1817 in 1938.

When bombing became intense [the Hall reported] classes were restricted to weekends: students worked at Toynbee in the hours of daylight and in the shelters at night. The students persisted in spite of raids, and on May 11th 1941, a number of them attended on the evening when the Settlement was still smouldering.[137]

Classes in art, speech, drama and ballet were the most popular subjects. The adult ballet class, in particular, became so popular that it was held on four evenings a week, and a children's class was held on two evenings. Throughout the worst weeks of the East-End bombing Theodore Wassilieff, known at Toynbee Hall as 'Maestro', a tall, straightbacked old man with 'a dancer's spring in his step', who had arrived in England in 1938, turned up unfailingly four times a week to take his ballet classes for war-workers; and along with Alice Lascelles, he founded a new School of Ballet which gave new life to the Toynbee Theatre. Alice Lascelles was the daughter of Mallon's 'Enquirer' friend, Edward Lascelles (joint author with Mallon of the book *Poverty, Yesterday and Today*, published in 1930).

Classes of all kinds continued for the rest of the war as 'the risks of the blackout' were deliberately accepted. The motto was 'There will be classes for all who need them.' And new needs were identified. Thus, a School of Social Studies was devised in 1943 to provide tuition for social and welfare war-time workers, promising 'theoretical and practical instruction in the operation both of the social services and of war-time legislation'.[138]

The rather erratic record of attendances at classes during the war years is interesting.

Year	Number of Students	Number of Classes
1939–40	1,173	74
1940–1	505	32
1941–2	834	40
1942–3	1,221	67
1943–4	1,414	80
1944–5	1,238	86

The arts flourished more consistently after the Theatre, which at first had fallen victim to the blackout, began to revive, and drama was in great demand as well as ballet. John Clements and Constance Cummings thrilled East End audiences, Austrian and Czech refugees danced and sang in national costume, German refugees, after they had returned from internment in the Isle of Man, produced *Iphigenia*.

There was a new development in 1942, when Mr. A. J. Duggan, a Toynbee Resident of long standing, began to organise drama festivals for companies of amateur players. Intended at first for young people, they proved so popular with audiences for whom playgoing was a novelty that their objectives were widened. Indeed drama began to be thought of as 'a curative influence in our damaged social life'.[139] In West Ham there were open-air performances. In Toynbee Hall four teams performed every Saturday afternoon during the eight-week run of the Festival, their performances judged by 'eminent actors and critics'. The best of them were then repeated in a special Saturday session. Sir Lewis Casson, who befriended the Festivals, described them 'as the most serious attempt which has yet been made to encourage and assist amateur productions'.[140]

In the middle of all this activity, in the spring of 1943, Mallon left the East End for a time and undertook a gruelling thirteen-week speaking tour in the USA and Canada for the Ministry of Information. He was asked to speak on 'The Impact of War on the British Social Services', a subject which it was felt would appeal to the social work organisations: 'The propaganda patter of the Ministry of Information in America emphasises social progress. R. L. Reiss had been talking on housing; Shena Simon is to talk on education; E. D. Simon on municipal government. I have to fill in the gaps.'[141]

> I do not like the idea of a long absence from East London [Mallon remarked after being asked to go]. There is no doubt that if and when the Germans disembarrass themselves wholly or partially of Russia they will come for us again. You will infer from this that I am not breaking with Toynbee which as you know is itself very much broken. Not its new building, however, in which a lot of activity is now concentrated.[142]

On the other side of the Atlantic Mallon spoke eloquently to his American audiences of the nightmare of the Blitz, of 'the memories we share of buildings collapsing and streets disappearing in the thunder and lightning of mighty explosions, of fire spreading to the horizon and seeming too vast and fierce ever to be subdued', and of 'a fantastic and fearful life, always producing new horrors and new problems'. Yet he could make fun of food in the shelters.

> When foods were various we advised the shelterers to prefer certain foods to others; we extolled soup and milk and the balanced diet. But very soon foods ceased to be various and we praised potatoes and carrots which were always abundant. We displayed a lighthearted notice which stated that carrots would not only cure night blindness but would increase beauty. A young woman who read this notice asked me whether I had ever tried carrots. I evaded the implication of her question by saying that I regarded my night blindness as incurable.[143]

On his return, Mallon broadcast a Sunday night postscript (with what he called a 'congregation' of 14 millions) on his experiences which included the sentence: 'I said that the reason why England did not abolish the House of Lords was because nearly all Englishmen are trying to join it.' And he kept up the banter. To

> a question which was put to me frequently, namely whether there were any methods of inducing the Germans to live peaceably after the war, I replied that a single and efficacious method would be to raise the school leaving age to 75.[144]

At least one of his listeners was capable of banter, too. Sergeant W. Gardner, of the Royal Engineers, wrote to him as

> one of the parasites who lived in the shade of your glamour. The word 'Toynbee Hall' was an open sesame in any circle, and I hung about for eleven years – as a Rover Scout there, curtain puller at the Ballet classes etc. A Great Life – Am wondering if you still smoke your cigars as you did when Churchill was still at the Woodbine stage. All the Lukis Rovers are at it some place. Carrying on Captain Lukis' work. I warn you that after the war the 13 of us (I hope 13) will continue to infest Toynbee with our company. It has been and ever will be our epic of social life in England.[145]

It is not surprising that Mallon, given his record, believed that even in the worst months of war 'reconstruction' should be a major concern there, and on Saturday 9 October 1943, several months after the Beveridge Report on Social Security had appeared, the *Eastminster Press and City Guardian* was able to report that 'Stepney Citizens and their friends everywhere will be glad to know that its Reconstruction Plans are now taking definite shape.' Indeed, Toynbee Hall 'under the experienced and expert guidance' of its 'notable Warden', 'from the first has taken a courageous lead'.[146] Almost two years before, following an inspiring address by the Borough Engineer and Surveyor at the Settlement Centre in Commercial Street, the Stepney Reconstruction Group had been formed, and since then it had been 'steadily at work, on somewhat original lines, on the complicated problems inevitably associated with a new East London'.[147]

One of the foremost figures in this Reconstruction Group was a young Oxford undergraduate economist, Denys Munby, who, answering Father Groser's call for help, had arrived in Dockland at one hour's notice in 1940 when the docks were on fire. He was able to help, but soon he found himself engaged in a very different kind of task, for Mallon commissioned him to do research on the changing structure of industry and employment in East London. The first result was a short book, *Living in Stepney*, which quickly sold out and might have gone on selling for months if the Paper Controller had been willing to grant paper for a reprint.[148]

Words were not thought to be enough, however, and an exhibition, 'Living in Cities', 'as simple, pictorial and factual as possible' was held at Toynbee Hall in an attempt to illustrate the problems which would be faced in building a new Stepney.[149]

Munby began to work at once on a detailed scheme which would take account of the 'gigantic social revolution' which had taken place in the area as the pre-war population had declined to a third;[150] and he and the Stepney Reconstruction Group went on to criticise sharply the LCC's Draft Plan, the famous Abercrombie Plan, for the Stepney/Poplar area:

> if there is one thing that the people of Stepney want at the end of the War [he wrote] it is a house and a garden; and conversely the one thing they do not want is a flat. To many people it is a deciding factor as to whether they will stay in Stepney. It is undoubtedly the only criterion by which many judge any scheme for post war reconstruction, and it would be a sad irony if the first glimpse of the new London that people saw would be the flats that they hate.[151]

He also complained that the acreage zoned for industry in the LCC's proposals was 'inordinately high' and spoke of 'atonement' to East London for what it had suffered in the past. 'We have to choose,' he concluded, 'between a rather glorified piece of slum clearance and a major social experiment. East London, and perhaps Stepney in particular, is all for the major experiment'.[152]

The war had been over for more than six years when Munby's survey was published in book form to receive enthusiastic notices in the *Architects Journal* and *The Times*:

> By an extremely thorough assembly of facts, in particular about industrial employment in the borough [the latter stated], Mr Munby shows that some of the conclusions of the Abercrombie scheme were founded on only a sketchy knowledge of the social and industrial circumstances in Stepney.[153]

The sub-title of the book was 'A Report presented to the Stepney Reconstruction Group, Toynbee Hall', and it was very much in the Toynbee Hall tradition that it could be described as 'sustained by an extremely thorough survey of Stepney's industrial enterprises'.[154] Already by then, however, it had become clear that Stepney was not to be rebuilt on Munby's lines. He prophesied, therefore, that at the end of the century it would still be sub-standard area, and that the opportunity of wiping out 'the stigma of the East End' would have been irrevocably lost.[155] 'Future generations will say we have missed our opportunities.'[156]

While environmental change was a main feature of all reconstruction proposals, the need for educational reorganisation and advance was also being insisted upon and promoted. The philosophy behind the Toynbee Hall proposals was the same, however, as that advanced for decades. It was significant, indeed, that the WEA, which was itself keenly interested in reconstruction, held its first annual general meeting since the outbreak of war at Toynbee Hall in 1944. There had been a substantial war-time boom in classes, parallelling the remarkable development of army education, and there were high hopes for the future of school education also, expressed, it seemed, in R. A. Butler's Education Act of 1944. In 1942 Mallon had quipped at a fringe meeting of the TUC Conference, 'Every time we have a war, we have an Education Act. If we were to reverse the process and have the Education Act first we might perhaps be spared the war.'[157] In more serious vein he had gone on to spell out the need for full access to the best secondary education, for more nursery schools, for the immediate raising of the school leaving age to 16 after the war ended, and for more facilities for continuing education.

It is fair to conclude that Mallon was one of the most alert of the many people who encouraged Butler to introduce an Education Act in war-time, when the thoughts of the Prime Minister were concentrated on the winning of the war. In 1942, for example, he chaired a public meeting on educational reconstruction at Toynbee Hall at which the resolution was passed demanding a new Education Bill, and he won the support of MPs of all parties, notably the Conservative reformer Hugh Molson, to speed up the process. He also drew into the movement the Earl of Lytton, who agreed to become Chairman of a Committee set up to assist Butler, who, it was said, feared that opposition to his Bill, while not 'intrinsically important', might act as a brake on its passage or to 'a lessening of the zeal of the Government to see the Bill enacted'.[158]

The Lytton Committee of Educational Reconstruction, composed of educationists, members of all major religious groups and political parties, leaders in industry and well-known figures in public life might have been a useful support to Butler but

> the truth is [Mallon wrote in March 1944], that there is nothing for my Committee to do. I am in touch with the Minister and the Parliamentary Secretary and they say their only trouble is the volubility of their supporters. If the educationalists in the House would dry up, the Bill would go through rapidly. It is their praises of it that make progress slow.[159]

'You will be pleased to note,' Mallon wrote to the son (in the Royal Air Force) of an old Toynbee Resident in February 1945 'that we stick to our inspiration and tradition and aim to be a centre and tabernacle of the liberal spirit.' And by then the V rocket attacks on London had tested the morale of East Enders yet again. Mallon felt that they were not as 'noxious' as the Blitz but that they 'affected a great many more people than the Blitz did'.[160] The war had lasted for a long time and stoicism was difficult to maintain. 'When the War is over,' Mallon's letter concluded, 'and we are now dreaming of the end, I hope that you will pay us a visit.'[161]

The end of the war soon afterwards brought relief from fear and, particularly after the General Election of 1945, hope for the future, but there was no quick escape either from austerity or from the memory of recent horror. 'The housing shortage is serious and the destruction affects every phase of life,' Mallon wrote to a friend in September 1945, 'London is dirty as never before and for this reason oppressive to the onlooker as never before.' Yet his humour did not falter: 'Let me end on a note of joy. I am glad to say that I am included in the Gestapo Black List. I am enormously stuck up in consequence.'[162]

War-damaged Toynbee Hall had its problems too, and they were not only problems related to war damage, like the loss of the library and the Warden's house. There was a mounting overdraft, there were no Residents, and the Warden himself, for all his energy and flow of high spirits was 72 years old. Mallon was determined, however, to secure the immediate future, with the assistance of a new Associate Warden, Major Lionel E. Ellis, a military historian, who had had a distinguished military career. He had experience of social work, too, for between the two wars he had helped to run the National Council for Social Service. 'The first year of peace finds Toynbee Hall reconstructing its activities,' Mallon wrote confidently in 1946, 'and is looking forward to a remoter prospect of reconstructing its lost buildings. All that was done before the War must be done again and more tellingly.'[163]

The New Building which had escaped the ravages of war inevitably became the centre of post-war activity, and there was no immediate change in the pattern of educational work carried out there. While the Enquirers' Club was revived – by Beveridge, Arthur Salter, Edward Lascelles and George Booth – the evening classes reassembled. The theme chosen by the Club in 1945 was 'The Question of Survival in Britain', in 1946 'Nationalisation'. The classes which attracted over 1,300 students each week, half of them living in East London or the City, many of them attending classes before they went home, covered all the old familiar subjects along with drawing and painting, music, ballet and other forms of dance and physical education, and some new subjects including the art of writing and film appreciation. One of the oldest subjects, philosophy, made its way back into the curriculum also. As in the past, special provision was always made for special circumstances: thus, a new feature in the Hall's life was the use of the premises in the day-time by Polish students who were being prepared for permanent settlement in Britain.

There seemed to be a particularly rosy future for the arts at a time when the war had proved their growing popularity, when there was talk of a cultural renaissance, and when in 1946 the Arts Council of Great Britain was established by Royal Charter. Toynbee's Drama School had survived the war under the direction of John Burrell, and provided opportunities for the ideas and methods of Michel St Denis of the pre-war London Theatre Studio to be tried out in the East End. And at the same time the Toynbee Drama Festival had restored to health and activity moribund amateur societies under Duggan's devoted, if idiosyncratic, leadership.

One of the most exciting post-war projects at Toynbee was a children's theatre, which was suggested by Suria Magito, who had conducted dramatic classes at Toynbee during the war, and who was to work closely with St Denis. 'Before the War this country had not gone far in providing an organised theatre for children,' Mallon wrote, pointing to experiments in Russia which had shown what might be done by professional actors specialising in such work;[164] and even before the war ended he engaged a professional company at Toynbee Hall which in 1966 presented *The Snow Queen* adapted from a Russian version, and subsequently shown to enthusiastic audiences of children in Liverpool, York, Chesterfield, Manchester and Wolverhampton.

Britain's first children's theatre thus came into being with the important rule that 'No adults may attend a performance unless accompanied by a child.'[165] From the start, however, it was gravely handicapped by lack of funds. Having looked in vain to local authorities, Mallon turned to his – and Toynbee's – old friend, Ellen Wilkinson, Minister of Education in the new Labour Government, who addressed a circular letter to the local education authorities commending the work of the Children's Theatre and stipulating that expenditure on the attendance of children during school hours could be included for partial reimbursement under Ministry Grant.

For prestigious support Mallon turned also to John Christie of Glyndebourne and to George Bernard Shaw. Glyndebourne supplied Rudolf Bing to be Director of Production, and Shaw made the offer first of *Androcles* without fee and then of all or any of his other plays 'at a fee of half-a-crown a month to be paid annually to my account', an arrangement which he later revised on the grounds that as

> a good Trade Unionist I must not undersell my fellow play-wrights. If the Children's Theatre cannot afford a shilling in the £ on the gross receipts it must pay me a fee equal to half of its profits on each performance. This arrangement should not be held to constitute a partnership. Its effect will be that when you lose I get nothing.[166]

Androcles was duly produced, and among other successes Alec Guiness's adaptation of *Great Expectations* played to packed houses at Toynbee Hall, at Cambridge, and at many provincial centres. Indeed, in two years of activity over 550 performances were seen by 300,000 children. It was not surprising that John Allen, the Administrator, wrote enthusiastically that such activity had succeeded because it was 'in step with one of the most exciting social, educational and artistic movements of our times'.[167]

The Christies hoped that their generous financial assistance would enable the work of the Children's Theatre to be developed to a stage at which an organic relationship between it, the Ministry of Education and the new Arts Council could be established;[168] and in 1948 an Arts Council grant of £3,000 was made. Yet the grant included the ominous proviso that 'this should not be regarded as recurrent in future years', and by then Ellen Wilkinson was dead and the new Minister of Education, George Tomlinson, was not prepared to give special help. Another children's theatre, that of the Young Vic, established eighteen months after Toynbee's pioneering effort, had begun to compete for grants, and it was this organisation which was destined to carry on the work of children's theatre in England.

Meanwhile, the Toynbee Hall Theatre, now given a full-time salaried Director, Bill

Prothero, and a salaried Manager, enjoyed a brief boom before the cost of necessary alterations to the building played havoc with its finances; and when Prothero left, the financial difficulties increased. The Toynbee Council hesitated to impose higher charges on the users of the Theatre, among them small local groups, themselves under financial pressure, and instead the use of the Theatre was curtailed. There was little consolation in the comment that

> perhaps the students are not too harshly treated, for though the present provision for their use of the Theatre is narrow it is ampler than that made for similar students in LCC Evening Institutes or even in the more exalted centre of evening study with which the Settlement compares itself.[169]

In fact, Toynbee Hall as a whole was in increasing financial difficulties and could take no more risks, however imaginative the project. Old friends and ex-Residents of Toynbee gathered around Mallon, as they had after the First World War, and Clement Attlee, now Labour Prime Minister, lent invaluable support by becoming President. The war-time tenants left, the older part of Toynbee was refurnished, a new domestic staff was engaged, and in 1949 sixteen young men came into residence, 'pleasant, high-grade, likeable fellows', most of them 'University men', and among them was the first Indian Resident.[170] Yet Mallon, hard though he tried, did not succeed in finding donors to assist him in his enterprises. They remained cold to his appeals for support to endow a new Student's Library, additional residential quarters, a new Warden's Lodge, a new wing with rooms for educational and social activities, a music room for 300 students, a new School of Art to cater for the hundred art students then enrolled, and rooms for 'a junior Toynbee Hall', where 'children of the neighbourhood would enter in a tidal wave'.[171]

In his appeals Mallon emphasised two main points – the importance of residence and the need even in a 'welfare state' (the term was now coming into fashion) to support voluntary initiatives – and although he was strongly supported on the second point by Attlee as well as Beveridge, he was disappointed, if not entirely surprised, by the response. 'Some of the employers are now sticky because of the Labour Government and heavy taxation,' Mallon wrote to a friend in 1945, quoting a businessman who suggested 'that we should turn to the Socialists, who are now in power and are taking everyone's money'.[172] And he noted how many old benefactors of Toynbee Hall struck a similar attitude. Nancy Astor wrote bewailing her desperate financial situation, while another prominent figure in the City was more brutally frank.

> I hope Toynbee Hall will in future receive its full share of resources which our present bureaucratic system under a totalitarian Government is robbing from the individual so that he can no longer enjoy the immense pleasure of supporting beneficent activities of this kind.[173]

It is interesting to compare this judgment with Attlee's own judgment that Britain had

> a tradition of voluntary effort that is not confined to any one class of the community. Alongside everything done by the local authority and by the state there are people who want to do a bit more. . . . This country will never become a people of an exclusive and omnipotent State. . . . I believe that we shall always have alongside

the great range of public services, the voluntary services which humanise our national life and bring it down from the general to the particular. We must keep stretching out to new horizons.

I will say one thing of Toynbee. It is always looking for new things. I have seen so many new ventures start at Toynbee. . . And I say this. The idea of our democracy does not mean that we sit down and have things done for us, but that we do things for ourselves. Toynbee in its time has been a great nurse of democracy.[174]

In a letter to Lord Leverhulme Mallon made the most of his other main point, emphasising the difference between Settlements and Community Centres of the kind now being provided by some enlightened local authorities. 'A Settlement is necessarily an experimenting and reforming body, whereas a Community Centre is concerned with things as they are.' 'Unless a standard is set for the Community Centre either by the Settlements or by some other body,' he went on, 'I think very meanly of their future.'[175]

As well as trying to raise funds for Toynbee, Mallon was also trying to raise £100,000 for the WEA, emphasising how important it was to keep it independent, and seeking to revive the Whitechapel Art Gallery and the People's Palace. When he was asked to raise money for the Council of Christians and Jews, he was forced to draw a line: 'I would gladly help you if I could,' he wrote to the Rev. Simpson. 'I don't see how I can. . . . I am made already to attack everyone I know. By this time my unpopularity is large and it is growing rapidly.'[176]

Finance was not, however, the only theme in these difficult but never dull years. When the Fascists made a reappearance in the East End again in 1947 and Jeffrey Hamm announced his intention of holding daily meetings in the Bethnal Green area, Mallon worked closely with the Board of Deputies of British Jews to try to control the situation. 'The redevelopment of anti-Jewish feeling is deplorable,' he wrote.

> During the War the evil effects of Mosley's agitation were obliterated. At Toynbee Hall and elsewhere Jews and Christians intermixed and played the part of good friends and neighbours. A Jewish manufacturer gave me thousands of camp beds to be used in shelters by whoever needed them. Local Roman Catholics and Jews exchanged gifts. The East End pulled together and was completely cordial. Now the Mosley virus is at work again and relationships are being poisoned.[177]

Yet Sidney Salmon, the Press Officer of the Board of Deputies of British Jews introduced a Mallon touch into his comment when he said of a plan to start a Mosley Book Club in Bethnal Green that he imagined that the number of 'literary gents' in Bethnal Green was somewhat limited. 'It will probably be merely a blind for a drinking club.'[178]

Mallon formed a Council of East London Citizens at Toynbee Hall to counter Fascist propaganda and in particular to fight anti-Semitism: he also asked the cartoonist David Low to produce his kind of commentary.[179] Throughout he found a staunch ally in Father Fitzgerald, an Irish priest of great influence in Stepney, who feared that since the post-war world was leaving a district like Stepney 'very much disillusioned', in such an atmosphere anything could happen.

And whereas 'No Popery' or 'Down with the Jesuits' was as good a racket as any about 100 years ago 'Perish Judah' or 'Down with the Jews' is a better winner for the phoney political boss of the 20th century.[180]

In fact, the immigrant issue in the East End was to take quite a different form as Jews gave way to Asians and West Africans. There was the first hint of their presence in an early post-war report which referred in language that would quickly become obsolete to 'English Classes for Coloured Colonials in Cable Street'.[181]

By 1951 the dangers of violent social conflict in the East End seemed to have passed. Yet it was now estimated that Toynbee Hall was running at a loss of around £2,000 a year and that an endowment of at least £150,000 was needed to secure its future. Mallon still felt that it was unwise to rely too heavily on the local authorities, and in consequence was persuaded that he had best turn for support to the land of free enterprise, the United States. Before he went, he told the Marquess of Salisbury that it would be unwise to seek more financial assistance from the local authorities.

> The recognition of our complete freedom from political or denominational bias has been precious to us in the past. It would be imperilled by the receipt of money from bodies all of which are now acutely political. I gladly add that we have cordial relations with all the Councils and co-operate with them in various ways. We do not wish however in any way or degree to depend on them.[182]

Laden with letters of commendation from Queen Mary, the Archbishop of Canterbury, Attlee, Lord Astor, Lord Halifax, Lord Woolton and – through a different line of descent – from the Master of Balliol and his predecessor in that office, Lord Lindsey, Mallon set sail across the Atlantic.

> You will, I am afraid, find your self-imposed task a rough one [Alfred Zimmern, an old friend of Toynbee Hall told him], although I agree with you that there are many Americans who owe more to Toynbee Hall (and to you personally) than a felicitous phrase of gratitude. . . . People tend to be over-impressed with the reported affluence of the working class and wonder why the people should not pay for the social and educational amenities they crave. Some of them will have read Rowntree's recent biassed report on the thoughtless spending of the English poor.[183]

Mallon was warmly greeted in America, but no funds were forthcoming. As he explained to a friend on his return,

> My American visit was, I am sorry to say, very much not successful. Everything was against me; increase of taxation, the preoccupation of the Jews with Israel, the multiplicity of other appeals, a certain exasperation with Britain occasioned in part by the late Government, and in part by the misbehaviour as it is deemed to be of our miners and our textile workers: added to all these sources of discouragement was a generalised feeling, understandable enough, that America is doing a damned sight too much for the world and that the world should do more for itself.[184]

Whatever the achievements or the problems, Mallon's own personal ascendancy was as obvious during these last years of his leadership as Barnett's had been after he ceased to be Warden in 1906 and became President. Thus, when Attlee was given a reception on 31 March 1947, attended by over 400 men and women who were prominent in business, politics, local government and social work in East London, he not only paid a tribute to the 'spirit of enterprise and mutual assistance for which Toynbee Hall stands', but recalled his own first somewhat uncertain assistance to Mallon in 1907 during the Anti-Sweating Campaign when Toynbee Hall was still in its pioneering years:

> There was a meeting of four unions to elect representatives on the Tailoring Board. There were four representatives from the Unions and I was Chairman. After the first ten minutes for two hours the proceedings were conducted in a language that I didn't know. I presided with great firmness and was told I wasn't at all satisfactory.[185]

Mallon, in such circumstances, was a consoling guide.

It was in a spirit of friendship that Labour and Conservative members of the LCC united in voting Toynbee Hall the bombed land on its Commercial Street frontage in recognition of Mallon's immense service to the East End. It was partly to be devoted to a pleasant garden, but it also made possible the addition of a new building to the Toynbee complex – the Attlee Building named after Mallon's friend.

At a later reception, this time for Mallon, Attlee described him as 'a very great citizen, a very great East Londoner and a most loveable man'. 'He was a bright young fellow' when they had first met; 'he still looks like a boy, and is always full of life and humour.'

> I think when he looks back at his achievements, he will say that his great achievement has been in personal relationship, and personal friendship. We have been rich in personalities at Toynbee and East London, but never have we had a more striking personality than Jimmy Mallon's, and I do not think there is any public figure that is more loved by everyone.[186]

In July 1952, the *Sunday Times* chose Mallon as the subject of its 'Portrait Gallery' feature. At the age of 77, he still suggested youth: indeed, 'to see him with young people is to realise that he is their contemporary, adored alike for his wisdom and his wit. He surrounds himself with laughter, and he would have life to be one long happy joke.' 'If there is more laughter and enjoyment of life in the East End now,' the article concluded, 'it has been led by Jimmy Mallon. . . . There were two things in life that he would never understand – envy and unkindliness.'[187]

The *East End News* corroborated what the *Sunday Times* had said:

> It is often the case that when a public worthy acquires national eminence the particular district in which he had previously laboured loses all contact with him, or at best is able to retain only a nominal connection. An outstanding feature of the life and character of Dr J. J. Mallon. . . is that although he has given much valued service to the country as a whole he has always remained close to the East End of which he became the 'adopted son' more than 40 years ago. He gives the same care and attention to the signing of a vaccination form for a worried mother as he does to problems which affect large numbers of workers throughout Britain.[188]

The Barnetts had deliberately 'settled in the East End'. Mallon simply lived there.

When in 1954, at the age of 80, and after thirty-five years at Toynbee Hall, Mallon decided to retire, Lord Waverley, the Chairman of the Toynbee Hall Council, wrote to him in deep gratitude, adding that to recall all he had done would mean a review of 'nearly half of the Settlement's long life and an excursion into the history of many other institutions and movements during a third of a century'.[189] Lord Francis Williams, close associate of Attlee, said the same. 'There are few good causes of the 'twenties and 'thirties [and he might have added most of the 1940s] in which his hand cannot be seen.'[190]

Mallon lived on for exactly seven years after leaving Toynbee Hall, winning the Margaret McMillan Medal in 1955, and in the same year seeing unveiled a bust of himself by Epstein. He died in hospital on 12 April 1961, having retained to the end his honorary secretaryship of the Wages Councils Advisory Committee and his membership of several trades boards, and while still working again on his autobiography, the first version of which had been destroyed during the war. 'If ever there was a life single-heartedly devoted to the services of others,' *The Times* obituary said of him, 'such a life was Mallon's,' and added, that he had been called 'the most popular man east of Aldgate Pump'.[191]

V
Unfinished Agenda, 1954–1984

Thirty years is the conventional span of a generation, and a whole generation has now passed since Mallon ceased to be Warden of Toynbee Hall. And if time is measured less precisely in terms of perpetually overlapping generations, this particular span of thirty years has encompassed probably greater changes in society and culture than any which had preceded it. At times there has been so much contrast between generations that the gulf between ages has been stressed even more than the gulf between classes.

The rhythm of technological change, including change in communications, has sharply accelerated, bringing new problems as well as achievements and opportunities in its way; and as we look back from the 1980s it is impossible to say whether or not the decade of the 1960s or that of the 1970s was the more significant in the history of change. In the former, there was a sense of challenge to all established institutions, including educational and religious as well as economic and political institutions, and in the latter there was a sense of challenge to the country as a whole – with the middle years of the decade seeing more alarming economic crises and sharper political divisions than in any previous decade, including the first decade, within the whole centenary span of existence of Toynbee Hall.[1]

Yet it was while Mallon was still Warden that an acute historian across the Channel was already pointing to a question which was already being asked in 1949, 'Why waste time on history when there are so many productive tasks to be carried out which require all our energy and mental powers?'[2] Many of the traditions which held through two World Wars were threatened more seriously ten years after the Second World War than they had been as a result of war experience itself, and many of the old social relationships which sustained them lost much of their vitality.

In retrospect, the year 1954, when Mallon left Toynbee Hall, was for a number of reasons one of the hinge years in British social history. On the one side of the mid-1950s divide, the prelude to the later and more publicised divides of the 1960s and the 1970s, was 'austerity', on the other side 'affluence'; on one side 'convention', and on the other side 'revolt'; on one side accepted British international power, and on the other side eroded national influence.[3] There were signs also of changes in individual motivation and in group behaviour. Yet the contrasts could be overdrawn, and in retrospect also there were obvious continuities. Poverty did not disappear in a period of affluence. Conventional values did not fade in a period of so-called 'permissiveness': some remained dominant, some were to return to favour. Nor did everything political change with Suez or with the break-up of the BBC's monopoly or with Harold Macmillan and Harold Wilson.

It was not until 1971 that Britain entered the European community, and not until later in the decade that the full implications of co-existence of unemployment and inflation began to be appreciated. Divisive debates centring on national economic and social politics of the kind that characterised the years 1974 to 1976 had not been predicted by Mallon, by Beveridge or even by Tawney, so that much that they had to say of England or London now seems dated, lost in a different world. There had been no more finality in the 'Welfare State' than in the old Poor Law of 1834. Nor was the 'traditional' industrial structure, which had shaped so much of British politics, to survive the advent of new technologies. It was not only Toynbee Hall, therefore, that had to adapt to change. A research body, like Political and Economic Planning, product of the 1930s – to which Mallon had belonged – had been forced to prepare a new agenda of its own before it became part of a new organisation, the Policy Studies Institute (PSI) in 1980.[4]

The new Warden of Toynbee Hall, appointed in April 1954, Dr Arthur Eustace Morgan, did not live long enough to see most of this change. Yet he was the first Warden who had to try to adapt an old institution to a new social pattern. Born in 1886, only two years after Toynbee Hall was founded, he was a graduate in English and French of Trinity College, Dublin. And he had had a distinguished academic career – first as Professor of English at Exeter and Sheffield Universities (though the former was not then a full university), then as the first Principal of the University College of Hull from 1927 to 1935, and after that as Principal and Vice-Chancellor of McGill University across the Atlantic, in Montreal, Canada.

In the best Toynbee Hall tradition Morgan, known to his friends as 'AE', had combined his academic interests with a concern for the underprivileged; and on his return to England this had led him to undertake large-scale surveys on behalf of King George's Jubilee Trust on 'The Needs of Youth' (1939) and 'The Young Citizen' (1943). He had been made a Life Vice-President of the National Association of Boys' Clubs and after a spell as District Commissioner, Special Areas (Durham and Tyneside) in 1939 – the kind of position that enabled him, again in the best Toynbee Hall tradition, to appreciate the needs of the unemployed – he had been an Assistant Secretary in the Ministry of Labour from 1941 to 1945. The problem of unemployment, which had dominated the 1930s, was solved then not through a wise and premeditated national policy but through the imperatives of war, though with the end of the war 'full employment in a free society', to use a Beveridge phrase, had become a deliberate national goal.[5]

Morgan's appointment was intended to be short-term, and he had a specific brief from the Toynbee Hall Council – objectively to assess what future role if any Toynbee Hall had to play in a changing society:

> It was most fortunate [the Council Minutes read] that a man so well qualified and of such distinction as Dr. Morgan was prepared to accept appointment on an experimental footing and to help Council in reaching the decisions as to the future which it would have to take in the next year.[6]

While the future of Toynbee Hall was so uncertain, no young man with the right qualifications would have accepted the post of Warden. Mallon had received no salary for many years, and had even tried to shore up Toynbee Hall with his own money. No suitable accommodation for a Warden now existed, and Morgan could only be offered the small sum of £500 a year. Moreover, of the Toynbee Hall salary fund £1,250 came not from London or Britain but from the American Friends of Toynbee Hall, an organisation, with Albert Einstein as Vice-President, which had been set up by Mallon on his last fund-raising trip to America. The gift seemed providential. 'Perhaps at length our bitter tide is turning,[7] J. S. Eagles, the Honorary Treasurer, had written to Mallon, when it was received. Eagles, who had piloted the finances of the Hall through many lean years, was in a position to know. He had made his mark as Director of Breweries and Public Houses in the Carlisle area during the First World War when the Lloyd George Government experimented in public ownership and had subsequently moved to Whitbread's great brewery in Chigwell Street. He remained Treasurer until 1970.

Since the war ended, it had remained impossible to obtain a sufficient addition to Toynbee Hall's income from voluntary sources to match the spiralling costs of the Settlement's work, even of its basic maintenance and management, and a run of annual deficits had had to be financed by loans from the Settlement's bankers. By 1954, a debt of some £20,000 had been contracted, a debt which seemed likely to increase almost inevitably by some £2,000 – £3,000 each year. It was little consolation that the value of the Settlement's fixed assets was greater than that of the debt, for if they were to be realised the Hall would cease to exist. And this, too, would be the outcome, it seemed to the Council, if the overdraft were allowed further to increase and accumulate. 'Unless a remedy is found,' it concluded, 'Toynbee Hall cannot survive.'[8]

Mallon, who had devoted so much of his energy to the building up of Toynbee Hall's educational programme, had become reluctantly convinced before his resignation that a shift of resources and energies away from the formal educational commitment of the Settlement would facilitate its continuance and development as a centre of social work and research. He felt too that greater financial resources would be necessary to make provision on an ampler scale for the care of the very elderly and very young, the most vulnerable groups in society. Given this approach, it seemed logical to him, as it did to many members of the Council, that the necessary course of action was to sell or to let the New Building so that the Settlement's annual expenditure could be substantially reduced and an additional income secured for activities which could then be conducted in the older buildings. Moreover, Major L. F. Ellis, his energetic Associate Warden, shared this line of thought:

> the transfer of the educational work in the New Building to the L.C.C. (if they will accept it) [he added] should be regarded as natural development, for it is a common progression for the public authority to take over responsibility for work which a voluntary organisation has so successfully pioneered that it has outgrown the strength of its parent body.[9]

The logic might have seemed irrefutable to Mallon, to Ellis and to Morgan – and efforts were made with 'some regrets' to sell the Educational Block to the LCC. Yet the

LCC was not persuaded of the logic, and in his last year as Warden, Mallon was forced to plead at County Hall for a breathing space of a year during which the LCC educational grant to Toynbee Hall would be increased by £1,500.[10] Margaret Cole, an old friend, who was now Chairman of its Further Education Committee, praising what she called 'your Daniel Act' wrote reassuringly to him that 'You will in the end get your £1,500 – you have the sympathy of the Leader and of the Chairman of the Finance Committees,'[11] and she was right, although Mallon was not so confident and felt that he was 'testing the ingenuity' of the LCC experts'.[12] What he had tested, of course, was their goodwill, and he deeply appreciated a warm letter from T. G. Randall, the Deputy Clerk of the LCC, written from County Hall.

> it was with special pleasure, as Stepney was my birthplace [Randall wrote] that I listened to your luminous exposition of the work and tradition of Toynbee Hall. Though I know nothing of it personally, I recall as a small child that the name was almost a talisman on the lips of my father and his friends.[13]

The long-term problem, of course, remained, and the LCC Comptroller, harder-headed than his colleagues, felt it necessary to add that 'valuable though the tradition of Toynbee Hall has been, the circumstances which had called for its work sixty years ago have disappeared largely due to the work which Toynbee Hall itself has done.' He hoped 'the authorities of Toynbee Hall would not exclude the possibility that a commercial letting of the educational block was after all the right course'.[14]

With no illusions about the precariousness of the financial situation, Morgan, as a new Warden, began at once to sound out old friends of Toynbee and local leaders – in search not only of money, but of inspiration. In response to Edward Lascelles's bold suggestion that the Hall might move lock, stock and barrel to one of England's new towns, he wrote anxiously and with 'an open mind' that his 'own feelings' were

> that we have got to think out the whole meaning and usefulness of Toynbee. . . . One must even, I think, face such extreme possibilities, though I hope not probabilities [he went on], of closing down, or, as you suggest, possibly of moving. . . . Clearly this cannot be done in a hurry and my own policy at the moment is to watch and listen and learn as preparation for deep consideration[15]

Margaret Cole was another friend who encouraged radical thinking. When Morgan suggested that whatever the changes, 'underlying principles may be the same' because 'Barnett builded pretty well', she replied sharply, 'Barnett may have builded well. But what he built mostly isn't there any longer, either socially or educationally. That is why new thought is needed.'[16]

Two old Toynbee stalwarts offered limited encouragement. Beveridge, Morgan reported to the Council, was

> most interested to hear about Toynbee, in which he maintains a real interest. . . . I put to him the idea of a survey of the possibilities of finding part-time employment for O.A.P.s and thereafter, if circumstances justified it, to set up an informal exchange. This he thought an excellent idea and well worth pursuing.[17]

Tawney, who may have been approached along different lines, was less precise.

He thinks that the real value of Toynbee is in having sent out men. . . . In an earlier day the struggle was against this or that social evil. Those fights have largely been won. He is imbued with a feeling that the forces of social science must be used to create joy and beauty.[18]

That indeed would have been a worthy task for Toynbee, whether or not Tawney was right in suggesting that the older fights had been largely won or that he himself had the secret of identifying 'joy and beauty'. The question, however, was not only how to fulfil a new task, but how to pay for it.

Sir Basil Henriques, a powerful influence, felt sure from the vantage point of the Bernhard Baron St George's Jewish Settlement in Commercial Road that 'there was still a place for a Settlement such as Toynbee in Whitechapel' provided that – and here he was following Mallon and Ellis's logic – it ceased to serve as an evening institute of the L.C.C.

> When Barnett founded the Settlement [he wrote to Morgan], there was no 'further education' being undertaken, except by voluntary social workers. The exact opposite is the case today, and if Toynbee kicked the LCC out of the magnificent premises which were built for the classes, you will have all the space you require for the different activities which could be undertaken.
>
> The problems of East End [Henriques went on at length] are as great as they ever have been in my time, but they are extremely different to what they were even 43 years ago, and I am confident that under inspiring leadership, an enormous amount could be done by the Residents in improving the moral conditions of the East End and in bringing happiness and friendship to those who need it most. . . .
>
> A Settlement ought to be a community centre to which local inhabitants can come and meet on terms of equality and friendship men of different education and background. The communal life of a Settlement such as Toynbee should not be confined to the Residents, but the Residents and the local community. The Cannon[sic], according to Mrs. Barnet [sic] did succeed in bringing together the East and the West to meet on the common ground at Toynbee. Although class distinctions are disappearing, cultural distinctions remain and there is a place for this kind of thing today.

Just as Toynbee Hall used to 'penetrate into the slums' and make its influence felt there, Henriques argued forcefully,

> so should the Residents of Toynbee penetrate into the new housing estates and form community centres in blocks of flats, and befriend the new inhabitants who are very often far more lonely than the street community of the old slums. There are so many gaps in the services of this welfare state. Toynbee has got to discover the gaps by research and exploration and fill them, if necessary, by legislation or by establishing voluntary organisations to do it.[19]

He might have used as an example *Family and Kinship in East London*, the sensitive and penetrating study by Michael Young (later Lord Young of Dartington), one of the most remarkable recent Residents of Toynbee Hall, and Peter Willmott.[20]

Two tasks were particularly challenging Henriques thought – 'the training of salaried social workers' and 'representation on the Borough Council and even on the London County Council'. The second was familiar enough: the first was being reorientated as increasing emphasis was being placed on the development of a new profession. *From Lady Bountiful to Social Welfare* was the title of one of the best historical studies to end with the 'new look'.[21]

> Toynbee in its earliest days was out for amelioration of existing ghastly conditions [Henriques concluded in moralising vein] – to-day, Toynbee should be out for the prevention of deterioration in the family life of the citizens of East London; the raising of moral standards; the cleansing of its streets of prostitutes; the meeting of the needs of the coloured population which has invaded it – we ought to be thinking of what is the right relationship between the white and coloured people. It ought to survey the needs of youth, what organisations exist, where the gaps are, which organisations require more manpower. It ought to be an experimenting in schemes such as Workrooms for the Elderly and what can be done to improve the life of the ever-increasing population of elderly people in the district and what can be done to make them more easy and happy.[22]

Other people approached by Morgan gave similar advice, and when one year after his appointment as Warden, he produced his 'first thoughts' for the Council, he rejected any suggestion that Settlements 'belonged to a bygone era' and that Toynbee should close its doors. For everyone who maintained that 'what Toynbee did so remarkably half a century ago' either was not needed or was done by 'the multifarious agencies which constitute our social machinery today', there were others, he pointed out, who maintained with equal vigour that however efficient that machinery was, or would be,

> it could never stimulate, or give, the friendship which is the cement of society, without which society will fall to dust. . . . To throw away the power for strengthening friendship, by the constant touch of human sympathy, which is the legacy of the Barnetts, their helpers and their successors, would surely be a desperate, even a wicked, surrender of a sacred trust.[23]

Morgan was abridging what Barnett had said and done, but he was in agreement with a number of Toynbee Hall Residents – there were twenty of them at the time, not all of them university graduates – in maintaining that while it was true that the people of the East End had, 'on the average', much more money than in the early part of the century and worked, on the average, for much shorter hours, it was 'doubtful whether their happiness' had 'increased to any greater extent' or whether 'they, in themselves' felt 'any more secure'.[24]

It is clear from such key passages that while Morgan wanted, if possible, to keep alive the 'formal educational work' of Toynbee Hall, he was more concerned – and this was even more true of the Residents – with the social rather than with the educational role of the institution. What mattered most to the Residents, in particular, was not so much the Education Act of 1944 and its implications as the existence of 'the Welfare State' in the form that it had taken shape between 1945 and 1948. The leading question was 'what did it *not* provide?' It offered listable benefits, but it did not offer 'quality of life'. At best, it made a better quality of life possible.

As far as research on the new social problems of the 1950s was concerned, Morgan believed with the Residents that there was 'no significant territory for social research' which professional research workers could not undertake. The day of the amateur was over. If research were to have a home at Toynbee Hall, it would have to be carried out by specialists on a full-time basis. What such specialists might not be able to offer, however, was care. The Hall still had an important function in the neighbourhood, therefore, if it served as a base for Residents and volunteers who would 'do citizen's duty in the neighbourhood'.[25] There were people in the East End who continued to need caring attention – particularly young people, who while they 'went to great lengths to demonstrate their self-sufficiency' demanded 'gentle direction and information from people of wider experience' and old people, large numbers of whom were 'living in real unhappiness, many of them alone'. Indeed, one of the most useful things Residents at Toynbee Hall could do was 'to be available to interpret the mysteries and services' of 'the Welfare State'. 'This district,' Morgan and the Residents concluded, 'can be really known and understood only by living in it and among the people one is trying to help.' They actually resented 'help and advice ... brought to them by people who do not normally live among them'. And, as in the nineteenth century, 'Residents active in the district – many of them coming from the Universities – could redress the unbalance of classes in the area.' New Residents 'should be carefully selected by the Warden personally and after an interview' and should be judged, as in the past, 'on the basis of what they are prepared to do for Toynbee Hall and the neighbourhood'.[26]

Such an endorsement of the principle and practice of Residency was of considerable importance at a time when most other Settlements had closed their residential accommodation. And so, too, was the optimistic conclusion to what Morgan called his 'tentative assessment':

> I believe the breeze can freshen again and again. Nor do I admit that no wind is blowing now. There are men among us who are devoting time and service in a variety of directions, and in the last year I have seen men coming and going and new actitivies emerging.

Given such a spirit, it was even possible, Morgan suggested, that the educational work at Toynbee might be saved, by which he meant children's education as much as adult education.

> There is a side of the educational work at Toynbee Hall [he wrote] which, as it owes nothing to the LCC might be called 'Pure Toynbee'; this is the educational work for children ... in Ballet, Piano and Recorder Playing and Drama Classes.[27]

Morgan was more gloomy about buildings than about people. The physical arrangement of rooms was 'unsuited for the development of a collegiate spirit'. The whole building was 'ill-designed and dilapidated'. The old Warden's Lodge had been destroyed. And while there was too little accommodation to meet all the demands on the Hall, the surroundings of 'obsolete poverty' were a constant burden. There was a 'lack both of money and of space'.[28]

It is not surprising that these difficulties persisted throughout the 1950s, although the increased LCC grant, treated by both sides as 'temporary', continued until 1958, guaranteeing that Toynbee's overdraft did not increase as alarmingly as it had done in previous years. The grant was renewed, however, only 'on the understanding that a policy review would be completed and the considered plans for the future transmitted to the LCC'.[29]

When in 1957 the Annual Accounts revealed an overdraft of £18,000, the Council emphasised that while during the past ten years only the most urgent repairs had been carried out, 'one of the most serious factors accounting for the deficit was the constant drain caused by age and decrepitude of much of the fabric'; and Morgan, now forced to choose, told his Council 'to shed all the adult evening work and realise the capital value of the Educational Block'. 'When Toynbee Hall ceases to be responsible for the large amount of adult education which it now conducts,' he added, 'it will be free to decide on its future policy.'[30]

For all the years of talk, what Morgan was now definitely recommending was an awkward kind of leap to an awkward kind of freedom, and when in January 1958 the leap was actually made, and the relinquishment of Toynbee's educational work was publicly announced, there was an inevitable outcry, with one member of the Toynbee Council, Edith Ramsay, a Stepney resident, fighting a bitter public campaign against the closure. There was Press criticism, too, of Morgan's 'remote' way of handling the issue, and he had to counter accusations of breach of trust and dispel rumours that the whole Settlement would soon close.

> For years we have been nothing more than agents of the LCC carrying on their educational work [he replied firmly]. Now the work will be carried on by them instead of us. . . . This is certainly not Toynbee dying, but Toynbee getting back to initial principles, laid down by Canon Barnett.[31]

In such difficult and contentious circumstances, Sir George Haynes, an ex-Resident and Director of the National Council of Social Service, intervened to suggest a new direction for Toynbee Hall which might secure its future. Aware that the Younghusband Committee on Social Workers was due to report, he advised that Toynbee's new function should be to develop pioneering forms of training for professional and voluntary workers in the social field. Toynbee could become a training centre and a conference centre for discussion of major social issues. Not surprisingly, Morgan took up the Haynes plan with alacrity.

> A scheme of this kind would be expensive [he wrote], but if it were boldly conceived and designed to meet a need which is recognised, the question of raising the necessary funds need not cause alarm. The sale of the New Building and the payment of War Damage which is due would go far to meet the initial cost.[32]

These discussions on Toynbee Hall's future were not exhausted by 1959, the year of publication of the Younghusband *Report on Social Workers in the Local Authority Health and Welfare Services*, which included the recommendation that a National Institute for Social Work Training should be set up.

There was an obvious national need at this time, following what the Report, published in May 1959, called 'a long history of failure to take vigorous action', both to classify social workers more systematically and to clarify the educational requirements, basic and specialised, for social workers of different kinds. Yet who should respond to the need was left open, with Foundations being urged to assist in stimulating action to provide a scheme of 'generic' training consisting of two years of full-time study with supervised field work taking up about half the students' time. There was even a backward glance at the Charity

Organisation Society, with a tribute to its emphasis on 'the importance of the family' and on knowledge of families gleaned through case work.[33]

Such ideas proved acceptable professionally, and sufficient Foundation support was forthcoming to enable a new Council for Training in Social Work to hold its first meetings in 1962. It envisaged twenty-five two-year courses in different parts of the country.[34] It was the successor to the Joint University Council for Social Studies and Public Administration, which included practical training as an integral part of the studies. Some public bodies, like the National Assistance Board and the Home Office still had their own individual training schemes.

Before the State itself accepted responsibility for general provision, the LCC decided almost at once to start a two-year course for social workers concerned with child care, and another early provisional course was backed not by a local authority but by the Joseph Rowntree Memorial Trust. The Nuffield Foundation backed the scheme also, and announced in 1960 that it had set aside £250,000 to launch it.

Toynbee Hall was at the centre of the Nuffield Foundation's deliberations about work in this field, although long before 1962 the Hall's Council Foundation had failed in its attempts to house and manage the new body in its own New Building. The issues were important, but the discussions with the Foundation, which appeared crucial to the future of the Hall, ended in anti-climax.

They had begun, however, in an atmosphere of optimism. At last, it seemed, Toynbee Hall had found a role – and the likelihood of the funds to activate it – and a Future Policy Sub-Committee was set up to negotiate with the Nuffield Foundation. The *Annual Report* for 1959 described cheerfully how the Council had decided to seek to convert the Hall into an Institute for the Training of Social Workers and how it had suspended discussions with the LCC about the purchase or leasing of the New Building.[35]

'The Council believe,' its minutes for September 1959 read, on the eve of the setting up of the new Sub-Committee,

> that Toynbee Hall as the first of all Settlements, with a long tradition and presitge as a centre of social thinking and social action for several generations, would give a weight to the new venture which a college started independently might lack. It is placed in an area which for historic reasons is served by a great variety of voluntary social organisations and a network of services provided by Government Departments, the London County Council and the East End Borough Councils. Consequently the area provides facilities for the field work necessary for training in special abundance. . . . As a living Settlement, Toynbee Hall has a body of Residents who are occupied in their professions by day and devote their spare time to social service of one kind or another. . . . The Training Courses would be rooted in a centre having living contacts with a large working-class area fraught with many of the personal and social problems which underlie the Younghusband Report.
>
> The new Toynbee Hall is conceived as a place in which the various elements of formal and informal courses, social activities, and the Residence itself will be integrated in the developing life of one Institution.[36]

This was the view of the future outlined also by the Toynbee Hall Council to Sir Geoffrey Gibbs, the Chairman of the Nuffield Foundation, and to Frederick (later Lord)

Seebohm, Trustee of the Rowntree Trust, who was to be Chairman in the late 1960s of the Committee which was to reshape the whole pattern of social work. When they visited the site for the first time to survey the possibilities there, they were left in no doubt of the enthusiasm of the Sub-Committee, though its members had stressed that the residential work of the Settlement should not be 'swamped' by the training scheme. The Sub-Committee itself consisted of men of independence and influence, among them Morgan, Haynes, Pimlott, then Honorary secretary of Toynbee Hall, Judge C. D. Aarvold, the Common Serjeant, and Lord Evershed, Master of the Rolls, who had just succeeded Waverley as Chairman of the Toynbee Hall Council in 1954.[37]

Almost at once, however, there was a snag. The Director of the Nuffield Foundation, Leslie Farrer-Brown, told Lord Evershed after the Gibbs and Seebohm visits that what he called 'the historic site in Commercial Street', which had 'furnished an abundance of opportunities for social work in the past', was 'too noisy and perhaps too typical of the last century to provide the kind of environment made for the social work training college of the future'. It would be better, Farrer-Brown suggested, to house the new centre 'in a less industrialised area which is well covered by social agencies and is reasonably near to academic and administrative centres'. Why not sell the whole site, therefore, he asked, and put up a new building in a new place? If the Council would do that, the two Trusts would guarantee to a new Toynbee Hall an income of £25,000 a year for ten years. Meanwhile, pending the completion of a new building, the old Toynbee Hall, not the New Building there, might be used temporarily.[38]

These proposals were very different from those which the Sub-Committee had had in mind, and they were bound to stir many members of the Council and many people outside it, including most of those who had connections with Toynbee Hall. Nor was the Council likely to be well disposed to the idea of managing the new institution through a bigger Council composed of representatives of professional organisations and of academic bodies along with Toynbee nominees.

At the time, the proposals were controversial; in retrospect, they look unconvincing. Social workers need to be near the people they serve. Administrative centres are not 'necessary' nearby facilities: they may get in the way. The East End seems exactly the kind of place where social work training could and should be carried out – and in its most compelling form. Moreover, a further argument used by the Foundations also looks dated as well as one-sided. It seemed too obvious to them that 'the new social problems are not those of the past' and that although there was 'a legacy of problems arising out of the unrelieved poverty or unremoved squalor, by and large, over the country as a whole they are only a part of the sum of social problems'.[39] In fact, the siting of Toynbee Hall raised every kind of issue concerning not only poverty but 'community'. And it was Eileen Younghusband herself who was to write two decades later of how 'community work had long been practiced in Settlements, Councils of Social Work and other settings', while only beginning to be identified as such during the late 1960s.[40]

For the most part, however, it was not so much deliberate considerations of this kind that accounted for the fierce opposition to the scheme on the part of people who knew Toynbee and its traditions, but the introduction of a new element into the discussions on the part of the Foundations – a possible merger with the Mary Ward Settlement in Bloomsbury.[41] What began in a mood of optimism ended, therefore, in a mood of bitterness. Nor did it make for easy discussion when the Foundations pointed out, as they were in a position to do, that if Toynbee would not meet their wishes, they were perfectly capable of going ahead with a quite different scheme of their own.

When Morgan started looking around for possible new sites to meet the Foundations' wishes, he was told firmly by Beveridge – and by Attlee – that they did not favour any move of location to a quite different area. Nor did Evershed.

> The move must not be to a site outside East London in which the good will of Toynbee is rooted. . . . the retention of Residents is an essential requirement if the Toynbee tradition is to make its influence felt on the proposed Institute of Social Work.

'I will do all I can,' he concluded, 'to maintain the Toynbee principle.'[42] And laconically as always – but decisively Attlee wrote to Morgan, 'I find myself in general agreement with Beveridge and Evershed.'[43]

In effect, these letters marked the end of the affair, although a further approach was made to the Foundations after the Planning and Valuation Departments of the LCC had told Morgan's son that there was a twelve-year plan for clearing and rebuilding around Toynbee Hall which would alter the whole appearance of the area. Whitechapel High Street would be broadened, and an island centre with three tall shopping blocks, connected by lower frontages, was to be built. As many people as possible would be rehoused in tall blocks of flats 'well separated by grass and formal gardens'.[44]

This vision in retrospect has an alarmingly cheerful wrongness of its own, particularly when it was used as an argument in the attempt to convince the Foundations that the East End would soon become like anywhere else. 'The general air of untidiness and down-at-heel quality of the neighbourhood will disappear and some of the new buildings, especially in Whitechapel High Street, will be of high quality.'[45] All that would be left would be the 'bustle' of which Booth had approved. Yet, whatever the twists of values, it was encouraging for Morgan to be told by the LCC architects that 'from a planning point of view' Toynbee Hall was 'in an eminently suitable locale to carry out the social and research work bearing in mind the good lines of communication and situated as it is at an entry point from the City of London to the East End'.[46]

On the basis of this new information, Evershed wrote to Farrer-Brown asking for a meeting with the Trustees,

> at which he would be accompanied by Lord Attlee and Lord Beveridge and some representatives of our Council; so that I could lay before the Trustees the contents and implications of the official of the Ministry of Housing and Local Government's Report.[47]

But the die had been cast – the new Institute was to be at Mary Ward. There was some talk of the possible collaboration, but it was vague. Toynbee Hall did not find a completely new role. The problem remained, therefore, of finding new purpose for the New Building which had stood empty while negotiations with Farrer-Brown dragged; and there was no lack of ingenuity as various uses were considered – a home for the Youth Theatre; a base and East End home for the arts for Arnold Wesker and others concerned in the establishment of Centre 42; an ITV studio. (It was, in fact, used briefly in the last of these ways.) Another possibility, that of converting it into a residence for young men, was sensibly rejected by the architect. Yet so long as the building, which had been the centre of so much purposeful activity since it was first constructed, stood idle it was bound to draw adverse (or even comic) comment. The Press, for example, even speculated that it might become a warehouse for bananas. Eventually, however, in 1964, a twenty-one year lease was negotiated with the LCC for the use of the Toynbee Theatre and the three floors of educational rooms.

By then there was a new Warden, for in spring 1963, now in his late seventies, Morgan retired to Bristol. In assessing the significance of his Wardenship it would be misleading to concentrate exclusively on the difficult negotiations in which he was almost perpetually involved and to overlook what was actually happening at Toynbee Hall during his nine-year tenure, a period when he was greatly helped by his able bursar, Doris Greening, and the Hall Secretary, Pam Williams. Morgan was particularly interested in the social needs both of the young and the old and made sure that they were welcomed at Toynbee Hall. 'Rarely is there a Saturday afternoon on which William (Billy) Dove, (one of the liveliest Residents) cannot be seen with a school party on an excursion to some place of interest in or around London,' it was reported in 1963.[48] Likewise, the Veterans' Club flourished: thirty-one voluntary visitors and helpers were mustered in its service, several of them Residents. By then there were twenty Residents, some of them switching courses and interests, like Denis Marsden who turned from chemical engineering to sociology, and Tony Lynes who moved from accountancy to social administration; and under Morgan the Council recommended that women should be added to their number, a step taken after his departure.

Toynbee Residents helped the Stepney Family Service Unit, while Joan Chapman served as Old People's Welfare Organiser and Ann Flynn ran a Citizens' Advice Bureau, reopened in 1963 after being closed since the late 1940s. In the first five months after its reopening it dealt with nearly 1,500 enquiries (32 per cent of them 'family and personal', 23 per cent relating to 'property and land').

The Toynbee Legal Advice Centre, practically self-supporting, was managed for ten years by James Dow, one of the most active Residents, and at the end of Morgan's Wardenship had a record number of clients, 767; many of them placed donations in a collecting box. Dow also edited for seven years the *Bulletin of the British Association of Residential Settlements*, and served on its Executive Committee along with two other Toynbee ex-Residents (and members of the Toynbee Hall Council) – Henry Smart and Eric Moonman. The latter, who was an elected member of the Stepney Borough Council, was Treasurer of the Association, and was to have a long and continuing connection with Toynbee Hall. In 1966 he was to become Labour MP for Billericay.

The President of the British Association of Residential Settlements in 1963 was Bever-idge, and his death in that year seemed to mark a far bigger turning point than the retirement of Morgan. In the words of Trevor Blount, an active Toynbee Hall Resident, he had been 'a legend in his lifetime'[49] and, whatever his other commitments, he always remained faithful to the Settlement ideal. His book on *Voluntary Action*, published in 1948, set out in new form all his youthful convictions. Human society should become a friendly society, like the National Deposit Friendly Society which commissioned the work.[50] There was no adequate substitute for mutual aid.

Almost sixty years before, Barnett had delegated Beveridge to write the twenty-first *Annual Report* of the Hall, and in it Beveridge had stressed in a highly practical way, with no touches of rhetoric, that 'locality has made and is making Toynbee Hall what it is.' His report was almost like a map.

> Toynbee Hall is, first and most obviously [he began simply], a group of buildings situated at 28 Commercial Street, London E. . . . The Bank of England is distant ten minutes by omnibus or fifteen on foot. . . . It is in easy communication with every part of the city and suburbs, north, east and west.

Yet, he went on, 'it is not, and never was intended to be, local in the way in which a parish church or a mission is local.'[51] He knew that Barnett, who would never have written a Report in this fashion, was in agreement with him.

Beveridge did not spell out his version of the special relationship between Toynbee Hall's local and national role. The way in which he conceived of the relatonship was to be spelt out by him not in words but in actions, and they were to encompass many other places besides Toynbee Hall – the London School of Economics, for example, and University College, Oxford. Yet for those concerned with the management of Toynbee Hall, the relationship between local and national always needed to be presented in a Toynbee Hall version. The first task for a new Warden in 1963, therefore, was to reconsider the implications of the historic relationship, bringing in the international relationship as well. There remained a second task, of course, that of finding new financial support, without which any such reconsideration would be academic. It is interesting in retrospect, indeed, to read a note preceding Beveridge's twenty-first *Annual Report* of 1905, the first note of its kind:

> The Council of Toynbee Hall [then presided over by Sir Charles Elliott] have never by advertisement or public meeting appealed for money. A body of subscribers – mostly dating from the foundation of the place – have year by year met the needs which follow the activities of the Residents who themselves more than pay for the upkeep of the House. Death, however, has made inroads on the list of regular givers. The Council . . . hope that new friends will come forward, either subscribing themselves or influencing others to subscribe, so that there may be no break in the progress which has gone on from the beginning.[52]

The first intimation of the shape of things to come may or may not have been studied by the writers of Beveridge's obituaries. It was very pertinent, however, as Morgan more than anyone else had known from the start.

When Morgan retired to Bristol, Lord Evershed sent out an urgent request to all former Residents, asking them to help him in the search for 'a youthful, energetic Warden.[53] Meanwhile, E. St. John Catchpool, who had been Sub-Warden during the 1920s, generously volunteered to act as Warden without salary until a new long-term Warden could be appointed.

Catchpool had long been a loyal friend to Toynbee Hall, and had remained active in the Workers' Travel Association as well as the Youth Hostels movement, which he saw through past its twenty-first birthday celebrations in 1950. It was while involved in setting up a Youth Hostels Association in Ghana that he had made the acquaintance of a young Quaker economist, Walter Birmingham, then working at the University of Accra, and he had been greatly impressed by his personality and outlook. Birmingham had since returned to England in 1961 to lecture in economics at Leicester University, where he became Sub-Dean of the Faculty of Social Sciences, and Catchpool, feeling that he had the right combination of adventure and commitment, invited him to visit Toynbee Hall to see whether he would be interested in becoming the next 'incumbent'.

For all its spirit, Toynbee Hall had become on first sight a doubtful inheritance, more so, indeed, than it had been when Morgan, an older man, had arrived. At first, therefore, Birmingham declined the offer of the Wardenship, but fortunately in November 1963 he changed his mind. There seemed to be more possibilities for action in being Warden of Toynbee than Senior Lecturer in Economics at Leicester; and Birmingham, a man of causes, was already enthusiastically engaged before he arrived at Toynbee in promoting a campaign to encourage 'developed countries' to devote 2 per cent of their gross national income to poor countries in the Third World. 'Freedom from Hunger' and 'War on Want' were causes which particularly appealed to him. The fact that Toynbee Hall was located in an area which itself was poor and where significant numbers of immigrants were now gathering from the Third World attracted him for reasons which more conventional men might well have deemed disadvantageous. There were still few references to them in the 1962–63 *Annual Report*, although one of the Residents, T. W. Casey, had attended a Conference on Race Relations at Utrecht as a representative of the Council of Citizens of East London (it was organised by the Council of Christians and Jews) and 15 per cent of the users of the Citizens' Advice Bureau were described as 'overseas callers'. There was also a note under the heading 'Council of Citizens of East London' of the publication of a booklet *Our East London*, launched at Toynbee Hall and designed to counter 'racial and religious' intolerance and of a lecture by Lord Walston on 'The Challenge of a Multi-Racial Society' at the Council's Annual General Meeting held in Toynbee Hall and presided over by Attlee.[54]

When he arrived in Toynbee Hall, Birmingham had taught economics at universities for twenty-one years and he had written a Penguin *Introduction to Economics*,[55] but his activities had never been confined to academia. Extra-mural teaching and social research had long been among his major interests, and during the 1940s he had organised a survey of social work in Cardiff for Nuffield College, Oxford, and had carried out a survey of the expenditure on food and housing of miners in a South Wales colliery for a Research Unit of the Medical Research Council.

He had also forged many international links during his academic career. In 1948–9, for example, he had been Associate Professor of Economics at Roosevelt University, Chicago, and he was invited to return there in 1958 as Professor of International Labour Studies. Finally, among his qualifications was an experience of Settlement work itself. He had been co-founder of a progressive school in South London, situated in a small co-operative community, and while at Cardiff he had joined in the development of a residential Settlement in the dock area. The activities of the Settlement there included a children's play centre, organisation of children's holidays on Barnett lines, a Women's Group, an Old Age Pensioners' Club, and WEA classes.[56]

Once installed in Toynbee Hall in 1964, Walter Birmingham and his able wife, Maisie, an Oxford graduate with experience of personnel management, factory inspection, social work and new town management, were able to radiate a feeling of warmth and of confidence, and the *Annual Report* for 1965 described how there were now thirty-seven Residents, how 'young people of different ages now have something going for them most nights of the week', and how 'the Friend and Neighbourhood service run by the Stepney Old People's Welfare Trust is now well settled at Toynbee Hall'.[57] The Inner London Education Authority had approved the appointment of a full-time Youth Officer, and a new Development Officer, Anne Evans, was concerned with community relations under the auspices of the Council of Citizens of East London and its subsidiary, the Council of Citizens of Tower Hamlets. 'Immigrants' now figured explicitly as the third of Toynbee Hall's 'major concerns'.

(The East London Society of Arts, founded in November 1964 – with Birmingham in the Chair – was sponsored by the *East London Arts Magazine*, and Ian Mikardo, MP for Poplar, became its first President. Its Chairman, Oscar Tapper was a keen enthusiast for the new venture which was said to be 'reliving some of Toynbee's history': by then, the Whitechapel Art Gallery was no longer holding exhibitions of the works of local artists and the People's Palace had been 'swallowed' up by Queen Mary College. The following year, however, Birmingham became Chairman of the Whitechapel Art Gallery's Finance Committee. Arts did not figure very prominently in the later 1960s, however, and it was said of the Art Club in 1971 that membership was static 'and we would welcome some new blood'.[58] The Toynbee Theatre, renamed the Curtain Theatre, was managed as a drama centre by the Inner London Education Authority, though a group of Toynbee Players put on Molière's *Tartuffe* in 1969 and there was one memorable cabaret a year earlier, *Anne in Toynbeeland*, making fun of Warden, Residents and staff.[59] The Residents' house journal *Channel* often did the same.)

There was life here and life with as distinctive a style as that of the 1890s. But if the institution were to be successful with Birmingham as Warden, it required the building of new Warden's accommodation as a matter of urgency. And this, too, had been forthcoming. Work on a new gatehouse began in July 1965, appropriately enough with a working party from the International Voluntary Service digging out the basement, and with the Prime Minister, Harold Wilson, turning the first sod. In March 1967 the new building was officially opened by the Archbishop of Canterbury, Dr Michael Ramsey.[60]

The completion of the Gatehouse, long-delayed successor to Barnett's Warden's Lodge, also made it possible to implement an imaginative plan devised by two ex-Residents, Cliff Tucker and James Dow, in the aftermath of the failure of the discussions with the Nuffield Foundation. They had suggested that the Hall should provide residential facilities for 'junior Residents', adolescents arriving in London who required the social setting of a supportive community. A new Resident, the Franciscan Monk, Brother Owen, supervised the new scheme, which was introduced in 1966. For the first two months the junior Residents were boarded out, and in November 1966, four months before the official opening, they moved into the Gatehouse. There was to be a Franciscan strain in Toynbee Hall's future, a different strain from the Quaker strain, and the older strain which led back through Toynbee and T. H. Green to J. R. Green and F. D. Maurice and before them to Coleridge.

Birmingham was not a historian, and, though he established a Toynbee archive, he thought more of the future than of the past. The Gatehouse was conceived of as the first building in a substantial 'redevelopment' of Toynbee Hall. Yet any 'redevelopment' would have been impossible unless new sources of funds had been tapped. And in this connection, there were two decisive changes in the history of Toynbee Hall following Birmingham's appointment: first John Profumo arrived at Toynbee Hall as a volunteer in 1964 – it was the indomitable Lady (Stella) Reading, founder of the Women's Voluntary Service, who put the idea to him. Second, Lord Blakenham became Chairman of Toynbee Hall Council in 1966: he was to remain in the post for fifteen years. Both men – and they were army friends in North Africa and Italy – had the political experience, the social contacts and, above all, the dedication of purpose that were essential qualities if the finances of Toynbee Hall were to be placed on a new basis. From the start Profumo was the most active of all volunteers, carrying out tasks, including the most menial tasks, which had nothing to do with finance at all. He knew little at first hand of the activities of Toynbee Hall before he arrived but soon he was completely at home. Blakenham, the brother of Lord Listowel, an ex-Toynbee Resident, was the kind of working Chairman of Council Toynbee most needed, and his personal experience, too, was specially valuable. He had been a highly successful Conservative Minister of Labour, who in Profumo's words, 'captured the affection of trade-unionists at a time of fragile industrial relations', and he had long had a deep interest in the problem of unemployment and in the care of the unemployed.[61]

The two newcomers worked closely together and, more important still, allowed Birmingham the necessary support for him to develop his ideas. The support was human as well as financial, but it must have been encouraging for Birmingham to see the financial situation improve in a way that would have delighted Mallon or Morgan. An appeal, which had been launched before Profumo arrived, now suddenly began to look realistic, though it was set at £185,000. The Lord Mayor of London agreed to conduct it from the Mansion House: that had never happened in the nineteenth century. Nor had there ever been such an untiring voluntary Appeal Secretary as May ('Billie') Lancaster. Judge Aarvold made Toynbee Hall the subject of a *Week's Good Cause* broadcast; Cliff Michelmore described it on television; and Queen Elizabeth attended a film première of Laurence Olivier's *Othello* at the Odeon, Leicester Square, in May 1966, 'delighting us all,' in Birmingham's words, 'with the warmth of her interest'. The old royal link with Toynbee Hall was reinforced. By 1967 when the Annual Account showed only a small deficit of just over £300 a grand Appeal total of over £150,000 had been promised.

It was in that year that Attlee, President of the Hall, died, another landmark in the history of the institution. By then Attlee was the main link with the past – he had been Secretary in 1909 – but he had written very recently about how he felt about the Hall in an article in *The Times* in 1964, under the title 'Toynbee Hall looks to the future'. In it he noted quietly how many of the 'advances pioneered by Toynbee Hall' had been 'generalised'. There was no touch of nostalgia in his account of his own long connection with it. Rather, he emphasised how it was 'right and natural' that a settlement should change with the times. No longer, he observed, was a Settlement 'an adventure into unknown territory inhabited by an entirely different stratum of society'. None the less, Attlee never referred to 'the Welfare State', like Beveridge, but, 'to what is called the Welfare State' and he did not suggest that all was well in the present. With the passing away of 'the old slums' there had also passed away 'a great deal of the cheerful life of old streets as I knew it'. Blocks of flats, he added tersely, are 'I think, less conducive to community life'. The concrete jungle was never part of his vision.[62]

> Despite Old Age Pensions and the abolition of the Poor Law [Attlee went on, almost thinking aloud], there is still the problem of the aged – despite the rebuilding of the area there is still much bad housing . . . despite all the excellent work done by girls and boys' clubs, the problem of young people is, I think, more difficult than in earlier days. There is, too, the problem of racial admixture. Stepney has always had a number of residents from countries inhabited by non-white people and has a fine tradition of tolerance, but the position still requires careful watching and active work to avoid incidents such as have occurred in other districts.

Attlee's final remarks were reserved, however, for the Hall itself, which he urged should 'set its own house in order'. 'A new building is required to house the Warden and six young men. A new venture will be a residential block for twelve young men from East London as part of an approach to dealing with the youth problem.' The old needed enlarged and modernised accommodation: 'buildings which in their day registered a big advance are now obsolete, some even condemned'.[63] He lived long enough to see the beginnings of change in the physical appearance of Toynbee Hall itself and its immediate neighbourhood, including a less dramatic but just as urgently necessary development as the Gatehouse itself – a bathroom extension to one of the old blocks of College Buildings and the modernisation of five flats. 'It will be good,' Birmingham wrote in the year Attlee died, 'to see some of our old tenants properly housed for the first time in their lives.'

Housing Associations were more numerous and increasingly active in the East End than ever before, but the local answer to housing problems depended on the policies followed by the Borough of Tower Hamlets and the GLC within the broader framework of national policy laid down by the Government. There was a shortage of housing and much of the housing available was in appalling condition. 'I don't know what fungus is, but they tell me that's what's growing on my floor,' a client of the Legal Advice Centre reported in 1965, and two years later another group of clients described their one-room home with a paraffin stove near the window as the only means of heating and cooking. The windows will not open 'and there are paying guests in the form of bugs, mice and an occasional rat'. The rent was £3.50 a week.[64]

The Toynbee Housing Society, with John Sinclair as Secretary, took interesting initiatives both inside and outside the East End, urging a proportion of the people it housed (from public funds) to take part in community activities. In 1966, a contract was signed for building an estate of eighty-four flats and maisonettes in a 3-acre former slum site, the Kidwall's Close Community, in the centre of Maidenhead.[65] Many of its tenants were drawn from the inner urban areas of London, with preference for East Enders. Meanwhile, a Tyne

Dr A. E. Morgan, his wife, and some Toynbee Residents, *c.* 1955

Toynbee Hall in the 1950s

Huw Wheldon, a Toynbee Resident, entertaining local children at a Christmas party in the Lecture Hall

Ballet classes in the Lecture Hall at Toynbee

Music classes in the New Building

Special provision was made at Toynbee Hall for old people left behind after the population exodus from the area

The Warden, Walter Birmingham, and his wife Maisie, discussing with John Profumo the Royal Film Premier, *Othello* on 2 May 1966, to raise funds for Attlee House

Harold Wilson, Prime Minister, after turning the first sod for the new Gatehouse, 23 July 1965

(*below, left*) Attlee with the Archbishop of Canterbury at the opening of the Gatehouse, 30 March 1967
(*below*) Her Majesty the Queen with John Profumo at the opening of Attlee House, 18 November 1971

The Queen Mother with Mrs Profumo, John Profumo and Lord Blakenham at the opening of Sunley House, April 1976

Some of the Sunley House children and helpers

(*below left*) The Children's Country Holiday Fund, a favourite activity of the Barnetts, is once again in operation from Toynbee Hall and organised with Anne Crisp and Bob le Vaillant

(*below*) A satisfied customer

Overseas visitors with the Warden, Donald Chesworth

Some Toynbee Hall volunteers, 1983

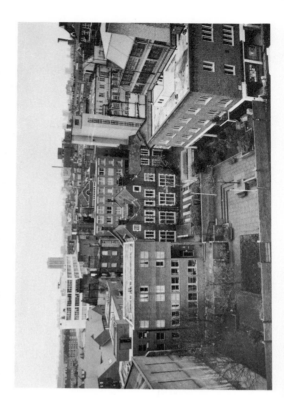

Toynbee Hall today

(*above*) Thrawl Street, the latest Toynbee Housing Association development

The scene in Whitechapel High Street: (*top left*) c. 1890, (*top right*) c. 1930, (*above left*) c. 1950, (*above right*) c. 1980

Street Project for a block of sixteen flats culminated in the opening of Evershed House, named after the former Chairman of Toynbee Hall's Council, in September 1970. The Prime Minister, Edward Heath, made an important speech on the occasion of its opening, when he also unveiled a plaque, to praise the work of housing societies.

> I believe the future will always provide room for a real partnership between State and voluntary bodies [he declared], and I am sure that voluntary effort will continue to add a vital element to the range of social services provided in the community.[66]

There was visual evidence of the partnership when alongside the new House there also was completed a new large GLC block. Old Castle Street was thereby given a completely new appearance.

As tenants of the 85-year-old tenement building, St George's House, were rehoused by the Greater London Council, successor to the LCC, Birmingham encouraged charities of various kinds to use the premises. The rents they paid were useful to the Hall but, even more important, the support the Hall could give to them, particularly when they were at the fledgling stage, greatly assisted their progress. By 1971 Community Service Volunteers, for example, was mobilising over 5,000 people, with the latest scheme 'a stamp out illiteracy' campaign – not for immigrants but for white Englishmen.[67] At a very different level of education Toynbee Hall was serving temporarily also as a base for Scholastic International which brought over American high-school students to Europe.[68]

The Community Service Volunteers were one of the first voluntary organisations to appear in St George's House. They arrived there, it was said, 'with joy', a favourite word with many of the new organisations of the 1960s.[69] They had been formed by Alec Dickson, who had pioneered the highly successful VSO (Volunteer Service Overseas), and they were granted their accommodation free. They were said to 'be teaching immigrants in schools, nursing in general and psychiatric hospitals, mothering deprived children at home, working with young delinquents in probation homes, approved schools and Borstals, and caring for gypsies, the mentally handicapped and the old'.[70] It was a list of which Barnett would have approved, and as Birmingham looks back he believes that the drawing in of such charities was one of the most useful of his achievements as Warden.

Another body, the Commonwealth Students' Children Society, was the inspiration of one man, Benjamin Boateng. Distressed by the lack of provision for children of Commonwealth students in Britain, he began a voluntary organisation in 1961 to inspect, approve, and pay child-minders, and when it faced wearing financial difficulties Birmingham offered him a flat and office facilities in 31, St George's in 1968.

In his report for that year, Boateng explained the scale of the problem his Society was trying to tackle.[71] British universities, hospitals, technical and training colleges were then attracting over 46,000 students from the Commonwealth, the biggest group of them 15,000 student nurses, on whom the National Health Service was coming to depend. Before they came they were usually unaware both of the housing shortage and of the views of many landlords on children and on colour. His Society was sending out information about housing conditions in Britain to prospective students before they left their countries of origin, finding suitable day-nurseries and reliable baby-minders to take care of young children while their mothers were working or studying, encouraging the formation of Housing Associations to provide homes for students where they could keep their children with them, and arranging for some children to go home when suitable arrangements could be made for them to be looked after by their parents' families. Finally, but only as a last resort, the Society was helping to find suitable foster-homes, the expenses of which would be paid for by the students. 'The more successful we are,' he concluded, 'the more we save local authorities the cost of taking the children into care.'

A full-time social worker, Mrs Pat Stapleton, was found to work with Boateng's Society, competent staff members were hired and financial support was secured from the Local Authority and the London Council of Social Service. The Society was well established, if still financially insecure, by the time it moved from Toynbee Hall.

Birmingham stayed on as Warden until 1972, by which time there was a new and distinctive shape to the pattern of activities in Toynbee Hall. It was not the case, however, that all the old activities disappeared: between 1965 and 1970 for example, one of the oldest of all the activities, the Children's Country Holidays Fund, sent 800 local children to the country. Likewise, the Legal Advice Centre was still much in demand – it had sixteen members of staff in 1970 – although the development of similar organisations in the neighbourhood reduced the load on it. In 1967 it provided an analysis of its records for a 'Law and Property Survey' undertaken by Professor Abel-Smith of the London School of Economics and Michael Zander, legal correspondent of the *Guardian*. The object of the survey was to find out what 'the poorer classes' knew of 'their rights under the law'; where, if anywhere, they would go for legal help if they needed it; what, if anything, they knew of the statutory Legal Aid and Advice Scheme extended in 1949 and again in 1964; and 'how effectively statutory, professional, and voluntary agencies are in fact serving the poorer classes'.[72]

This was pioneering work to fit a new situation. In many cases, however, the need for the new activities at Toynbee Hall had been spelt out first by previous Wardens, particularly by Mallon when he drew a distinction between a community centre and a Settlement: Toynbee Hall should not only serve the local community, a changing community, but the whole community. Birmingham echoed his cry that 'it should also identify areas of need, national and international, as well as local'. He echoed Barnett, too, when he stated in his final message that in eight exciting years at Toynbee he and his family had been given the opportunity to 'learn something of the true meaning of life, to understand what damage deprivation and privilege do together [and Barnett would certainly have linked these two] and yet how triumphantly some can overcome their circumstances'.[73]

At the same time, Birmingham, who was Warden in a decade when the adjective 'new' enjoyed one of its recurring, if brief, spells of popularity in England, saw himself as an innovator. In 1966, for example, the *Annual Report* was describing as an 'innovation' 'a series of coffee evenings to discuss selected problems' of urgent importance 'such as poverty among children, industrial relations and housing'.[74] It might have added immigration to the list, for the topic began to hit the headlines, and although it did not immediately assume the same kind of priority that work with the Jewish community had assumed during the middle years of Barnett's Wardenship, this was because in many ways it was far more difficult. At the last census before Birmingham left, that of 1971, the proportion of residents of Tower Hamlets born outside the United Kingdom was still relatively low (12.2 per cent) compared with the figure for the GLC areas as a whole (14.9 per cent). Yet the outflow of white inhabitants was to continue and the immigrant proportion was to increase. Meanwhile, the first efforts to improve community relations had not all been successful.[75]

The first hopes were focused, if not on the possibility of integration, at least on the elimination of prejudice; and a prize-winning essay on the subject 'What is Prejudice?', in a competition sponsored by one of the new organisations, the Council of Citizens of Tower Hamlets, caught the spirit of the early immigrant wave:

> As a little girl in Guyana [the prize winner wrote] I visualised England as a land of tall, white buildings, rich rolling estates and wealthy people. All of this grandeur was ruled over by a gracious lady, the Queen. In school we were taught to regard England as our 'Mother country'. We people of the Caribbeans were the children of 'Mother England'. So, when my family decided to come to England, though I was sad to be leaving my own land, I looked with happy anticipation to seeing the England which I imagined to be so wonderful.
>
> In Guyana the white people were given the kind of jobs that they were qualified for and were treated with respect and humanity. I thought it would be the same for us when we were in England which to my mind was a kind of Eldorado.
>
> I was sadly disappointed. It never occurred to me although there were some folk who would accept me and be friends, there were others who would not.
>
> In England I saw the tall stately buildings but no homes for people like us. Back home we were not too well housed, but we were given a fair chance of getting accommodation when it was available. It seems strange to me that coloured people should be barred from getting good homes simply because they are coloured. Why should Negroes and Indians be categorised as being dirty? Surely there are as many slovenly white housewives as coloured ones? Among all human beings there is a fair mixture of good and bad. The proportion does not depend on the colour of the skin.[76]

There must have been many early immigrants who shared such feelings, but as their number increased, the sense of shocked surprise diminished and the problems focused less on individual reactions than on the unequal fortunes of families and groups. In such circumstances discrimination could be blatant and prejudice raw, and a new Campaign against Racial Discrimination, set up in February 1965, would have found it difficult to work nationally without the premises provided 'on a generous basis' by Toynbee Hall. Its object was 'the elimination of prejudice and its effects in the community by means of education on the widest possible basis.'[77] None the less, education was a long-term hope, and the importation of overseas politics into race relations – particularly after the separation of Bangladesh from Pakistan in 1971 – meant that there were many barriers besides languages or religion in the way of understanding immigrant attitudes. Inevitably in such circumstances the emphasis shifted from doing something for immigrants and their families to providing the right opportunities for them to do things for themselves. And to do things quickly.[78]

In the early period of Birmingham's Wardenship a multi-racial pre-school play group was started in July 1966, and an international leisure centre was opened at St George's a month later. There was also a survey, which attracted much interest in the press, on housing with the title *Sorry, no coloured*. It was then, too, that classes in English began. By the end of Birmingham's Wardenship however, the opportunities and the problems were far bigger. When disaster and flood swept the Ganges Delta in 1971, it was Bangladeshi leaders who went to Birmingham to ask him to help to organise a public appeal for funds. He acted as Treasurer, and £10,000 was collected in ten weeks. Meanwhile, the Hall was opened to all Asian immigrants for meetings for 'mutual support and prayer.'[79]

Birmingham was approached not only as Warden of Toynbee Hall, but as Chairman of the Council of Citizens of East London and Tower Hamlets, a body set up in 1966 as a result of the White Paper on Immigration which had been published in 1964. The Archbishop of Canterbury presided, and it had every kind of official support. It was perhaps for this reason that it found it increasingly difficult, as the years went by, to reach grass-root opinion. The year 1971 was designated the United Nations 'Year for Racial Harmony', but there was less of it in Tower Hamlets and Whitechapel than there had been in 1963.

One of the most successful new activities relating to immigrants had links with old ones. Thus, the setting up of a Workers' Education Centre at Toynbee Hall in 1965 had its origins in an approach by the African and Asian Association, an early immigrant organisation, to the WEA, and through the WEA to Toynbee Hall. The early opening of the centre was 'beyond the wildest expectations of the organisers', wrote Preetash Singh, its President, who was anxious that his fellow immigrants should learn English as quickly as possible, with the help of, among others, Toynbee Residents. They were hosts, very necessary hosts, as well as teachers as they took them on visits to cinemas and theatres – and Parliament – as well as taught them in classrooms. About 150 immigrants were enrolled by the middle of 1965 – Indians, Pakistanis, Saudis, Sudanese, Nigerians and West Indians. 'They do not waste a minute of their time,' claimed Preetash Singh proudly, adding that their most creditable attribute is that 'they give up Saturday and Sunday leisure week after week, for the sake of gaining knowledge.'[80]

The failure of the Farrer-Brown scheme did not mean that Toynbee Hall lost its interest in social work. In 1966 Birmingham was reporting that students in training had visited Toynbee Hall from Swansea, Liverpool and the London School of Economics and that he had directed a course for the training of social workers from overseas at the Barking College of Technology. The eighteen students came from Africa, the West Indies, the Middle East and the Far East.

Perhaps Birmingham and his wife's biggest innovation, however, was the devotion of a special part of their life to so-called difficult 'problem cases'. They gave marriage guidance counselling, and they tried to help the kind of young people who could not find a place in the Gatehouse. In 1968, a series of Saturday evening House discussions, introduced by Birmingham with the question 'Well – whither Toynbee?', turned quickly in the second discussion to what Simon Purcell, who introduced it, called 'the Inadequates' – 'how best to help the many methylated spirit drinkers, transients, homeless and drug addicts who are drawn to this area.'[81] They were, in fact, and long had been a significant proportion of the population. The Simon Community Trust, which linked a cluster of projects to deal with such people in different parts of the country, almost entirely staffed by volunteers, found a base in the Hall at the end of the 1960s; and it was volunteers who organised a 'soup run' from Toynbee Hall to provide 'the Inadequates' with human contact as well as nourishing soup. Among the volunteers were a group of Sandhurst Cadets who made a survey of sixty 'rough sleepers' in the neighbourhood.[82]

It was at one of the Birmingham coffee meetings, called in 1965 to discuss 'selected problems', that Professor Abel-Smith of the London School of Economics gave a talk on poverty among children, which led directly to action.[83] He had been engaged with his colleague, Professor Peter Townsend, in a series of controversial studies which had replaced concepts of absolute poverty tied to the idea of subsistence levels (as in the Booth and Rowntree surveys) with concepts of relative poverty, relating the poverty line to the rising economic and social standards of society. According to Abel-Smith and Townsend, an individual was poor to the extent that he or she could not control the resources available to the average person. Taking such a view of poverty, they estimated that 14 per cent of the population, 7½ million people in all, were below their poverty line, and that for all the talk of the 'abolition of poverty' this figure had actually risen since the early 1950s. They were particularly concerned about the effects of such poverty on families and the life chances of the children who from the start were absolutely as well as relatively deprived.[84] The Toynbee Hall meeting was a momentous one, and led to the setting up there of the Child Poverty Action Group.

The Group needed a constitution if it were to be recognised as a charity, and Maisie Birmingham, as resourceful as Henrietta Barnett would have been in such circumstances, by-passed the tedious task of drawing one up by visiting the Guildhall, selecting a short and intelligible constitution, that of the Yorkshire Footpaths Society, and substituting the name CPAG throughout for YFP. The Charity Commissioners, who even in 'Welfare State' days were dealing with over 20,000 charities, approved and registered the new organisation within forty-eight hours.

Birmingham was Treasurer of the Group and the then Labour MP for Hounslow, Frank Field, a graduate of Hull University, was to become its Director in 1969. Meanwhile, a vigorous campaign to highlight the problem of poverty and advocate new policies to deal with it was launched. The Group was to undermine a good deal of the complacency which characterised attitudes to poverty during the 1950s and early 1960s as it focused attention on 'the poor and the poorest', stressing inequalities as much as privations.[85]. One of the main arguments of the Group, following earlier work by Richard Titmuss, was that in spite of social and incomes legislation, greater equality of income was not achieved between the mid-1950s and 1970. On the contrary there was a shift in the reverse direction.[86]

The Group claimed that the biggest single cause of poverty in Britain at that time was the discrepancy between incomes and needs in families with young children, where the earnings of a single 'breadwinner' (not as appropriate a term as it had been in Rowntree's time) were low. There were half a million children in Britain, the Group calculated, who were living at standards below the minimum tolerated by the National Assistance Board and only bigger family allowances could improve that position.[87]

Tony Lynes, a former Toynbee Resident, gave up his appointment at the London School of Economics to manage the Group's first campaign which coincided deliberately with the General Election of 1965. A poverty election manifesto was published by the Group, and, poverty – and family allowances – became major electoral issues. The timing was right, and political support was won at the highest level. A meeting with Harold Wilson, by now familiar with Toynbee Hall, was arranged; and he agreed to draw attention to the Group in his election broadcast to the nation. Likewise, Edward Heath, his Conservative opponent, accepted the CPAG argument that family allowances should be increased. Action followed after Wilson's victory. In 1967 family allowances were raised to 15s and 17s for the second and subsequent child, and in the following year they were further increased to 18s and 20s respectively. At the same time, personal tax allowances were lowered to meet part of the cost of increased family allowances, thus linking cash and tax allowances in a way proposed by the Group. Two years later Field, now Director, wrote to Birmingham thanking him for support from Toynbee Hall at a critical stage: 'Toynbee Hall,' he explained, 'has a long tradition of helping in the foundation of new movements and then leaving them to make their own mark on the fabric of society.'[88] Although he recognised that 'much remained to be done', his pressure group had more than justified its existence.

While the Child Poverty Action Group was focusing attention on the particular problems of children in poor families, there were major changes during the 1960s in attitudes to children and to youth, and Toynbee Hall Residents, who had adapted themselves to an earlier shift of attitudes during the 1890s and the first decade of this century, were trying hard to respond to them – and to changes in styles which assumed a new importance in a more fashion-conscious culture. A new 'Planets' club was created in 1964 for small children with separate facilities for the under and over-11s – and a new Youth Club which met from 7 to 9 p.m. on Sundays was formed soon afterwards. (The first meeting of the latter took place in the Aves Room.) Once again, as in the past, it was an enthusiastic Resident, Peter Wilson, who initiated these activities.

The first members of the Youth Club, more determined than some of their predecessors, decided against having elected officers, except for a Treasurer. They preferred to delegate different jobs when they had to be done. By the end of the decade, however, there was one full-time Youth Leader in charge of general direction, backed by two part-time Leaders, and a very varied programme had been organised which included a 'Discodive Club Night' for adolescents and an 'Ace of Clubs' Club for 12 to 15-year-olds. The story of the development of youth cultures during the 1960s has never been fully told, yet it is clear that while Toynbee Hall was doing no more than touch the surface it was aware of the reasons why it was difficult to do more. Sweeping changes were made in 1966, when it was discovered belatedly that the interests of young people between the ages of 11 and 18 did not converge, and even after these changes had been made two years later, the *Annual Report* noted that 'the intermediate club' (12 to 15-year-olds) had never 'really had a firm basis' and had had to be reorganised. It was noted, too, how the coffee bar had had to be rebuilt and 'other amenities essential to this type of club provided'.[89]

There were different signs of the times when the Scout Troop was dissolved around 1960 and, more positively, when one of the most successful new ventures, a Spitalfields Field Workers' August Project, was introduced in 1970 to organise daily 'play' activities for 200 to 250 school children during their holidays. The word 'play' was itself revealing, for there was still an exceptionally small section of the local school population passing on either to higher or post-secondary education of any kind.[90] For the young, adventure playgrounds were another great success, and a permanent playground was opened at Christchurch, Spitalfields, in 1970.

It was one of a series of new developments which changed the appearance of Spitalfields. Yet Birmingham was disappointed when he failed to secure another and bigger change, the building of a Rehabilitation Centre for the Hall. The City Parochial Foundation and the Gulbenkian Foundation had offered to provide funds to replace the Hall's buildings along Gunthorpe Street by a set of new buildings, one of which would have housed the Centre, but Tower Hamlets Borough Council, while sympathetic, was not prepared to approve a Centre for more than nineteen people. Birmingham felt that this was too small a size to be viable economically – he wanted room for sixty – or to provide a prototype to be copied on a national scale, and the project had to be abandoned. The whole of the plans for the site had to be abandoned also and a new comprehensive scheme prepared and submitted which included the replacement of the war-destroyed library and the construction of a new wing.

The climax of Birmingham's Wardenship was the opening of a new building, Attlee House, in 1971, although it was Profumo's idea that a new building should be constructed on the site of the old library as a memorial to him, and the idea had been put to Attlee before he died. When Wilson broke the news to him at an official function in Whitehall and elaborated at length on the possibilities for the Memorial, his only reply, 'Quite', was properly taken by those acquainted with him to indicate his complete approval. Lord Longford was the first Chairman of the Foundation, and it was through this connection that Lady Longford was to deliver a scintillating centenary address on 'The Toynbee Hall Adventure' at the Royal Society of Arts in 1983.[91] The first Director was Captain John Brown, an able administrator, who ensured that this particular adventure was highly successful.

Yet the history of the building of Attlee House was more troubled than had been contemplated, for the first builders failed financially and work had to be stopped and the second builders found it difficult at one stage to find bricks – and bricklayers. Only on Opening Day did all the delays seem at last worthwhile. There was room in the building for thirty-six new Residents and six single old people, each provided with a one-room flatlet, and there was room, too, for the offices of the Attlee Memorial Foundation, alongside the St Leonard's Housing Association for ex-prisoners on the top floor. The Old People's Welfare Service was also housed in the building.

There were two main initial Attlee Foundation projects – the first, provision for young people (advice and help) along similar lines to those already offered in the Gatehouse Flat. Richard Pentney, a former Resident, was the Director, and he, his wife and four daughters were among the first people to settle into the Attlee Building. Project II was concerned with drug addiction, and assistance was given to addicts at a Day Community Centre at Camberwell, a Residential Rehabilitation Centre, and Phoenix House, in South East London. Drugs were not a new problem in the 1960s – indeed, Dickens had explored the drug centres in the back streets of the East End when he wrote *Edwin Drood*, long before Toynbee Hall was founded – but there were more addicts and much more talk of a 'drug culture' in the Press and on television[92] The more affluent society of the twentieth century encouraged the proliferation of sub-cultures distinguishable from mainstream culture and the traditional sub-cultures of the past.[93] It is interesting to note, too, that an Alcoholics Anonymous Group had been started at Toynbee Hall in 1966, and that when its co-founder moved to Australia he intended to start a new group there, to be called 'Toynbee Two'.[94]

By the time Attlee House was opened, the financial means at the disposal of the Hall had greatly improved as a result of Profumo's drive and the careful attention of Blakenham. In 1963/4 subscriptions and donations amounted to £1,067 6s 1d.: in 1971 after decimalisation, they stood at £2,852.62p. The Appeal fund in its early stages in 1963/4 amounted to £18,480 8s. 8d.: in 1971, the balance had reached £151,830.93p. There was only a bare intimation then of the dimensions of future inflation in the 1970s – it was not referred to in the 1971 *Report* – but there could be reasonable satisfaction at what had been accomplished, and the original Appeal target of £185,000 was near to being realised. Of course, expenditure had grown too. In 1963/4 staff salaries amounted to just over £1,505: in 1971 they were over £4,452, still a very small share of the total annual expenditure of £20,398. This was still difficult finance, backed by willing voluntary effort, and although the Appeal target was reached under Birmingham's successor, by 1977 it was being stressed once more that 'with continually rising costs it is becoming increasingly difficult to meet the bills for the Settlement's upkeep' and that 'failure to do so would necessitate curtailing worthwile activities while our aim is expansion.'[95]

Birmingham's immediate successor as Warden, Tony Locke, the father of a young family, held the position for only four years. He had been associated with a number of universities, the last of them Leeds, before arriving at Toynbee Hall, and had been a teacher for three years and an Organiser for Further Education for two. Not surprisingly, he was interested in the needs of young children at the beginning of the educational process – he started a toy library at Toynbee and an Adventure Playgroup in Thrawl Street – and in the campaign to get rid of adult illiteracy, now recognised openly as a national problem for the first time since the Education Act of 1870. Yet out of these interests – and out of a study of gaps in the public provision of educational and social services – he developed bigger schemes. An ambitious Arts Workshop, opened in October 1973, was designed to offer creative leisure facilities for children from 4 to 14, the starting age for statutory Youth Service provision; and Deborah Gardner from Bank Street College of Education in New York came over to run it. There were difficulties in 1975, however, when the basement of the Gatehouse which housed the Workshop had to be closed. Asbestos was coming loose on a crumbling ceiling. Yet it soon reopened thanks to a grant from the Gulbenkian Foundation. And the BBC took up the adult literacy plan.[96]

Meanwhile, a Special Families Centre for the Mentally Handicapped was opened in a new building, Sunley House, in December 1974. It was on the site of the condemned tenement block of St George's and Booth House, and consisted of an office and large activities room with a small adjoining room. It also included eighteen flats for old people. The service set out to be therapeutic, informative and educational, and to provide facilities not available elsewhere in an integrated manner. The fund-raising had been masterminded by Profumo, and the first Director of the Centre, Rosalind Wyman, had the experience and the skill to establish it. In 1978 the Boroughs of Tower Hamlets and Hackney took over a larger part of the funding. Once again, a gap in the public provision of social services had been identified and action taken. This, indeed, was still conceived of as one of the main tasks of Toynbee Hall, by Locke as much as by Birmingham 'I still think,' Locke wrote in 1983, 'that the support to the small new, voluntary independent organisation is one of the most effective ways that Toynbee can help'.[97]

There were two other interesting new local schemes – a Money Advice Centre, operating entirely with voluntary help and open once a week, and a Telephone Service for the Elderly – while the Toy Library was so successful that Locke urged its more general adoption and became Vice-Chairman of the Toy Libraries Association, a new national body. He was also associated with the Association for All Speech Impaired Children, a body which always had to operate on a shoestring, and dreamed of the Telephone Service growing into a country-wide network. In fact, however, he ceased to act as Warden before these dreams could be realised, and in a difficult interregnum Marion Press, the Deputy Warden, became Acting Warden.

The present Warden of Toynbee Hall, Donald Piers Chesworth, who has been described aptly as 'a man whose private and professional lives are completely merged', was appointed in 1977 at the age of 55. He had behind him a wealth of experience, both of voluntary and public service. As a young man he wanted to be a politician, and he stood as a Labour candidate at the General Election of 1945. Later he turned to local government, being elected to the LCC in 1952. As an LCC member for North Kensington he took a special interest in social matters, being particularly concerned with Child Care committees, the amelioration of race relations, and the countering of 'Rachmanism', the exploitation of poor tenants. Later he became an active – and radical – co-opted member of the ILEA Education Committee. Yet these London interests were interwoven with international interests, particularly in the Third World. Thus, he had worked as a Labour Adviser in Tanzania and Mauritius, and in Geneva with the Economics Branch of the International Labour Organisation. It seemed fitting, therefore, that on his return to Britain he became Chairman of 'War on Want', which under his chairmanship, he has stated, became 'the most radically minded of the voluntary aid agencies'.

Chesworth was also Director of the Notting Hill Social Council in an area of London where there had been much-publicised racial disturbances, and Chairman of the Association for Neighbourhood Councils. Appropriately, it was Chesworth's close friend, Trevor Huddleston, a former Bishop of Stepney, who, aware of the extent of his commitment and the breadth of his experience, urged him to come to Toynbee Hall. His belief in voluntary action grew out of his own experience, but he and the Toynbee Council were sustained in it at the time of his appointment by the publication of the Wolfenden Committee Report on the Future of Voluntary Organisations and a Government White Paper on Policy for the Inner Cities. For Lord Wolfenden, a former member of the Toynbee Hall Council – and Chairman of the University Grants Committee – there was an urgent need to look afresh at the whole pattern of social and environmental administration, and Chesworth felt, like him, that there was a strong case for treating bodies from the 'voluntary and informal sectors' as major providing agencies.[98] There were signs at this point, therefore, of a reassessment – and it came from the left as well as from the right – of the role of the state, perhaps as significant a reassessment in historic perspective as that which had pointed in the opposite direction seventy and eighty years before.

There was, of course, a further consideration which was presented by Wolfenden in the form of an elegant understatement.

> Over the next 25 years we cannot see any likelihood that public expenditure on the social and environmental services will continue to grow as fast as it has done during the last quarter of a century. Nor can we see any likelihood of a diminution in the rate at which additional services will be expected and demanded.[99]

In such circumstances Toynbee Hall would fit into a different context and, not surprisingly, there were two meetings at Toynbee on the initiative of the Warden between representatives of the Hall and Stephen Hatch, the Senior Research Officer of the Wolfenden Committee. There were also other meetings to discuss the problems of inner cities, one of them led by the Secretary of State for the Environment, Peter Shore, who was also MP for Tower Hamlets (since 1974, after ten years as MP for Stepney) and, like Ian Mikardo (MP for Bow and Poplar), a frequent visitor to the Hall.

As Warden, Donald Chesworth worked selflessly, endeavouring to strengthen and maintain the Toynbee community, which had grown in size from the original fifteen to twenty Residents to about fifty, the greater part of them 'between 20 and 30 years old . . . and dividing pretty equally among men and women'. Some of them, but only a few, still came from Oxford, and many of them were engaged in voluntary work – from escorting District Nurses on their rounds, taking handicapped children to special schools, and assisting patients to Sunday services at London Hospital to serving on local voluntary bodies and participating in Toynbee activities like the Citizens' Advice Bureau, the Legal Advice Centre, the Mallon Club, and the Grand. They spanned 'almost every conceivable background and interest', 'some coming from distant parts of the world'. There was a Cambridge as well as an Oxford link in arrangements made for a number of Cambridge postgraduate students to live at Toynbee during their teaching practice.[100]

Volunteers as well as Residents continued to give invaluable support to the Legal Advice Centre which was dealing still with as many as 400 new cases a year, and the Toynbee Citizens' Advice Bureau, the largest of five Citizens' Advice Bureaux in Tower Hamlets, which now had on its staff a full-time organiser, Jane Gross, and a Bengali-speaking worker, Manzoor Hasan. More than one-third of the Bureau's clients were Bangladeshi. In 1982/3 the Bureau dealt with 14,232 queries, with immigration and nationality problems and social security problems as two most difficult and time-consuming case categories.

The Senior Care and Leisure Centre, under the highly capable supervision of its Organiser, Olive Wagstaff, besides being a club for the thirty-five elderly people living within the Toynbee complex, was also used by others living within walking distance. The average age in 1980/1 was said to be 'a youthful 78', and membership ranged from sixty to ninety-two. New skills, including playing the piano, were learnt in a variety of classes supplied most days by tutors from the Tower Hamlets Adult Education Institute; and members of the Centre were encouraged and helped to remain independent to give mutual support to each other. The Centre also provided a training ground for students, particularly those who intended to work with older people. The Report for 1981 described how the Prime Minister, Mrs Thatcher, on a visit to Toynbee in July 1980 'showed her talent with a tambourine when confronted with the members of our Percussion Band', and how the Speaker of the House of Commons, now Lord Tonypandy, admitted, 'I ought to take to armchair exercises.'[101]

Other community activities included the Special Families Centre, still providing services for families with handicaps, the pre-school playgroup – with a greatly extended range of facilities – and the Mallon Club which had over fifty or sixty elderly members and met, as in the past, on Monday evenings. There is a plan to demolish College East, Barnett's model housing, and construct eighteen flats for elderly people.

The Attlee Foundation, chaired by Arthur (Lord) Bottomley and directed first by Brown, then by Chesworth and at present by the indefatigable Billy Dove, long a Toynbee Resident and volunteer, continues to pioneer and raise funds for special projects. In 1982/3 there were six of them, one international, the support of 'eye camps' in India under the auspices of the Royal Commonwealth Society for the Blind. The plan was taken up to celebrate the hundredth anniversary of the birth of Attlee, Prime Minister when India secured independence. A commemorative evensong in Westminster Abbey was attended by two other former Prime Ministers, Lord Home and James Callaghan, and more than sixty members of Attlee's family were present. There has remained an international flavour to Toynbee Hall also. It has housed the Secretariat of the International Federation of Settlements, and the Warden with his unremitting concern for international understanding, has welcomed official delegations, including the Social Affairs Minister of Denmark and a group from Kobe, Japan. The Secretary of the International Federation, Tom (Lord) Ponsonby, was maintaining a long family association with the Hall.

By the late 1970s, much of the attention of Toynbee Hall was already being focused on its own hundredth anniversary celebrations, and a special sub-committee of Council was set up to prepare for it. There had already been substantial changes in the administration of the Hall, beginning in 1978 with the launching of an administrative review, planned by Sir Charles Johnston, a Member of Council since 1974. Johnston, a distinguished diplomat and from 1965 to 1971 High Commissioner to Australia, was in a line of highly versatile as well as constructive members of Council: he had just completed a translation of Pushkin's *Eugene Onegin*.[102]

The administrative review was entrusted to Sir Harold Atcherley, Chairman of the Armed Forces Pay Review Body, and Walter Birmingham, and covered resources as well as tasks. Its first fruits were seen when John Crisp was appointed as Administrator in 1979. He had served for thirty years with the Metropolitan Police and had retired at the early age of 53 with the rank of Deputy Assistant Commissioner. In the same year a new Accountant, Jack Raby, was also appointed. Such changes were necessary in a period of increasing financial pressure, but there was a great loss in 1982 when Lord Blakenham suffered a severe stroke from which he never recovered. His place as Chairman of Council was very properly filled, however, by John Profumo, whose memorable eighteen years at Toynbee Hall, culminating in his Vice-Chairmanship, already represented a distinctive era in its history. Lord Henniker, who was already Chairman of the Centenary Sub-Committee, became Deputy Chairman, thereby starting a new partnership with the Chairman. The role of the Council was of crucial importance at this point in the story.

Lord Henniker was a former diplomat and for four years he had been Director-General of the British Council. He knew something, therefore, of the kind of problems that were besetting race relations during the 1970s. They were set out in detail in relation to the Tower Hamlets area in a Report of the Commission for Racial Equality which had noted in 1977 that race relations in the East End, especially in Tower Hamlets, were 'less than satisfactory', and which two years later published *Brick Lane and Beyond, An Inquiry into Racial Strife and Violence in Tower Hamlets*, an important document which 'tapped' the views and feelings of residents in the area through interviews in depth. The reactions included the views and feelings of the Bengali community, but those of other groups were studied also. There had been serious disturbances at Spitalfields, in particular, between January and June 1978 – with much violence directed against Bengalis – and the Commission was anxious to go beyond diagnosis to making 'appropriate recommendations'. 'Tower Hamlets [a community worker maintained] is a touchstone of the deepening racial conflict and violence which has come to characterise the relationship between "oppressed" blacks and many whites whose present life style and future welfare are severely threatened by the spate of economic and industrial crises.'[103]

The same point was made in the Toynbee Hall Report of 1980/1 in which the Warden described how 'almost all the adult Bengalis taking part in Toynbee activities, including Residents, have been abused and assaulted whilst peacefully engaged in the neighbourhood.'[104] The Council of Citizens of Tower Hamlets had been able to do little to alleviate this intolerable position, and it was clear to the Warden that a major Toynbee Hall contribution was essential if the local community, now largely Bengali, were to have any chance of becoming a happier place. The Bengalis were 'the modern heirs, economically as well as residentially, of the nineteenth-century European Jews': they were even said to share the passion for gambling.[105] Yet life in Whitechapel was too much of a gamble. And there were some young activists in the Bengali community who were uninterested in what Toynbee Hall was offering – or might offer. They did not want to communicate.

Various initiatives were taken by the Warden. Thus, Shiv Banerjee, Volunteer Coordinator, was appointed to encourage and monitor voluntary work in 1982 and 1983 (before joining the ILEA Welfare Service); a number of Residents, several of whom were Bengali, continued to teach English; a Bengali Health Service, set up in 1978, helped with the awkward problem of advice and communication; a Bengali Mother Tongue School was created; and the Toynbee Language Club was revived. Kumar Murshid planned 'computer camps' and there was a Bengali Music Club. At festival times the Toynbee basement was turned into a Hindu temple.[106] Immigrants of all nationalities were always made welcome in the Warden's Gatehouse flat.

Immigrant happiness – and the happiness of a new generation of Asians, West Indians and Africans born in the East End – depended in the first instance, of course, on housing and employment, and here the position was deteriorating during the late 1970s. The Toynbee Housing Association, still a separate entity, was active in the area, undertaking a village-style development to be known as 'Flower and Dean' on a 3½-acre site immediately north of Toynbee Hall (on land leased from the Borough Council), but there were massive housing problems which no single Housing Association could tackle.[107] As for employment, in 1982, when unemployment in Tower Hamlets had reached a figure of over 20 per cent – as against a GLC average of 11 per cent – any contribution that Toynbee Hall could make was, once again, limited. Lord Henniker became Chairman of a new Toynbee Hall Committee, appointed in that year, to examine ways of contributing, particularly in the field of training. The idea of training workshops was advanced, including workshops specifically for Bengalis and for the handicapped, and a site was selected on land in Gunthorpe Street belonging to the Tower Hamlets Borough Council, which also provided financial assistance. There were also discussions with the Manpower Services Commission. David Sarre, who had first come to Toynbee Hall (as a young barrister) to help the Poor Man's Lawyer Scheme, served as a co-ordinator, and played an important part in the discussion on this project, taking advantage of the experience he had acquired as Personnel Director of British Petroleum. Sir Harold Atcherley, with wide business experience also, prepared useful working papers, and Maurice Machin and Kenneth Slater carried out necessary research. They were all volunteers. Because of difficulties in implementation, they had to possess patience as well as sympathy.

It was not a new recipe. Indeed, there are many resemblances between the present situation in Whitechapel and that when Barnett first arrived there. The district is still deprived. Yet there is immense wealth in the 'Square Mile' of the City of London which is adjacent to it. The social mix is still strictly limited. There is a large immigrant population, although, unlike the late-nineteenth-century Jews, they are not political refugees. Outside the East End there is still ignorance about the life there; most visitors go only to the markets or the restaurants. And within the area Spitalfields has been recently described by Honor Marshall in her book *Twilight London* – a Victorian title – as the 'single most impoverished square mile in the A to Z'.[108] Social workers often confirm the impression. A cluster of welfare services has taken the place of the Victorian Poor Law, but there are constraints on or cuts in the expenditures both of local and of national government which limit social spending. Voluntary action is being canvassed again – for different and often contradictory reasons; and there are efforts on the part of local voluntary groups, many of them radical, to change the situation. Through the politics the 'bitter cry' can often be heard.

Of course, there have been important changes in the pattern both of economics and of politics, in the structure of local government, and in the styles both of research and of action. An active, if now divided and locally challenged Labour Party was absent in 1884. Nor was a great Borough of Tower Hamlets envisaged. There were far fewer 'experts' in 1884 than there are now. Yet the expert can be treated with suspicion today. Moreover, there is a clearer recognition now than there was during the 1880s that Spitalfields, for all its problems is, in the words of a draft local plan prepared in 1977, 'an area of great character and potential'. 'The quality of historic buildings and the variety of building form and style make it potentially more attractive than those parts of the Borough of Tower Hamlets rebuilt in the fifties and sixties.'[109]

Such a judgment is compatible, of course, with the more obvious judgment that the area is an 'Action Area' riddled with social problems; and the statistics bear out the latter judgment without the need for commentary. For example, the average life expectancy of a child aged 5 in Tower Hamlets is 63.4 years, the lowest of all London boroughs and three years lower than the London average. The percentage of elderly people living alone has increased to 35 per cent – over 8,500 people. The latest local *Spitalfields Survey* of housing and social conditions was published in July 1981: it was the work of a militant local pressure group – the Spitalfields Housing and Planning Rights Service, supported by the Catholic Housing Aid Charity. There was a further Report by the Service in 1981 after its existence had been threatened when an urban aid grant to it was withdrawn. It was called *The Law, The Homeless and the Council in Tower Hamlets.*

Another Report of 1980, prepared by the Service, was discussed at a public meeting held in Toynbee Hall in 1980. *What's Happening to West Spitalfields?* dealt with the smaller area of 50 acres with which Toynbee Hall was directly and intimately associated. It named nineteen voluntary organisations which were associated with the Service, ranging from the Spitalfields Project to the Bangladesh Youth Front and including the Toynbee Citizens' Advice Bureau; and among its controversial themes were 'the growth of office development at the expense of privilege rented housing'; the role of developers and the methods they had used 'to exploit the area'; 'the falling level of services'; and 'the failure of the GLC's development schemes'.

The small area of West Spitalfields had lost a higher proportion of its population between 1961 and 1979 – 41 per cent – than Tower Hamlets as a whole. Yet it had retained most of its 'traditional industries' – the rag trade, breweries and printing – during a period when the dock area just outside it had lost its livelihood. Its markets attracted large numbers of people from outside: Booth's lurid gas flares had gone, but there was no shortage of colour or drama. Yet the range of goods on offer had changed and there was less market responsiveness to purely local needs. Despite all this, significant numbers of the inhabitants of the area wanted to stay there. Others wanted to go at almost any cost. Inside the area there was exceptional mobility. When the 1981 Census was taken, seventeen out of a hundred of those aged 1 year or more had changed their accomodation within the previous year. There was also an exceptionally high proportion of young people, with a quarter of the population under the age of 25.

Housing conditions are often appalling – with overcrowding and lack of amenities – and this was one reason for the mobility: in one small and particularly dilapidated group of twenty-one houses at the end of the 1970s, 77 per cent of the occupants had no use of hot water and 70 per cent had to share an outside toilet. Low rental accommodation had been sharply reduced – the number of streets in private ownership had fallen from 923 in 1961 to 195 in 1979 – and there had been a decline in the number of streets with public housing from 1,972 to 1,560. The official policy then and later had been to encourage office development, although in 1977 it had been stated explicitly that the Tower Hamlets Borough Council had 'a general presumption against purely office schemes, but will consider mixed-use proposals offering some form of 'planning gain'.[110]

The views expressed by pressure groups, particularly tenant groups, were often distinctly different from those expressed by the local authorities, although the local authorities made no effort to conceal the seriousness of the issues. Housing associations, whatever their history, were inevitably aware of the extent of general need. They were inevitably aware, too, of the relationship between housing and work and of the distinctive features of the employment pattern which determined family incomes.

A topic paper, *Employment*, produced officially in the mid-1970s as a key paper in the preparation of a 'Borough Plan' for the new borough of Tower Hamlets, surveyed the distribution of industry, commerce and offices in the whole borough, noting the presence of many 'old and outworn' premises 'not suited very well to the needs of industry today'. There were very small firms facing difficulties; 76 per cent of all firms had less than ten employees. At that time, the population of Tower Hamlets was 2 per cent of the total population of the London of the Greater London Council, and the proportion of unemployed in the borough was already 5 per cent. It was thought to be very high then. Now, eight years later, it is four times as great. It has been more difficult in some respects also to introduce palliative recovery than it was during the 1930s. Thus, a Special Temporary Employment Scheme (STEP), funded by the Manpower Services commission in 1979 and based at Toynbee, was dropped on the grounds that it provided too much 'training' and too little 'work'.[111]

The limited social mix is still stressed as much as it would have been in the mid-1870s, and still preoccupies some Toynbee Hall Residents who choose to live in the area because of its distinctive social characteristics.

> In comparison with other boroughs, Tower Hamlets is within the lowest five boroughs for resident professional workers, employers and managers and intermediate non-manual workers, whilst it is in the top five boroughs with resident foremen, and supervisors, personal service waiters and unskilled manual workers.

The other London boroughs with which it has most in common include Barking, Hackney, Newham and Southwark.

Turning to other social indicators, the borough has a lower rate of car ownership than any other London borough, only just over half the GLC average. Moving around largely depends on public transport as it had done before the invention of the motor car. Of all Tower Hamlets residents, 56 per cent work in Tower Hamlets and 12.5 per cent in the City, but 4.6 per cent make the journey to Westminster as Barnett had done, 38.5 per cent of Tower Hamlets workers live in Tower Hamlets, with another 23 per cent coming from North East London.[112]

The Report dealt with categories of the local unemployed essentially within the same framework as Beveridge had come to do, noting, in particular, the high unemployment rate among unskilled workers and the difficulties of young people. Adding to the unskilled pool, 62 per cent of school leavers left school with no academic qualification of any kind. There was also a category of 'unemployable'. There were not enough people entering re-training, though there was a range of possible options, wider than would have been the case a hundred or even fifty years before.

The environmental powers of the Council were stated explicitly in a table which showed how recent some of them were, and how dependent they were on financial assistance from government.[113] There was little intimation then, however, that not only would full employment cease to be an object of national policy, but also that the spending powers of local government would come to be challenged. The policy turns of the late 1970s and the early 1980s will stand out in history as sharply as the policy turns of the late 1940s.

As Toynbee Hall looks into its own future during the next hundred years, it has to take stock not only of what it has achieved but of what it has not been able to do. Moreover, it has to consider not only society as it is today but society as it is likely to become or might become. There is no one single option. The conditions of the time suggest that the time is ripe for a new set of initiatives, concerned with how best to deal with heavy unemployment, financial pressure on statutory social services, discontent with the fiscal system; continuing environmental problems, beginning with housing; and on the positive side, the desire to be of service, not least on the part of many university graduates. The fact that a far larger share of the unemployment is structural rather than cyclical, bound up with the development of new technology rather than with 'depression', challenges long-accepted attitudes to the organisation of work and to the balance between work and leisure. Meanwhile, the paradox is that while there are large numbers of people looking for work there is much necessary work that is not being done. The fact that the statutory social services are under constant governmental scrutiny with a view to cutting costs at a time when what they were devised to secure is not being secured not only provokes resistance but forces a reassessment both of need and of 'machinery'. Attention is inevitably focused on the position of the volunteer – and of the trade unionist. The existence of an alternative economy, 'hidden' or 'informal', has become possible because of the fiscal system, and has developed its own modes and norms of behaviour. The fact that an increasing visual awareness of the built environment and of the social purposes it is designed to serve still co-exists with soul-less building on the one hand and vandalism on the other is a challenge to every kind of planner. And the idealism of those who are anxious to serve can easily be either blunted or frustrated, not least when, unlike the first Residents, they are seeking to share the life of families not unlike those into which they were themselves born.

There can be no cosy agreement on policies, for there are conflicts of interest and values in society and culture which are just as sharp as those of the 1880s. Moreover, there are still potent philosophies of conflict which can attract and convince, particularly when in conventional politics the long-term implications of short-term policies are often almost deliberately ignored. In such circumstances, there is continuing need for independent social research on most of the topics on this kind of agenda, research which will take account both of the underlying economics and the psychology.

Placed as it is, Toynbee Hall is a sounding board. But it is also, as Profumo has described it, a 'social workshop' which needs Residents among its workmen.[114] Placed as it is, it must be sensitive to grievances, but with the purposes that it has it must also be open to ideas. Yet it, too, has its paradoxes. As Lord Henniker put it in a letter of February 1983,

> It is a sad paradox that at a moment when innovation and new thinking about the provision of social services and help for the deprived is more than ever necessary [and he might have added more items to his short list of two] it is ebbing. Why? Because as charities have to carry experiments for a longer period, the costs of these experiments increase year by year, and there is no relief from statutory sources

in sight. There is another factor – when statutory money was in generous supply, so, too, were would-be social innovators. Now they are far fewer, because whereas once they could start on a financial shoe-string, inflation and the uncertainty of the future have made this impossible; the innovators are discouraged because they see no sufficient help in sight, and the charities, which are put to it to keep their established and proven clients afloat, are not, as before, out looking to anything like the same extent for innovations to support.[115]

Toynbee Hall is established as an institution. It will only be innovatory in its projects, however, provided that those who direct its fortunes have the imagination and the drive first to find the right people to carry them out and, second, to give them the required resources. 'Do not imagine that Toynbee has finished its work,' Beveridge once wrote. 'As long as men and women have problems, so long will Toynbee have a job to do.'[116] Yet the job, it is now recognised, must be realistically as well as imaginatively assessed. No institution can solve the problems of society. It can at best try to discover through research and experiment how to tackle them and through education – to which Barnett rightly attached such fundamental importance – to try to help people both to understand and to act.

The role of education – not least, social education – may have been somewhat neglected at Toynbee in recent years, partly because it was assumed that the local authorities were providing it, under lease, after the 'New Building' passed into the hands, first of the LCC and most recently of ILEA. There was an increase of activity in the late 1970s, however, particularly in the field of community education, which did not feature in the activities of the 'New Building' and there are good foundations to build on – in co-operation with other bodies, including polytechnics as well as universities. It was an interesting development, too, which would have appealed to Barnett, when the National Association of Gifted Children started its life in the East End at Toynbee Hall in 1981 before moving to the Tower Hamlets School for reasons of space. There was a special need to give such children the right kind of guidance in an area with the smallest proportion of children gaining graded passes in public examinations. Indeed, the proportion of children staying on at school after the age of 16 was only 23 per cent. Whatever educational activities are carried on at Toynbee Hall in the future, they will have to be of a very varied kind and there are very varied views about what they might be.

As part of the Centenary programme, an Educational Working Party has been set up – in the knowledge that the lease of the 'New Building' expires in 1984. It includes Charles Johnston, who is re-developing the Library, and Cliff Tucker, one of the most dedicated of all twentieth-century Residents. There has already been co-operation with Queen Mary College and with the City of London Polytechnic on a joint diploma in Social Policy, and there have been – and will be – explorations as to how Oxford, a very different Oxford from that of Barnett's time or Beveridge's, can be brought into the picture.

The sense of an unfinished agenda is strong, but not new. It was put with characteristic economy by Clement Attlee in 1964. In his article 'Toynbee Hall looks to the Future' he ended – or almost ended – with Churchill's slogan 'give us the tools and we will finish the job.' He had his own version, however. His own last words were 'carry on, not finish, for wars finish, but there is no foreseeable end to the campaign for social advance.'[117]

Appendix

Wardens of Toynbee Hall

Samuel Barnett   1884–1906
T. E. Harvey   1906–1911
Maurice Birley   1911–1914
J. St George Heath   1914–1917
Eldred Hitchcock   1917–1919
J. J. ('Jimmy') Mallon   1919–1954

A. E. Morgan   1954–1962
E. St. John ('Jack') Catchpool   1962–1963
Walter Birmingham   1963–1972
Tony Locke   1972–1976
Donald Chesworth   1977–

Chairmen of Toynbee Hall

Philip Lyttleton Gell   1885–1895
Lord Peel   1896–1897
Lord Herschell   1897–1898
Sir Charles Elliott   1899–1912
Lord Milner   1912–1925
Lord Burnham   1925–1933

Lord Lang   1933–1945
Lord Waverley   1945–1958
Viscount Monckton   1958–1959
Lord Evershed   1959–1966
Lord Blakenham   1966–1982
John Profumo   1982–

Notes

I Time and Place: the Victorian Prelude

1 N. Williams, *Chronology of the Modern World* (1966), p. 333.
2 W. S. Churchill, *Lord Randolph Churchill*, Vol. I (1906), pp. 268–9.
3 R. H. Gretton, *A Modern History of the British People* (1913), p. 11.
4 Dilke Papers, Add. MSS. 43937, f. 174.
5 Lord Salisbury, 'Labourers' and Artisans' Dwellings' in the *National Review*, November 1883.
6 Dilke Papers, Add. MSS. 43938, f. 53.
7 J. Chamberlain, *The Radical Programme* (1885), pp. v–vii.
8 R. Woods, *English Social Movements* (1892), p. 173.
9 See the valuable recent edition of the pamphlet and related commentary, including some critical assessments, edited with introduction and notes, by A. S. Wohl, (Victorian Library, Leicester University Press, 1970). For Sims, see the articles written in *The Pictorial World* earlier in 1883 and other pieces reprinted in *How the Poor Live and Horrible London* (1889).
10 W. T. Stead, *Pall Mall Gazette*, 16 October 1883.
11 Quoted in J. A. R. Pimlott, *Toynbee Hall, Fifty Years of Social Progress, 1883–1934* (1935), p. 30. See also the new periodical, which first appeared in that year, the *Oxford Magazine* 31 October 1883. Half the sermons reported in the *Magazine* in 1883 dealt with social issues.
12 The full address is reprinted as the first appendix, in Pimlott, *op. cit*, pp. 266 – 73. For its prophetic appeal, see Henry Scott Holland in *Commonwealth*, July 1913.
13 *Illustrated London News*, 22 December 1883.
14 T. Okey, *A Basketful of Memories* (1930), p. 56.
15 See L. Stephen, *Letters of John Richard Green* (1901); and K. S. Inglis, *Churches and The Working Classes in Victorian England* (1961), pp. 143–75.
16 Denison's ideas on the subject were set out in the cheap edition of his *Letter and Other Writings*, published (significantly) in the year 1884. Denison had died in 1870.
17 *The Times*, 27 March 1882. For a recent study of Green, see M. Richter, *The Politics of Conscience: T. H. Green and His Age* (1966): Green died on 26 March 1882. For Toynbee, see his *Lectures on the Industrial Revolution in England, Popular Addresses and Other Fragments*, with a reminiscence by Alfred Milner (1894). See also Milner to G. W. E. Russell, 10 March 1883, on Toynbee's death: 'The sight and thought of human suffering and sin tortured him and he was too clear-headed and too fair-minded to find the relief that some men, equally sensitive, have found in mere denunciations or in the construction of Utopias' (Toynbee Hall Papers) and A. Kadish, *The Oxford Economists in the Late Nineteenth Century* (1982).
18 Toynbee to L. R. Phelps, 8 April 1882 (Phelps Papers).
19 S. Ball to P. L. Gell, 5 November 1883 (Gell Family Papers).
20 Toynbee, *op. cit.*, p. 245.
21 A phrase of Barnett, quoted in M. B. Reckitt, *Maurice to Temple: The Social Movement in the Church of England* (1947), p. 118.
22 Toynbee, *op. cit.*, p. 273.
23 R. L. Nettleship (ed.), *The Work of T. H. Green*, Vol. III (1885–8) 1888, p. cxii. See also his *Memoir of Thomas Hill Green* (1906).
24 S. A. and H. O. Barnett, *Towards Social Reform* (1909), p. 285.
25 Letter of 7 March 1873 (Barnett Papers).
26 W. F. Aitken, *Canon Barnett* (1902), p. 76. See also A. F. Young and E. T. Ashton, *British Social Work in the Nineteenth Century* (1956); C. L. Mowat, *The Charity Organisation Society, 1869–1913* (1961); and M. Roote, *A Hundred Years of Family Welfare* (1972).

27 See his article in the *Saturday Review*, 28 December 1867.

28 See her 1869 paper, 'The Importance of Aiding the Poor Without Almsgiving', read to the Social Science Association. See also E. Moberly Bell, *Octavia Hill* (1942).

29 See U. Cormack, *The Welfare State* (1954) and K. Woodroofe, *From Charity to Social Work* (1962).

30 See G. B. Shaw, *Plays Pleasant and Unpleasant* (1898).

31 See the interesting essay by Stephen Yeo on Thomas Hancock in M. B. Reckitt (ed.), *For Christ and the People* (1968).

32 F. Harris, 'The Housing of the Poor in Towns' in the *Fortnightly Review*, October 1883.

33 The article appeared in the *Nineteenth Century* in May 1883, and the books in 1894 and 1915. See a further letter of 11 May 1902, quoted in M. B. Reckitt, *Maurice to Temple op. cit.*, p. 118.

34 Letter of 30 January 1894, quoted in H. O. Barnett, *Canon Barnett: His Life, Work, and Friends* (1918), p. 163.

35 See his address 'Are Radicals Socialists?', 'delivered to an audience of workmen and employers' in 1882 and reprinted in his *The Industrial Revolution*, pp. 219–38. See also M. E. Sadler, 'Owen, Lovett, Maurice and Toynbee' in the *University Review*, July 1907.

36 *Oxford Magazine*, 21 November 1883. See also J. Rae, *Contemporary Socialism* (1884) and S. Webb, *Socialism in England* (1890). For a recent survey, see J. W. Mason, 'Political Economy and the Response to Socialism in Britain' in the *Historical Journal* (1980).

37 See the *Pall Mall Gazette*, 25 and 27 October 1883, for the comments both of Stead and others.

38 Introduction to Toynbee's Industrial Revolution, *op. cit.*, p. xxvi. See also H. Perkin, 'Individualism and Collectivism in Nineteenth-Century Britain, A False Antithesis' in the *Journal of British Studies* (1977). Milner had lectured on Socialism in the East End in 1882. The lectures were reproduced after his death in the *National Review*, January-June 1931. For different views, see K. Willis 'The Introduction and critical reception of Marxist thought in Britain, 1850–1900' in the *Historical Journal*, 1977.

39 Quoted in H. O. Barnett, *op. cit.*, p. 340.

40 P. L. Gell, 'The Work of Toynbee Hall' in his *Arnold Toynbee* (Johns Hopkins University Studies in History and Political Science, 1889), p. 58.

41 *Oxford Magazine*, 21 November 1883.

42 Barnett Papers: *Cambridge Review*, 18 February 1885.

43 Quoted in Pimlott, *op. cit.*, p. 39.

44 See *Work for University Men Amongst the London Poor* (1884) and an appeal by the Warden of Keble, E. S. Talbot, in *The Times*, 21 January 1891.

45 See H. Henley Henson, 'The University Settlements in the East End' in *Some Urgent Questions in Christian Lights* (1889).

46 Toynbee to Barnett, 18 February 1879 (Barnett Papers).

47 A. Milner, *Arnold Toynbee: A Reminiscence* (1895), p. 36.

48 Barnett to Frank Barnett, March 1884 (Barnett Papers).

49 See J. Adderley, *In Slums and Society* (1916) and *A Little Primer of Christian Socialism* (1909), p. 27. See also S. Mayor, *The Churches and the Labour Movement* (1967).

50 See *British Weekly*, 24 December 1896, quoted in Inglis, *op. cit.*, p. 159.

51 See W. S. Peterson, *Victorian Heretic* (1976).

52 Quoted in H. W. Nevinson, *Changes and Chances* (1923), p. 78.

53 Quoted in H. O. Barnett, *op. cit.*, p. 421.

54 Letter from Milner to Gell (Gell Family Papers).

55 Note by Barnett, 19 July 1884 (Barnett Papers).

56 Letter of October 1860, quoted in C. Kent, *Brains and Numbers* (1978), p. 73.

57 See A. Briggs, *Victorian Cities* (1963), Ch. VIII, 'London, the World City' and G. Stedman-Jones, *Outcast London* (1971). See also P. Waller, *Town, City and Nation* (1983), Ch. 2.

58 A. Sherwell, *Life of West London* (1902), p. 100.

59 Quoted in P. Thompson, *Socialists, Liberals and Labour, The Struggle for London, 1885–1914* (1967), p. 100.

60 C. Booth, *Life and Labour of the People in London* Vol. I, (1892 edn) pp. 29–30.

61 *Ibid.*, p.66

62 See V. D. Lipman, *Social History of the Jews in England, 1850–1950* (1954), p. 90; Jewish Historical Society, *Proceedings of the Conference on the Jewish East End, 1840–1939* (1980); and L. P. Gartner, *The Jewish Immigrant in England, 1870–1914* (1960).

63 See C. Booth, *Life and Labour*, Vol. I (1889

edn), pp. 566–90; Jack London, *People of the Abyss* (1903).

64 See C. Russell and H. S. Lewis, *The Jew in London* (1901) and L. Mocatta, *Out of the Ghetto* (n.d.).

65 See J. White's fascinating *Rothschild Buildings* (1980); *Hansard*, Vol. LXXII (1900), col. 277; and A. S. Wohl, 'The Housing of the Working Classes in London, 1815–1914' in S. D. Chapman (ed.), *The History of Working Class Housing* (1971).

66 For an early example, see W. Wilkins, *The Alien Immigration* (1892). Jewish immigration was blamed for economic problems also. See Stedman Jones, *op. cit.*, p. 125.

67 Interview quoted in White, *op. cit.*, p. 136.

68 See *ibid.*, pp. 25–6.

69 For the genesis of Booth's enquiry, see E. P. Hennock, 'Poverty and Social Theory in England: the Experience of the 1880s' in *Social History*, Vo. I (1874), and C. Booth, 'The Inhabitants of Tower Hamlets' in the *Journal of Royal Statistical Society* (1887). For the role of the Barnetts and of Aves, see T. S. and M. B. Simey, *Charles Booth, Social Scientist* (1960), pp. 64, 124. See also A. Fried and R. M. Elman, *Introduction to Charles Booth's London* (1968).

70 See C. Booth, *Life and Labour*, Vol. I (1892 edn), p. 172.

71 *Ibid.*, p.66.

72 See H. McLeod, *Class and Religion in the late Victorian City* (1974); D. Rubenstein, *School Attendance in London, 1870–1914* (1969); and G. A. N. Lowndes, *The Silent Social Revolution* (1937).

73 *East London Observer*, 30 August 1896.

74 Quoted in T. S. and M. Simey, *op. cit.*, p. 117.

75 *Ibid.*, p. 90.

76 Quoted in H. O. Barnett, *op. cit.*, p. 233.

77 For different views of the East End, see G. Stedman-Jones, *op. cit.*, esp. Ch. 16, 'The Threat of Outcast London' and his 'Working-Class Culture and Working-Class Politics in London, 1870–1900: Notes on the Remaking of a Working Class', in the *Journal of Social History* (1974).

78 Toynbee Hall, *8th Annual Report* (1892). For William Booth and 'the submerged tenth', see William Booth, *In Darkest England and the Way Out* (1890).

79 Presidential Address to the Royal Statistical Society, published in its *Journal* (1893).

80 See R. E. Park, *Human Communities* (1952 edn), Ch. I, 'The Cry!'

81 See A. I. Abell, *The Urban Impact on American Protestantism* (1963).

82 Quoted in I. Howe, *The Immigrant Jews of New York* (1976), p. 400. See also J. Riis, *How the Other Half Lives* (1980).

83 Quoted in S. A. Barnett, 'Distress in East London' in the *Nineteenth Century*, November 1886.

84 *Ibid.*

85 W. Besant, *East London* (1901), pp. 7–9.

86 See P. J. Keating, *The Working Class in Victorian Fiction* (1970).

87 Quoted in E. P. Thompson, *William Morris* (1955), p. 390.

88 Quoted in R. Johnson, 'Educational Policy and Social Control in Early Victorian England' in *Past and Present* (1970).

89 M. Loane, *The Common Growth* (1911). See also H. Bosanquet, *Rich and Poor* (1898) and C. S. Yeo (ed.), *Social Work in London 1869–1912)* (1973 edn).

90 See the important article by R. I. McKibbin, 'Social Class and Social Observation in Edwardian England' in *Transactions of the Royal Historical Society* (1978).

91 A. W. à Beckett, *London at the End of the Century* (1900), p. 209.

92 'From Oxford to Whitechapel' in the *Spectator*, 17 January 1885.

93 Article in the *University Review* (1905), quoted in H. O. Barnett, *op. cit.*, p. 311.

94 *Ibid.*, p. 326.

95 Address delivered by Lord Milner at Toynbee Hall, 9 December 1912, printed in Toynbee Hall *Annual Report*, 1913 p. 14. See also, T. H. O'Brien, *Milner*, 1979.

96 Quoted in Pimlott, *op. cit.*, p. 37. There is a brief note in the *Builder*, 14 February 1885, which deals more with the purpose of the building than with its architecture.

97 Elizabeth Longford, 'The Toynbee Hall Adventure', 9 November 1983, Royal Society of Arts Lecture.

98 N. Pevsner, *London, except the Cities of London and Westminster* (1952), p. 423.

99 For Ashbee, see below, pp. 34–5.

100 Letter of Barnett to Frank Barnett, March 1884 (Barnett papers).

101 Quoted in Pimlott, *op. cit.*, pp. 38, 73–4.

102 London Borough of Tower Hamlets, *Brick and Mortar* (1975, for European Architectural Heritage Year) with a Foreward by G. Fletcher.

103 Quoted in Commission for Racial Equality,

Brick Lane and Beyond, An Inquiry into Racial Strife and Violence in Tower Hamlets (1979).
104 Avram Stencl, 'Shakespeare at Whitechapel' in *This is Whitechapel*, A Companion to an Exhibition of Photographs (Whitechapel Art Gallery, 1972).
105 *Daily Chronicle*, 12 April 1901.
106 Exhibition cover of 1885, Whitechapel Art Gallery Archive.
107 *Ibid.*

II Samuel Barnett and his Friends, 1884–1913

1 Beatrice Webb, *My Apprenticeship* (1926), p. 219.
2 Reprinted in Toynbee Hall *Annual Report*, 1913, p. 21.
3 J. A. Spender, *Life, Journalism and Politics* (1927), p. 46.
4 H. Spender, *The Fire of Life, A Book of Memories* (1926), p. 69. See also his 'Barnett the Sower' in the *Contemporary Review*, January 1919.
5 See G. Lansbury, *My Life* (1928), pp. 129–30.
6 Quoted in L. Stephen, *Letters of John Richard Green* (1901) p. 136.
7 H. O. Barnett, *Canon Barnett: His Life, Work and Friends* (1918), p. 45: letter from Henrietta Barnett to Jane Addams, 25 January 1919, the anniversary of her wedding (Barnett Papers).
8 Address at Henrietta Barnett's funeral, 15 January 1936 (Hampstead Garden Suburb Archives, Press Cuttings).
9 Note by T. E. Harvey (Toynbee Hall Papers).
10 Note by J. J. Mallon (Toynbee Hall Papers).
11 See N. Mackenzie (ed.), *The Letters of Sidney and Beatrice Webb*, Vol. I (1978), pp. 35, 48.
12 Text of speech by Henrietta Barnett (Toynbee Hall Papers): *City and East London Observer*, 7 May 1932.
13 H. O. Barnett, *Canon Barnett*, p. 326.
14 *Ibid.*, p. 160.
15 P. L. Gell, 'The Work of Toynbee Hall' in his *Arnold Toynbee* (Johns Hopkins University Studies in History and Political Science, 1889), p. 58.
16 For an account of activities at St Jude's prior to the opening of Toynbee Hall see *Report of Parish Work, 1883–4* (Toynbee Hall Archive, GLC).
17 See W. Goldman, *East End, My Cradle* (1940).
18 J. A. R. Pimlott, *Toynbee Hall, Fifty years of Social Progress, 1883–1934* (1935), pp. 92–3.
19 *Ibid.*, p. 57.
20 *Ibid.*, p. 58.
21 *Toynbee Record*, October 1902, p. 5.
22 See J. F. C. Harrison, *A History of the Workingmen's College* (1954) and his later book, *Learning and Living* (1961).
23 Toynbee Hall *Annual Report*, 1890, p. 8.
24 For the 'fixed place or permanent home', see Toynbee Hall *Annual Report*, 1886. For class composition, see *Toynbee Record*, October 1888, p. 10. For teachers, see Barnett, a letter of 29 October 1887, describing a party given for them (Barnett Papers).
25 Toynbee Hall *Annual Report*, 1886, p. 22.
26 *Toynbee Record*, October 1888, p. 12.
27 *Toynbee Record* October 1893, p. 3.
28 Toynbee Hall *Annual Report*, 1890. p.14.
29 Toynbee Hall *Annual Report*, 1889, pp. 21–2.
30 *Toynbee Record*, February 1891, p. 50, and *Toynbee Record*, April 1891, p. 71.
31 Pimlott, *op. cit.*, p. 63.
32 *Ibid.*
33 *Toynbee Record*, April 1891, p. 77.
34 *Toynbee Record*, December 1888, p. 33 and *Toynbee Record*, September 1888, p. 132.
35 Letter of Barnett to Frank Barnett, 25 October 1887 (Barnett Papers).
36 See A. Acland, *A Devon Family* (1981), pp. 121 ff. See also J. H. Higginson, *Selections from Michael Sadler* (1979), Section I.
37 *Toynbee Record*, November 1893, pp. 25–6.
38 See F. Rogers, *Labour, Life and History: Some Memories of Sixty Years* (1913), p. 88.
39 See H. R. Dent (ed.), *Memoirs of J. M. Dent* (1928), p. 52.
40 See J. M. Dent, *House of Dent, 1888–1938* (1938).
41 A letter from Fox's son to J. J. Mallon, 15 January 1945 (Mallon Papers).
42 Toynbee Hall *Annual Report*, 1889, p. 24. For the origins of the Travellers' Club, see *Toynbee Record*, October 1892, p. 5 and Toynbee Hall *Annual Report*, 1892, pp. 20–1. For Bolton King, see R. Bolton King, J. D. Browne and E. M. H. Ibbotson, *Bolton King, Practical Idealist*, Warwickshire Local History Society, Occasional Paper, No. 2, 1978.
43 Pimlott, *op. cit.*, pp. 158–9; J. A. Symonds, *Life and Papers* (ed. H. F. Brown, 1923), p. 100.
44 T. Okey, *A Basketful of Memories* (1930), p. 67.

45 See *Records of the Toynbee Travellers' Club* (Toynbee Hall Papers and Toynbee Archive).
46 Dent, *op. cit.*, p. 100.
47 The Workmen's Travelling Club was still flourishing in 1914.
48 *Toynbee Record*, October 1893, p. 3.
49 Toynbee Hall *Annual Report*, 1886 p. 12. For the origins of the Adam Smith Club, see *Toynbee Record*, October 1892, p. 5.
50 See A. Toynbee, *Lectures on the Industrial Revolution in England* (1884), p. 1.
51 Gell, *op. cit.*, p. 58.
52 *Toynbee Record*, December 1888, p. 26, and *Toynbee Record*, November 1892, p. 22.
53 See Margaret W. Nevinson, *Life's Fitful Fever* (1926), p. 80.
54 Pimlott, *op. cit.*, p. 49. See also *Toynbee Record*, March 1894, pp. 82–3.
55 Pimlott, *op. cit.*, p. 77.
56 *Ibid.*, p. 67.
57 Gell, *op. cit.*, p. 58.
58 Toynbee Hall *Annual Report*, 1891, p. 19.
59 Toynbee Hall *Annual Report*, 1896, p. 18.
60 See C. R. Ashbee, *Journals* (Library, King's College, Cambridge).
61 *Ibid.* Poem by C. R. Ashbee, 'Suggested Report of Toynbee Hall, November 1886', read at Toynbee Hall.
62 See C. R. Ashbee, *The Building of Thelema* (1910).
63 See H. W. Nevinson, *Changes and Chances* (1923), pp. 78–92.
64 *Ibid.*
65 *Ibid.*
66 See Helen Bosanquet, *Rich and Poor* (1898). See also her *Social Work in London* (1973 edn, with Introduction by C. S. Yeo) and R. I. McKibbin, 'Social Class and Social Observation in Edwardian England', in *Transactions of the Royal Historical Society* (1978). See also A. Briggs, 'The History of Changing Approaches to Social Welfare' in E. W. Martin (ed.), *Comparative Development in Social Welfare* (1972).
67 Letter of Barnett to Frank Barnett, n.d. (1888) (Barnett Papers).
68 Letter of Barnett to Frank Barnett, 12 April 1890 (Barnett Papers).
69 See also T. S. and M. B. Simey, *Charles Booth, Social Scientist* (1960), p. 64.
70 Toynbee Hall *Annual Report*, 1888 p. 19.
71 *Toynbee Record*, May 1889, p. 96.
72 H. O. Barnett, *Canon Barnett*, Vol. 2, p. 266.

73 Letter of Barnett to Frank Barnett, March 1884 (Barnett Papers).
74 See the *Charity Organisation Review*, August 1895, pp. 338–42 for a paper read by Barnett in July 1895, to the COS Council. See also, for the other side, B. Bosanquet (ed.), *Aspects of Social Problems* (1895).
75 See the *Westminster Gazette*, 20 September 1895, for comment on Loch's reply. See also the *Toynbee Record*, March 1891, p. 59.
76 See the evidence of Alfred Marshall to the *Royal Commission on the Aged Poor*, 1893; Minutes of Evidence, Q. 10210.
77 Toynbee Hall *Annual Report*, 1913, p. 21.
78 Letter of Barnett to Frank Barnett, October 1889 (Barnett Papers).
79 Letter of Barnett to Frank Barnett, n.d. (1887) (Barnett Papers).
80 Letter of Barnett to Frank Barnett, n.d. (1902) (Barnett Papers).
81 Letter of Barnett to Frank Barnett, 19 June 1904 (Barnett Papers).
82 Letter of Barnett to Frank Barnett, 27 May 1905 (Barnett Papers).
83 *Nation*, 21 June 1913, p. 443.
84 Toynbee Hall *Annual Report*, 1898, p. 12.
85 Quoted in P. N. Backstrom, *Christian Socialism and Cooperation in Victorian England* (1976), p. 177.
86 Toynbee Hall *Annual Report*, 1886, p. 28.
87 Toynbee Hall *Annual Report*, 1889, p. 30.
88 *Toynbee Record*, November 1889, p. 16.
89 *Toynbee Record*, November 1889, pp. 16, 24.
90 See J. Gorman, *Banners Bright* (1973), pp. 12, 53.
91 Charles Dickens, 'Travels in the East', in *All the Year Round*, 1859–68, Part VI, pp. 92–8.
92 *East London Observer*, 1 February 1896. See the useful brochure by R. Beer, *Match Girls' Strike*, Museum of Labour History, 1979. See also A. H. Nethercot, *The First Five Lives of Annie Besant* (1960), pp. 252 ff.
93 Letters of A. P. Laurie, A. J. L. Rogers, H. Llewellyn Smith and A. S. Stevenson (the last not a Resident) to *The Times*, 12, 14, 17 July 1888.
94 *Pall Mall Gazette*, 18 July 1888.
95 B. Tillett, *A Dock Labourer's Bitter Cry*, (1887) with a preface by G. Blaiklock.
96 Letter of Barnett to Frank Barnett, 15 April 1889 (Barnett Papers). See, for the attitudes of Bolton King, an old Resident, J. D. Browne, 'A seat lost to the Government is a seat gained by the Boers' in *Warwickshire History* (1981–2).
97 Barnett, Notes for Lectures in Bristol

Cathedral, 1894 (Barnett Papers). The lectures were much criticised on the grounds that they enouraged working men to be 'discontented with their lot'. See H. O. Barnett, *Canon Barnett*, Vol. II, pp. 212 ff.

98 *Church Times*, 6, 13 September 1889; C. Tsuzuki, *H. M. Hyndman and British Socialism* (1961) p. 95. See also Hyndman's *Recount of an Adventurous Life* (1911).

99 *Toynbee Record*, September 1889, p. 130.

100 *Toynbee Record*, September 1889, p. 130.

101 See Tom Mann, *Memoirs* (1923), p. 79.

102 *Toynbee Record*, October 1889, pp. 8–10.

103 For Manning's 'interference' see also *Guardian*, 23 July 1890; S. Leslie, *Henry Edward Manning* (1953 edn). For the strike see J. Lovell, *Stevedores and Dockers* (1969). See also V. A. McClelland, *Cardinal Manning, his Public Life and Influence, 1865–1892* (1962).

104 *Toynbee Record*, October 1889, p. 7.

105 Letter of Barnett to Frank Barnett, n.d. (1889) (Barnett Papers).

106 See Norman and Jeanne Mackenzie (eds), *The Diary of Beatrice Webb*, Vol. I (1982), p. 291.

107 Ben Tillett, *Memoirs and Reflections* (1931), p.112.

108 *Toynbee Record*, December 1889, p. 34.

109 See H. Llewellyn Smith and Vaughan Nash, *The Story of the Dockers' Strike* (1889) and Mann, *op. cit.*, p. 78. For a history of the docks see John Pudney, *London's Docks* (1975).

110 Toynbee Hall *Annual Report*, 1890, pp. 27–9.

111 *Toynbee Record*, October 1889, p. 8.

112 *Ibid.*, November 1889, p. 15.

113 Toynbee Hall *Annual Report*, 1891, p. 43.

114 Toynbee Hall *Annual Report*, 1890, pp. 27–9.

115 *Ibid.*

116 *Ibid.*

117 *Toynbee Record*, February 1890, pp. 66–7.

118 Toynbee Hall *Annual Report*, 1891, p. 30, and *Toynbee Record*, January 1891, p. 48.

119 Pimlott, *op. cit.*, p. 87. See, for the trade union background H. Clay, A. Fox and A. Thompson, *History of British Trade Unions, 1889–1910* (1964); E. Hobsbawm, *Labouring Men* (1964); and K. D. Brown, *The English Labour Movement, 1700–1951* (1982).

120 Toynbee Hall *Annual Report*, 1892, pp. 17–18.

121 Pimlott, *op. cit.* p. 161.

122 *Ibid.*, p. 103.

123 *Toynbee Record*, July-September 1913, p. 147.

124 Toynbee Hall, *Annual Report*, 1897, p. 11.

125 Pimlott, *op. cit.*, pp. 117–19.

126 Toynbee Hall *Annual Report*, 1913, p. 35.

127 Letter of Barnett to Frank Barnett, 18 February 1888 (Barnett Papers).

128 Letter of Barnett to Frank Barnett, 25 February 1886 (Barnett Papers).

129 Letter of Barnett to Frank Barnett, 12 October 1901 (Barnett Papers).

130 See Albert Mansbridge, *University Tutorial Classes* (1914), p. 16.

131 Letter of Barnett to Frank Barnett, 30 November 1895 (Barnett Papers). For Morant, see B. M. Allen, *Sir Robert Morant* (1934).

132 Letter of Barnett to Frank Barnett, 30 December 1895 (Barnett Papers).

133 See Sir John Gorst, 'Settlement in England and America' in J. M. Knapp, *The Universities and the Social Problem* (1895). See also Sir John Gorst, *The Children of the Nation* (1906).

134 Letter of Barnett to Frank Barnett, 12 May 1900 (Barnett Papers). See also E. Eaglesham, 'Planning the Education Bill of 1902' in the *British Journal of Educational Studies* (1960).

135 *Ibid.*

136 See an article by J. J. Mallon on 'Toynbee Hall' (Toynbee Hall Papers).

137 Barnett, *Notes on Education* (Barnett Papers). See also E. Eaglesham, 'Implementing the Educational Act of 1902' in the *British Journal of Educational Studies* (1962).

138 For Barnett on local government see Toynbee Hall *Annual Report*, 1899.

139 Toynbee Hall *Annual Report*, See P. J. Waller, *Town, City and Nation* (1983), Ch. 2. See also S. Webb, *The London Programme* (1891) and A. G. Gardiner, *John Benn and the Progressive Movement* (1925).

140 H. O. Barnett, *Canon Barnett*, pp. 396–8. See also T. Kelly, *History of Public Libraries in Great Britain, 1865–1965* (1973), pp. 450, 495 for the London chronology.

141 Marie Eyquem, *Pierre de Coubertin, L'Épopée olympique* (1966), pp. 46–48.

142 See *Daily Chronicle*, 14 December 1896 and see also A. Briggs, *The Birth of Broadcasting* (1961).

143 See W. Bowman, 'Lenin in London' in *Contemporary Review* (June, 1957), pp. 336–8.

144 Notes by Lord Ponsonby on a meeting organised in 1905 by Barnett at Toynbee Hall (Private Papers of Lord Ponsonby). For the background, see H. Pelling and F. Bealey,

Labour and Politics, 1900–1906 (1958) and P. P. Poirier, *Advent of the Labour Party* (1965).
145 Letter of Barnett to Frank Barnett, 20 January 1906 (Barnett Papers).
146 S. A. Barnett, 'Labour and Culture' in the *Tribune*, January 1906.
147 Letter of Barnett to Frank Barnett, 28 November 1900 (Barnett Papers).
148 H. O. Barnett, *Canon Barnett* p. 500.
149 Toynbee Hall *Annual Report*, 1886, p. 27.
150 Letter of Barnett to the Bishop of London, April 1882 (Lambeth Palace Archive).
151 Pimlott, *op. cit.*, p. 168.
152 H. O. Barnett, *Canon Barnett*, p. 555.
153 *Daily Chronicle*, 15 March 1897.
154 Letter of G. F. Watts to *The Times*, 16 April 1897.
155 *Punch*, 24 April 1897.
156 *Daily Chronicle*, 12 April 1901.
157 *Manchester Guardian*, 7 February 1901.
158 *Ibid.*, 23 November 1903.
159 *Evening News*, 13 March 1901.
160 *Daily Chronicle*, 13 April 1894.
161 Pimlott, *op. cit.*, p. 174.
162 Toynbee Hall *Annual Report*, 1905 p. 8.
163 H. O. Barnett, *Canon Barnett* p. 437.
164 Toynbee Hall *Annual Report*, 1913, p. 18; *Toynbee Record*, March 1914, pp. 87–91.
165 See A. H. Halsey (ed.), *Traditions of Social Policy*, 1973. See also C. V. Butler, *Barnett House 1914 to 1964: A Record for its Friends* (Private circulation, n.d.).
166 Barnett House was first at the corner of Turl and Broad Street in Oxford. It is now in Wellington Square, Oxford.

III Beveridge and After, 1903–1919

1 Letter of Beveridge to his father, 28 April 1903 (Beveridge Papers).
2 Letter of Beveridge to his mother, 11 May 1903 (Beveridge Papers).
3 *Ibid.*
4 Letter to his father, quoted in Lord Beveridge, *Power and Influence* (1953), p. 17. His father had used the phrase 'soup kitchens' and 'genial smiles bestowed on horny-handed mechanics' in a letter of 28 April 1903 (Beveridge Papers).
5 Letter of Beveridge to his mother, 25 January 1903, quoted in *Power and Influence*, p. 9.
6 Quoted in *ibid.*, p. 14.
7 Quoted in *ibid.*, p. 17.
8 Letter to his mother after going to Toynbee Hall, 28 November 1904, quoted in *ibid.*, pp. 30–1.
9 Letter to Frank Barnett, 9 May 1903 (Barnett Papers).
10 Beveridge *Power and Influence*, p. 24.
11 See J. G. Lockhart, *Cosmo Gordon Lang* (1949).
12 Letter of Barnett to Frank Barnett, 28 February 1903 (Barnett Papers).
13 Toynbee Hall *Annual Report* 1903, p. 8.
14 Letter of Barnett to Beveridge, 21 May 1903 (Beveridge Papers).
15 Letter of Sir William Markby to Annette Beveridge, 12 May 1903 (Beveridge Papers).
16 See M. Freeden, *The New Liberalism* (1978). The change is described also in M. Ginsberg (ed.), *Law and Opinion in England in the Twentieth Century* (1959).
17 Letter of Henry Beveridge to William Beveridge, 29 January 1903 (Beveridge Papers).
18 A remark of the new Liberal Prime Minister, Henry Campbell Bannerman, quoted in C. W. Pipkin, *Social Politics and Modern Democracies*, Vol. I (1931), p. 41.
19 Beveridge *Power and Influence*, p. 20.
20 Letter of Barnett to Beveridge, 25 August 1903 (Beveridge Papers).
21 *Toynbee Record*, October 1903, p. 5.
22 Beveridge *Power and Influence*, p. 24.
23 *Ibid.*, p. 25.
24 Letter of Beveridge to his mother, 22 September 1903 (Beveridge Papers).
25 Toynbee Hall *Annual Report*, 1906, p. 13.
26 *Toynbee Record*, July – September 1906.
27 *Toynbee Record*, May 1904, p. 117.
28 Toynbee Hall *Annual Report*, 1906, p. 15.
29 Beveridge, *Power and Influence*, p. 27.
30 Letter of Beveridge to his mother, 25 October 1905.
31 *Toynbee Record*, April 1903, p. 87; *Toynbee Record*, February 1903, p. 58; *Toynbee Record*, November 1904, p. 25.
32 W. H. Beveridge, *Unemployment. A Problem of Industry* (1909). For its place in the history of attitudes to unemployment see the indispensible study by J. Harris, *Unemployment and Politics* (1972), pp. 21–6.
33 Letter of Beatrice Webb to Beveridge, n.d. (Beveridge Papers).
34 *Toynbee Record*, February 1903, p. 58.
35 *Toynbee Record* December 1903, p. 42. See also T. Brown, Charles Booth and labour colonies, 1889–1905, in the *Economic History Review* (1968) and Stedman-Jones, *Outcast London* (1971), pp. 303–8.
36 Beveridge, *Power and Influence*, pp. 23–4.
37 *Ibid.*, p. 24.

38 *Toynbee Record*, January 1907, p. 132.
39 *Toynbee Record*, December 1904, p. 43.
40 Letter of Beveridge to his mother, 5 November 1903 (Beveridge Papers).
41 *Toynbee Record*, January 1904, p. 52.
42 *Notes of Committee on Unemployment* (Beveridge Papers).
43 *Ibid.*
44 *Toynbee Record*, October 1904, p. 9.
45 *Ibid.*, p. 14.
46 Letter of Beveridge to his father, 10 February 1905 (Beveridge Papers).
47 Letter of Beveridge to his mother, 4 March 1905 (Beveridge Papers).
48 *Ibid.*
49 Toynbee Hall *Annual Report*, 1907, p. 19.
50 Letter of Beveridge to his mother, 20 November 1905 (Beveridge Papers).
51 *Hansard*, Vol. 151, 3–10 August 1905.
52 Toynbee Hall *Annual Report*, 1907, p. 25. See also *Toynbee Record*, October 1906, p. 7, and *Toynbee Record*, January 1907, p. 132. See also, Llewelyn Smith, 'The Labour Department and Government Growth, 1886–1909' in G. Sutherland (ed.), *Studies in the Growth of Ninteenth Century Government* (1972).
53 Letter of Beveridge to his mother, 25 October 1905 (Beveridge Papers).
54 Letter of Beveridge to his father, 23 November 1906 (Beveridge Papers).
55 Toynbee Hall *Annual Report*, 1904, p. 22.
56 Beveridge, *Power and Influence*, p. 29.
57 Letter of R. H. Tawney to Beveridge, 8 September 1903. There is no evidence that at that time Tawney thought, as he did later, that the methods of the Charity Organisation society were too 'inquisitorial' (T. S. Ashton, 'Richard Henry Tawney, 1880–1962' in the *Proceedings of the British Academy* (1962), p. 462.
58 Unsigned article, 'The Call of the Wild' in the *Toynbee Record*, July-September 1904, p. 148. R. Terrill in his useful *R. H. Tawney and his Times* (1973) is wrong in describing this as 'a slightly arrogant spoof'.
59 Quoted in G. Himmelfarb, *The Idea of Poverty, England in the Early Industrial Age* (1984), p. 3.
60 Letter from Tawney to Beveridge, 20 September 1906 (Beveridge Papers).
61 Article in the *Daily News*, 'Religious Census of London', quoted in the *Toynbee Record*, March 1904, p. 87.
62 Beveridge, *Power and Influence*, p. 52.
63 See Bernard Jennings, 'Albert Mansbridge' (Mansbridge Memorial Lecture, University of Leeds, 1973).
64 Quoted in H. Begbie, *Living Water* (1918), p. 187.
65 See Albert Mansbridge, *The Trodden Road* (1940), p. 60.
66 *Yorkshire Post*, January 1904 (Mansbridge Papers).
67 See Mansbridge, 'Democracy and Education' in the *University Extension Journal* (1903) and *University Tutorial Classes* (1913), Ch. 2.
68 Mansbridge, *University Tutorial Classes, op. cit.*, p. vii.
69 See Mary Stocks, *The Workers' Educational Association, the First Fifty Years* (1953), p. 35.
70 See Bernard Jennings, *Knowledge is Power, A Short History of the W.E.A., 1903–1978* (1979), pp. 13–14.
71 See Mansbridge, *University Tutorial Classes*, p. 17.
72 *Ibid.*, pp. 23, 27.
73 *Tribune*, 18 January 1906.
74 Letter of Beveridge to his father, 2 March 1906 (Beveridge Papers).
75 Report of the Joint Committee, *Oxford and Working-Class Education* (1908).
76 J. W. Headlam and L. T. Hobhouse, *Tutorial Classes*, Board of Education Special report on certain classes in connection with the Workers' Eductional Association (No. 2) (1911).
77 H. O. Barnett, *Canon Barnett: His Life, Work and Friends* (1918), p. 724.
78 See R. B. Nevill, *Scouting in London, 1908–1965* (1966), pp. 123–32. For the background, see J. Springhall, *Youth, Empire and Society, British Youth Movements, 1883–1940* (1977).
79 *Toynbee Record*, October 1908, p. 12. See also *Toynbee Record*, May 1909, p. 125.
80 Toynbee Hall *Annual Report*, 1906, p. 19.
81 Toynbee Hall *Annual Report*, 1913, p. 37.
82 *Ibid.*, p. 12.
83 Letter of Henrietta Barnett to Milner, 23 May 1913 (Toynbee Papers).
84 *Toynbee Record*, April 1914, p. 110.
85 Beveridge, *Power and Influence*, p. 37.
86 *Toynbee Record*, June 1911, p. 127.
87 Letter of Henrietta Barnett to Milner, 23 May 1913 (Toynbee Papers).
88 *Toynbee Record*, July–September 1906, p. 1.
89 *Ibid.*, p. 139.
90 *Toynbee Record*, May 1906, p. 138.
91 *Toynbee Record*, November 1911, p. 19. For

the background, see G. Dangerfield, *The Strange Death of Liberal England* (1936).
92 *Toynbee Record* October 1911, p. 3.
93 Toynbee Hall *Annual Report*, 1912, p. 11.
94 *Ibid.*
95 For the background, see R. Price, *An Imperial War and the British Working Class* (1902).
96 Toynbee Hall *Annual Report*, 1910, p.
97 Records of the Enquirers' Club (Toynbee Hall papers).
98 *Ibid.*
99 *Ibid.*
100 W. J. Braithewaite, *Lloyd George's Ambulance Wagon* (1957). See also J. Grigg, *Lloyd George, The People's Champion* (1978), pp. 345–6.
101 For the background, see B. B. Gilbert, *The Evolution of National Insurance in Great Britain* (1966).
102 Records of the Enquirers' Club (Toynbee Hall Papers).
103 *Ibid.*
104 *Ibid.*
105 *Toynbee Record*, February 1904, pp. 71–3.
106 E. J. Urwick, *A Philosophy of Social Progress* (1912).
107 L. T. Hobhouse, *Social Evolution and Social Theory* (1911), p. 83. For the background, see P. Clarke, *Liberals and Social Democrats* (1978) and M. Freeden, *op. cit.*
108 *Toynbee Record*, May 1912, p. 119.
109 Toynbee Hall *Annual Report*, 1912, p. 25.
110 Letter to the *Toynbee Record*, October 1911.
111 Memorandum of Residents, 1913 (Toynbee Hall Papers).
112 *Ibid.*
113 *Ibid.*
114 *Ibid.*
115 Letter of Henrietta Barnett to Milner, 20 September 1913 (Toynbee Papers).
116 *Ibid.*
117 See *The Land, The Report of the Land Enquiry Committee*, 2 vols. (1913, 1914).
118 Letter of 26 June 1912, quoted in A. Briggs, *A Study of the Work of Seebohm Rowntree* (1961), p. 65.
119 See, for the contributions of a number of Toynbee men, P. B. Johnson, *Land Fit for Heroes* (1968).
120 Toynbee Hall *Annual Report*, 1915, p. 21.
121 *Ibid.*, p. 22.
122 *Toynbee Record*, December 1915, p. 9.
123 Letter of Heath J. St George Heath to Milner, 17 September 1917.
124 Letter of Henrietta Barnett to Milner, 15 November 1917 (Toynbee Papers).
125 Toynbee Hall *Jubilee Report*.
126 *Toynbee Record*, January 1915, p. 37.
127 *Memorandum on Future Policy*, January 1919 (Toynbee Hall Papers).

IV The Mallon Years, 1919–1954

1 *Daily Express*, 20 October 1919.
2 *Evening Standard*, 21 October 1919.
3 Toynbee Hall *Report*, 1916–19, p. 8.
4 See B. B. Gilbert, *British Social Policy, 1914–1939* (1970), pp. 25 ff.
5 See A. Henderson, *The Aims of Labour* (1917); Labour Party, *Report of the Executive Committee* (1918) and *Report of the Twentieth Annual Conference* (1920); R. Mckibbin, *The Evolution of the Labour Party, 1910–1924* (1974); and M. Cowling, *The Impact of Labour, 1920–1924* (1971).
6 *Manchester Guardian* 1 November 1955.
7 See M. Stocks, *Fifty Years in Every Street* (1956), p. 33.
8 *Ibid.*
9 Foreword by J. J. Mallon to *ibid.*
10 See M. A. Hamilton, *Mary Macarthur* (1925), p. 56. As early as 1889, a Select committee under Lord Dunraven had recommended inspection and registration of industries, and Sir Charles Dilke introduced private members' bills on the subject in 1904 and 1905. See Pipkin, *Social Politics and Modern Democracies*, vol. I, (1931), Ch. 6.
11 See his fascinating collection of articles *The Pillars of Society* (1916) which incorporated pieces from *Prophets, Priests and Kings* (1906) and S. Koss, *A. G. Gardiner and the Daily News, Fleet Street Radical* (1973).
12 R. H. Tawney *The Establishment of Minimum Rates in the Chain-making Industry* (1914) and *The Establishment of Minimum Rates in the Tailoring Industry* (1915).
13 See R. Terrill, *R. H. Tawney and His Times* (1973), p. 98.
14 'The Sweated Industries Exhibition' in the *Toynbee Record*, June 1906.
15 Sir Frederick Banbury in the House of Commons, quoted in Pipkin, *op. cit.*, p. 131. He had described an earlier bill of 1908 as 'the thin end of the socialist wedge'. (*Ibid.*, p. 130.)
16 For the relationship between Churchill and the Webbs see Gilbert, *op. cit.*, pp. 251–2.

17 J. A. R. Pimlott, *Toynbee Hall, Fifty Years of Social Progress, 1883–1934* (1935), p. 141.
18 *Toynbee Record*, July 1917, p. 59.
19 P. B. Johnson, *Land Fit for Heroes* (1968), pp. 48, 158.
20 P. Clarke, *Liberals and Social Democrats*, (1978), p. 191.
21 Memorandum to Lloyd George, 28 January 1917, printed in K. Middlemas (ed.), *Thomas Jones, Whitehall Diary* (1969), p. 21.
22 Mallon Papers, Toynbee Hall.
23 K. Middlemas, *op cit.*, p. 37.
24 *Ibid.*, p. 36; Clarke, *op. cit.*, p. 198.
25 Quoted in Clarke, *op. cit.*, p. 235.
26 Election Manifesto of 1922 (Toynbee Hall Papers).
27 Report of the Chairman of the Finance Committee, 11 October 1919 (Toynbee Hall Papers).
28 Letter of J. A. Dale to Milner, January 1823 (Toynbee Hall Papers).
29 Toynbee Hall *Jubilee Report*, p. 8.
30 Toynbee Hall *Annual Report*, 1920, p. 12. and *Annual Report*, 1921, p. 15.
31 Toynbee Hall *Annual Report*, 1921, p. 12.
32 Toynbee Hall *Annual Report*, 1920, p. 10.
33 See J. A. R. Pimlott, *The Englishman's Holiday* (1947) and *The Englishman's Holiday; a Social History* (1976).
34 Toynbee Hall *Annual Report*, 1922, p. 15.
35 Toynbee Hall *Annual Report*, 1926, p. 38.
36 Mallon papers, Toynbee Hall.
37 Toynbee Hall *Annual Report*, 1926, p. 6.
38 Toynbee Hall *Annual Report*, 1930, p. 19.
39 *Ibid.*, p. 7.
40 Toynbee Hall *Annual Report*, 1926, p. 10.
41 *Ibid.*, pp. 10–11.
42 *Ibid.*
43 See Toynbee Hall *Report* 1935–8, p. 37, with a reference to an article in the *Manchester Guardian* dealing with the Swedish experience. the writer, a former Resident at Toynbee, according to the Report, made out 'a good case for experiments on these lines in England'.
44 *Scouter*, August 1933.
45 Toynbee Hall *Report*, 1935–8, p. 29.
46 Toynbee Hall *Annual Report* 1926, p. 15.
47 *Ibid.*, p. 16.
48 Toynbee Hall *Report* 1935–8, p. 35.
49 Toynbee Hall *Annual Report*, 1926, p. 20.
50 Toynbee Hall *Report*, 1935–8, p. 30. See also the *Report of the Children's Branch of the Home Office* (1938).
51 Toynbee Hall *Annual Report*, 1930, p. 16.
52 *Evening News*, 22 December 1934.

53 See J. Catchpool, *Candles in the Darkness* (1966), p. 122.
54 Toynbee Hall *Annual Report*, 1926, p. 20.
55 *Ibid.*, p. 33.
56 *Ibid.*
57 *Ibid.*
58 Tonybee Hall *Annual Report*, 1921, p. 8.
59 Toynbee Hall *Annual Report* 1922, pp. 7–8.
60 See Kenneth Lindsay, *Social Progress and Educational Waste* (1926).
61 H. Llewellyn Smith, *New Survey of London Life and Labour* (1930).
62 Toynbee Hall *Annual Report*, 1926, p. 28, and Toynbee Hall *Jubilee Report*, 1935, p. 24.
63 Toynbee Hall *Annual Report*, 1930, p. 9.
64 Toynbee Hall *Annual Report*, 1926, p. 28.
65 *Ibid.*, p. 30.
66 *Ibid.*
67 *Ibid.*, p. 27.
68 *Ibid.*
69 Toynbee Hall Papers, unsigned.
70 Toynbee Hall *Annual Report*, 1926, p. 5.
71 *Ibid.*
72 *Ibid.*
73 'Notes on the General Strike' by Stephen Wilson, a Toynbee Hall Resident.
74 Toynbee Hall *Annual Report*, 1925–6, p. 6.
75 *Wilson, op. cit.*
76 Toynbee Hall *Annual Report* 1925–6, p. 8.
77 Wilson, *op. cit.*
78 Toynbee Hall *Annual Report*, 1929–30.
79 Toynbee Hall *Jubilee Report*, 1935, p. 19.
80 *Ibid.*, p. 24.
81 *Ibid.*, p. 27.
82 *Ibid.*
83 *Ibid.*, p. 10.
84 *Ibid.*, p. 7.
85 *Ibid.*, p. 10.
86 *Ibid.*, p. 6.
87 Jane Addams Papers, Swarthmore Peace Collection, *The Times*, 27 December 1934.
88 *Evening News*, 22 December 1934.
89 *Morning Post*, 24 December 1934.
90 *Spectator*, 21 December 1934.
91 For an early forecast of this development, see G. Wallas, *Human Nature in Politics* (1908).
92 *Spectator*, 21 December 1934.
93 *Ibid.*
94 J. A. R. Pimlott, 'The Mother of Settlements' in *The Times*, 21 December 1934.
95 *Ibid.*, 27 December 1934.
96 *Guardian*, 20 December 1935.
97 *Daily Telegraph*, 14 December 1935.
98 Toynbee Hall *Report*, 1935–8, Introduction by Mallon.

99 *Star*, 24 November 1938; *Hackney Gazette*, 23 November 1938; *Illustrated London News*, 3 December 1938.
100 See C. Cross, *The Fascists in Britain* (1961), p. 78.
101 *Star*, 4 October 1936.
102 Cross, *op. cit.*, p. 161.
103 Toynbee Hall *Report*, 1935–8, p. 18.
104 Article by Mallon (Mallon Papers, Toynbee Hall). See also Mallon's letter to the Editor of the *Manchester Guardian*, 20 October 1936.
105 Toynbee Hall *Report*, 1935–8, p. 18. See the *Jewish Chronicle*, 28 December 1934, for an assessment of Toynbee Hall, which concluded, 'We cannot recognise too warmly the practical sympathy and cooperation which our Community receives from the good-hearted labours of our fellow-citizens at Toynbee.' See also *The Jewish Bulletin*, May, 1942 for an article by Mallon on 'Jews and Gentiles in East London'.
106 Toynbee Hall *Report*, 1935–8, p. 19.
107 *Ibid.*, p. 19.
108 *News Chronicle*, 3 November 1938.
109 Toynbee Hall *Jubilee Report*, p. 15.
110 See B. Simon, *The Politics of Educational Reform, 1920–1940* (1974), p. 198. For Mallon's ability to work through groups of politicians of different persuasions, see A. Marwick, 'Middle Opinion in the Thirties: Planning, Progress and Political Agreement' in the *English Historical Review* (1964). Mallon was a signatory of the proposals set out in *The Next Five Years, An Essay in Political Agreement* (1935).
111 Mallon Papers, Toynbee Hall.
112 Toynbee Hall *Report*, 1935–8, p. 19. See also A. Vallance, *Hire Purchase* (1939).
113 Toynbee Hall *Report*, 1935–8.
114 *Weekly Illustrated*, 28 May 1936.
115 *Solicitor's Journal*, 25 December 1937.
116 *Daily Sketch*, 5 May 1938. See also *Picture Show*, 18 June 1938.
117 *Daily Herald*, 20 May 1938.
118 *Birmingham Gazette*, 7 May 1938.
119 See Alexander Hartog, *Born to Sing* (1982).
120 Toynbee Hall *Report*, 1935–8, p. 24.
121 Letter of Professor John Mars to Anne Macartney, 22 December 1983.
122 Report of the first years of the war (Mallon Papers, Toynbee Hall), and Toynbee Hall *Report*, 1938–46, p. 10.
123 Letter of Lilian Todd to Mallon, 22 July 1940 (Mallon Papers, Toynbee Hall).
124 Account by Edith Ramsay (Mallon Papers, Toynbee Hall).
125 Toynbee Hall *Report*, 1938–46, p. 11.
126 *Ibid.*, pp. 11–12.
127 *Ibid.*, p. 14.
128 *Ibid.*
129 *Ibid.*, p. 12–13.
130 *Ibid.*, p. 12.
131 Letter of Mallon to Stella, 9 May, 1941, lent by Mallon's niece, Mrs Anne Johnston.
132 Letter of Mallon to Victor Cullen, 20 May 1941 and letter of Mallon to Pilkington Turner, 22 June 1941 (Mallon Papers, Toynbee Hall).
133 *Ibid.*
134 Letter of Mallon to David Garley, 20 December 1941 (Mallon Papers, Toynbee Archive).
135 Toynbee Hall *Report*, 1938–46.
136 *Ibid*, p. 13. See also a Paper on CAB activities (Mallon Papers, Toynbee Hall).
137 Toynbee Hall *Report*, 1938–46, p. 15.
138 Report for 1943 (Mallon Papers, Toynbee Hall).
139 Toynbee Hall *Report*, 1938–46, p. 22.
140 *Ibid.*
141 Letter of Mallon to Mrs Hope Graham, 28 September 1942 (Mallon Papers, Toynbee Hall).
142 *Ibid.*
143 Mallon Papers, Toynbee Hall.
144 *Ibid.*
145 Letter of Sergeant W. Gardner to Mallon, 3 March 1943 (Mallon Papers, Toynbee Hall). For the background see A. Calder, *The People's War* (1969).
146 *Eastminster Press and City Guardian*, 9 October 1943.
147 *Ibid.*
148 See Denys Munby, *Living in Stepney* (1945).
149 *Westminster Press and City Guardian*, 9 October 1943.
150 *Ibid.*
151 Draft Report by Denys Munby on the LCC Plan (Toynbee Hall Papers).
152 *Ibid.*
153 See Denys Munby, *Industry and Planning in Stepney* (1952). For reviews see the *Architects Journal*, 17 April 1952, and the leading article in *The Times* 25 September 1951.
154 *The Times*, 25 September 1951.
155 *Ibid.*
156 Denys Munby, *Industry and Planning in Stepney, op. cit.*
157 Mallon Papers, Toynbee Hall.

158 *Ibid.*
159 *Ibid.* Letter of Mallon to Earl of Lytton, March 1944 (Mallon Papers, Toynbee Hall).
160 Letter of Mallon to Mrs Hope Graham, 21 June 1944.
161 Letter of Mallon to Flt Lt C. H. Fox, 3 February 1945 (Mallon Papers, Toynbee Hall).
162 Letter of Mallon to Mrs Hope Graham, 16 September 1945 (Mallon Papers, Toynbee Hall).
163 Toynbee Hall *Report*, 1938–46 p. 25. See also *Journal of the Royal Society of Arts*, 13 February 1948; L. F. Ellis, *Toynbee Hall and the University Settlements*, (1948), p. 167.
164 Toynbee Hall *Report*, 1938–46, p. 24.
165 *Everybody's*, 13 January 1945.
166 Letter of George Bernard Shaw to Mallon, 20 April 1948 (Mallon Papers, Toynbee Hall Archive).
167 Mallon Papers, Toynbee Hall.
168 *Ibid.*
169 *Ibid.*
170 Typescript Report for 1949–50 (Mallon Papers, Toynbee Hall).
171 Mallon Papers, Toynbee Hall.
172 Letter of Mallon to Alice Crompton, quoting a remark of L. E. Mather, n.d. 1945 (Mallon Papers, Toynbee Hall).
173 Letter of Sir Robert Waley Cohen to Mallon, 3 October 1946 (Mallon Papers, Toynbee Hall).
174 Speech of Attlee at a special reception for him at Toynbee Hall, 31 March 1947 (Toynbee Hall Papers).
175 Letter of Mallon to Lord Leverhulme, 26 April, 1945 (Mallon Papers, Toynbee Hall).
176 Letter of Mallon to Reverend Simpson, 1 March, 1945 (Mallon Papers, Toynbee Hall).
177 Letter of Mallon to the Board of Deputies of British Jews (Mallon Papers, Toynbee Hall).
178 Letter of Sidney Salmon to Mallon, 24 April, 1947 (Mallon Papers, Toynbee Hall).
179 Letter of Mallon to David Low, n.d. (Mallon Papers, Toynbee Hall).
180 Paper by Father Fitzgerald on race relations, n.d. (Mallon Papers, Toynbee Hall).
181 Report on *English Classes for Coloured Colonials*, n.d. (Toynbee Hall Papers).
182 Letter of Mallon to the Marquess of Salisbury, 1 June, 1949 (Mallon Papers, Toynbee Hall Archive).
183 Letter of Alfred Zimmern to Mallon, 11 October, 1951 (Mallon Papers, Toynbee Hall).
184 Letter of Mallon to Sir Harold Hewitt, 22 January, 1952 (Mallon Papers, Toynbee Hall Archive).
185 Speech of Attlee at a special reception for him at Toynbee Hall, 31 March 1947 (Toynbee Hall Papers).
186 Speech of Attlee at Mallon's retirement, 18 May 1954 (Toynbee Hall Papers).
187 *Sunday Times*, 6 July 1952.
188 *East End News* (Press cutting, Mallon Papers, Toynbee Hall).
189 Letter of Lord Waverley to Mallon, 12 April, 1954 (Toynbee Hall Archive).
190 Mallon Papers, Toynbee Hall.
191 *The Times*, 13 April 1961. See also *East London Advertiser*, 14 April 1961.

V Unfinished Agenda, 1954–1984

1 For the background, see A. Marwick, *British Society Since 1945* (1982) and A. Briggs, 'Social History' in R. Floud and D. McClosky (eds), *The Economic History of Britain Since 1860* (1981).
2 Lucien Febvre, 'A New Kind of History' in the *Revue de Metaphysique et de Morale*, reprinted in translation in P. Burke (ed.), *A New Kind of History from the Writings of Febvre* (1973). pp. 27–44.
3 See H. Hopkins, *The New Look* (1963); M. Sissons and P. French (eds), *The Age of Austerity* (1963); V. Bogdanor and R. Skidelsky *The Age of Affluence* (1970).
4 See J. Pinder (ed.), *Fifty Years of Political and Economic Planning* (1981).
5 See W. H. Beveridge, *Full Employment in a Free Society* (1944). For a note on Dr Morgan, see *Annual Report of the National Association of Boys' Clubs* (September 1972).
6 Toynbee Hall Council Minutes, 15 March 1954 (Toynbee Hall Papers).
7 Letter from Eagles to Mallon, 18 March 1954 (Toynbee Hall Papers).
8 Toynbee Hall Council Minutes, 15 March 1954 (Toynbee Hall Papers).
9 Note by Ellis, October 1953 (Toynbee Hall Papers).
10 Letter from Mallon to the LCC, 19 October 1953 (Toynbee Hall Papers).
11 Letter from Margaret Cole to Mallon, 2 February 1954 (Toynbee Hall Papers).
12 Letter from Mallon to Lord Waverley, 21 January 1954 (Toynbee Hall Papers).
13 Letter from T. G. Randall to Mallon, 2 March 1954.
14 Notes of a Meeting at County Hall, 2 March 1954 (Toynbee Hall Papers).

15 Letter of Morgan to Edward Lascelles, 26 November 1954 (Toynbee Hall Papers).
16 Letter of Margaret Cole to Morgan, 14 October 1954 (Toynbee Hall Papers).
17 Report by Morgan to the Council of conversation with Beveridge, Council Minutes, February 1955 (Toynbee Hall Papers).
18 Letter of R. H. Tawney to Morgan, November 1955 (Toynbee Hall Papers).
19 Letter of Basil Henriques to Morgan, 8 June 1955 (Toynbee Hall Papers).
20 See M. Young and P. Willmott, *Family and Kinship in East London* (1954).
21 See also K. Woodroffe, *A History of Social Work in England and the United States* (1968).
22 Letter of Henriques to Morgan, *op. cit.*
23 Report of Morgan to the Toynbee Council, July 1955 (Toynbee Hall Papers).
24 Residents' Memorandum, 1955 (Toynbee Hall Papers).
25 *Ibid.*
26 *Ibid.*
27 Report of Morgan to the Toynbee Council, July 1955.
28 *Ibid.*
29 Letter from the LCC to Morgan, 29 December 1955 (Toynbee Hall Papers).
30 Morgan to Toynbee Hall Council, Memorandum on Lines of Future Development, 1957. See also Minutes of a Meeting of Toynbee Hall Council, 30 April 1957.
31 Letter of Morgan to the *East London Advertiser*, 14 February 1958. See also Warden's Letter, March 1958 (Toynbee Hall Papers).
32 Minutes of Toynbee Hall Council, December 1957 (Toynbee Hall Papers).
33 See the Younghusband *Report of the Working Party on Social Workers* (1959) and E. Younghusband, *Social Work in Britain, 1950–1975* (1978) Vol. I, Ch. 14.
34 Memorandum sent to the Nuffield Foundation, September 1959 (Toynbee Hall Archives).
35 Toynbee Hall *Report*, 1959 (Toynbee Hall Papers).
36 Minutes of a Meeting of the Council, September 1959 (Toynbee Hall Papers).
37 Minutes of a Meeting of the Sub-Committee, 7 December 1959 (Toynbee Hall Papers).
38 See a letter of 23 May 1960, Farrer-Brown to Morgan (Toynbee Hall Papers).
39 *Ibid.*
40 E. Younghusband, *The New Profession* (1981), p. 28.

41 Note of a Meeting, 28 September 1960 (Toynbee Hall Papers).
42 Letter of Beveridge to Morgan, 23 July 1960 (Toynbee Hall Archives).
43 Letter of Lord Attlee to Morgan, 18 July 1960 (Toynbee Hall Archives).
44 Letter of Jack Morgan to Morgan, 22 September 1960 (Toynbee Hall Papers).
45 Letter of H. Bennett to Morgan, 10 October 1960 (Toynbee Hall Papers).
46 *Ibid.*
47 Letter of Lord Evershed to Farrer-Brown, 11 October 1960 (Toynbee Hall Papers).
48 Toynbee Hall *Annual Report* 1963, p. 41.
49 *Ibid.*, p. 14.
50 See W. H. Beveridge, *Voluntary Action* (1948).
51 Toynbee Hall *Annual Report*, 1905, pp. 11–18.
52 *Ibid.*
53 Toynbee Hall *Annual Report*, 1963, p. 8.
54 *Ibid.*, p. 21.
55 See W. Birmingham, *Introduction to Economics* (1955).
56 For a post-war history of the WEA, See B. Jennings, *Knowledge is Power, A Short History of the W.E.A., 1903, 1978* (1979).
57 Toynbee Hall *Annual Report*, 1965, p. 10.
58 Toynbee Hall *Annual Report*, 1971, p. 37.
59 Toynbee Hall *Annual Report*, 1969, p. 33 and 1968, p. 7.
60 Toynbee Hall *Annual Report*, 1967, p. 14.
61 Lord Blakenham's obituary. Address given by John Profumo, Toynbee Hall *Annual Report*, 1982, pp. 7–9.
62 See also C. R. Attlee, *As it happened* (1954) p. 166: Full employment and the development of the Social Services are, of course, the principal factors: but there are many others.
63 Appeal by Lord Attlee on behalf of Toynbee Hall printed in *The Times*, 2 July 1964.
64 Toynbee Hall *Annual Report*, 1965, p. 8 and Toynbee Hall *Annual Report*, 1967, p. 35.
65 Toynbee Hall *Annual Report*, 1966, p. 8.
66 *Daily Telegraph*, 24 September 1970.
67 Toynbee Hall *Annual Report*, 1971, p. 34.
68 *Ibid.*, p. 35.
69 Toynbee Hall *Annual Report*, 1965, p. 17.
70 *Ibid.*
71 Toynbee Hall *Annual Report*, 1968, pp. 33–4.
72 Toynbee Hall *Annual Report*, 1967, p. 33.
73 Toynbee Hall *Annual Report*, 1971, p. 6.
74 Toynbee Hall *Annual Report*, 1966, p. 6.
75 For the early background, see R. Glass,

Newcomers (1966), p. 339; S. Collins *Coloured Minorities in Britain* (1957); and R. Desai, *Indian Immigrants in Britain* (1963). See CPAND 2739 (1965).

76 Toynbee Hall *Annual Report*, 1967, p. 45. See also Campaign Against Racial Discrimination, *The White Paper: A Spur to Racialism* (1965).

77 Toynbee Hall *Annual Report* 1966, p. 33.

78 See N. Deakin (ed), *Colour and the British Electorate, 1964* (1965) and E. J. B. Rose and Associates, *Colour and Citizenship* (1969).

79 Toynbee Hall *Annual Report*, 1971, p. 5.

80 Toynbee Hall *Annual Report*, 1966, pp. 35–6.

81 Toynbee Hall *Annual Report*, 1968, p. 8.

82 Toynbee Hall *Annual Report*, 1969, p. 31.

83 Toynbee Hall *Annual Report*, 1966, pp. 35–6.

84 Toynbee Hall *Annual Report*, 1967, pp. 33–4.

85 Toynbee Hall *Annual Report* 1965, p. 5.

86 See R. M. Titmuss, *Income Distribution and Social Change* (1962). See also P. Townsend, *The Family Life of Old People: An Inquiry into East London* (1957); B. Abel-Smith and P. Townsend, *The Poor and The Poorest* (1965); and F. Field, *An Income Policy for Poor Families* (1973).

87 For the fullest statement of the argument see P. Townsend, *Poverty in the United Kingdom* (1979). For relative deprivation, see W. G. Runciman, *Relative Deprivation and Social Justice* (1966). See also A. B. Atkinson, *The Economics of Inequality* (1973) and G. C. Figehen, P. S. Lansley and A. D. Smith, *Poverty and Progress in Britain, 1953–1973* (1977).

88 Letter of Frank Field to Walter Birmingham, 4 May 1970 (Toynbee Hall Papers).

89 Toynbee Hall *Annual Report*, 1968, p. 24. For the background of social change, see A. Briggs *A Social History of England* (1983), Ch. 13.

90 Toynbee Hall *Annual Report* 1970, p. 14.

91 Elizabeth Longford, 'The Toynbee Hall Adventure' 9 November 1983, Royal Society of Arts Lecture.

92 For reports of Attlee House see Toynbee Hall *Annual Reports*, 1971 onwards.

93 See J. Nuttall, *Bomb Culture* (1968). See also Briggs *A Social History of England, op. cit.*, Ch. 13.

94 Toynbee Hall *Annual Report*, 1968, p. 39.

95 Toynbee Hall *Annual Report*, 1977, p. 20.

96 Toynbee Hall *Annual Report*, 1975, p. 6.

97 Letter of T. Locke to A. Macartney, n.d. (1983).

98 For Wolfenden's own account of his life, see his *Turning Points* (1976).

99 Toynbee Hall *Annual Report*, 1977 p. 8.

100 Toynbee Hall *Annual Report*, 1983, pp. 22–4.

101 Toynbee Hall *Annual Report*, 1981, p. 27.

102 Alexander Pushkin, *Eugene Onegin*, translated by Charles Johnston (1977).

103 Commission for Racial Equality, *Brick Lane and Beyond, an Inquiry into Racist Strife and Violence in Tower Hamlets* (1979), p. 4. See also Rose, *op. cit.*; W. Daniel, *Racial Discrimination in England* (1968); and D. J. Smith, *Racial Disadvantage in Britain* (1977).

104 Toynbee Hall *Annual Report*, 1981, p. 9.

105 Commission for Racial Equality, *Brick Lane and Beyond*, 1979, p. 27.

106 Toynbee Hall *Annual Report*, 1983, p. 33.

107 *Ibid.*, p. 37. See also the *Guardian*, 23 November 1983.

108 H. Marshall, *Twilight London: A Study in Degradation* (1971) and see also W. J. Fishman, *The Streets of East London* (1979).

109 Planning Department, Directorate of Development, Tower Hamlets, *Towards a Local Plan for Spitalfields*, Interim Report, February 1977.

110 *Ibid.*

111 Toynbee Hall *Annual Report*, 1981, p. 28.

112 Tower Hamlets Borough Plan: *Employment* (1976).

113 *Ibid.*

114 *The Times*, 28 February 1984. See also Devitte Haskins and Sells, *Quarterly Review*, No. 3, 1983/4, pp. 17–18.

115 Letter of Lord Henniker to David Sarre, February 1983.

116 Toynbee Hall *Annual Report*, 1963, p. 23.

117 *The Times*, 2 July 1966.

Index

Note: *All sub-headings are arranged chronologically. Headings for Toynbee Hall are arranged chronologically and correspond to the chapters of the book.*

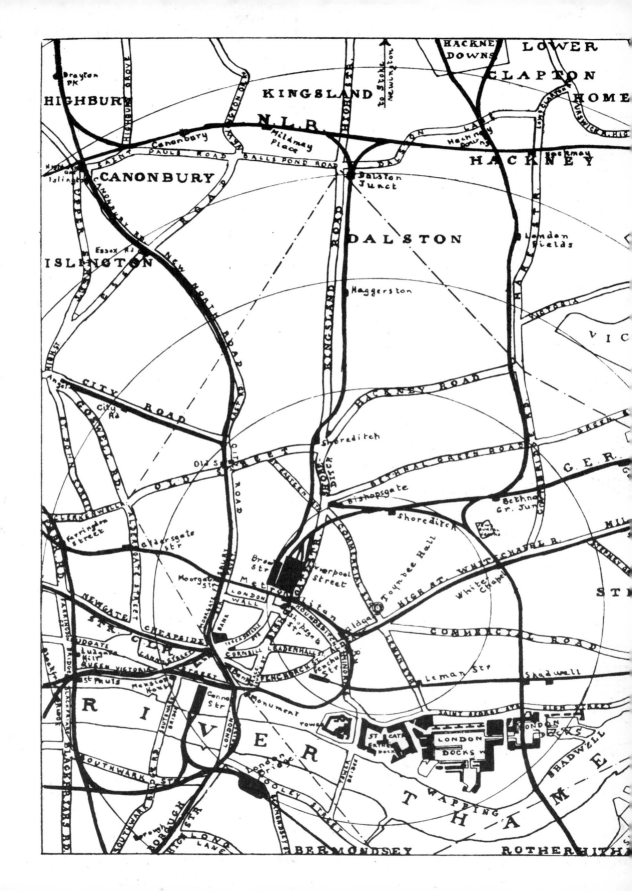